Copyright © 2025 by *Glenn Blythe*. All rights reserved.

ISBN: 978-0-6455071-2-6 Softcover

Yi Chi Li Theory Of Tai Chi

No portion of this book, except for brief review, may be reproduced, stored in a retrieval system, or transmitted in any form or by any means - electronic, mechanical, photocopying, recording, or otherwise - without written permission from the copyright owner.

Email: yichilioftaichi@gmail.com

Published by
Glenn Blythe

To order additional copies of this book
www.taichischoolofyichili.com.au

Other books by the same author:
"Yi Chi Li of Opening and Closing and the Five Loosening Exercises of Tai Chi"

DEDICATION

This Book is Dedicated to my Family

My wife Lindy and my son and daughter, William and Sarah.

Acknowledgements

I mention here not only the people who helped me to create this book, but also the people who have supported me throughout my time in Tai Chi, giving me the ability to put into words the knowledge acquired over many years.

Firstly, Lindy my wife who has supported me from the time I begun teaching Tai Chi full time in 1983, all those years ago. The life of a Tai Chi teacher's wife is not an easy one. She has stuck by me through the few easy times, and mostly hard times. From sneaking photocopies of my Tai Chi fliers from her office job, to helping with classes, and everything in between. **Thank you..........so much.**

Listed in chronological order are some of the people who have guided and encouraged me to continue my love of practising and teaching Tai Chi.

I would like to thank Vincent Leo who gave me the strong foundations on which I've used throughout my time in Tai Chi, and for life in general. He showed me that hard training and a positive outlook can change the negative attitude of a teenager.

It was an incredibly lucky day indeed when Katherine Richardson walked into my school. Introducing me to the teachings of Master Sheng-Shyan Huang, creating a sequence of events that led me to where I am now.

A very big thank you to Tony Ward who was responsible for my early training in Master Sheng-Shyan Huang's teachings. His help was critical in giving the me the foundations that I still use today, and which are used extensively throughout this book. I would like to thank Roger Cotgreave, a senior student of Tony's, who was so generous and giving with his time to me, the newbie, even allowing me to stay at his home numerous times when training in Sydney.

I would also like to thank Adele Walker for her contribution to the graphic art featured in this book.

Joey Zhou, was such a big help with the Chinese translation. Paul Turner, thank you for your invaluable help with my many Tai Chi and IT problems. I also would like to thank the following people who helped me in the editing and their generous advice. They are Marcello Abbate, Sarah Blythe, Paul Turner, Angela Conway, Richard Best, June Flavel, Joe Martinello, Jeffrey Guishard, Anthony Woad and Dennis Woodland.

Last, but definitely not least, I express profound gratitude and thanks to my teacher of 33 years, Wee Kee Jin. Without exaggeration you have been the very source of my knowledge and understanding of Tai Chi. Always patient, friendly and giving with his knowledge, never holding back. Always encouraging me to think outside the square. I would like place on record, my most sincere appreciation and gratitude for the time and effort that you gave me.

Preface

We've all been there, having read a Tai Chi book that promised so much, but delivered so little, leaving you more confused, than when you started. I have dozens of these Tai Chi books on my book shelves collecting dust, attesting to this. Having read these books, you're often left wondering which aspects and qualities to train. One book tells you to focus on relaxation, another book tells you to focus on circulating the chi, the next book tells you to focus exclusively on the Dan Tien. Another, the breath. Conflicting advice abounds. We read that all power comes from the Dan Tien, then later told power is developed by the legs, or strength is released from the spine. The Tai Chi Classics further contribute to this confusion, offering seemingly contradictory and ambiguous guidance, full of double meanings and riddles. The Classics promote conflicting ideas such as; "Only when one is truly soft can one be truly hard" *(aren't we supposed to be soft all the time?)*. Another Classic suggests; "If the opponent doesn't move, I don't move. If the opponent moves, I move first" *(how is it possible to move first, when your opponent has already moved?)*. Paradoxical advice is everywhere in the Classics.

Tai Chi by its nature is counter intuitive. It's as if Tai Chi was developed in a parallel universe. Where muscle is weakness and softness is strength. This results in a fragmented landscape of disjointed theories that no longer coalesce into a cohesive whole. Each individual theory is now a theory unto itself, with no relationship to other supplementary theories of Tai Chi. For theories to be effective, they must work harmoniously as a whole. Aristotle described this process 2,300 years ago when he said, "The whole is Greater than the Sum of its Parts". To add to the confusion, Qi Gong and Traditional Chinese Medicine has been added to the mix, often used to fill gaps often found in Tai Chi theory, turning Tai Chi into a patchwork of theories stitched together from different disciplines and arts. No wonder Tai Chi lacks coherency and consistency, resulting in an incoherent mishmash of theories. Tai Chi theory is made up of a collection of integrated theories, which mutually reinforce and support each other, like a garment held together by various threads. Pull on an important thread, such as Wu Wei *(Non-action)*, and the whole garment falls apart. If theories appear to contradict each other, these contradictions are not inherent; they need to be resolved and can't be simply swept under the rug for another day. Often what prevents us seeing the inter connectivity of these individual theories is our preconceived bias of strength, power, speed and movement we bring to our Tai Chi.

The purpose of writing this book is to bring clarity and qualification to individual theories, such as: power, strength, external movement, internal movement, speed, health and martial aspects all unified under the banner of Taoist philosophy. Upon clarifying and qualifying individual theories, they are then brought together into a seamless, homogeneous entity called Tai Chi. Tai Chi is half science *(quantitative)* and half art *(qualitative)* and like any art and science, by their nature it is a work in progress. Rarely does a week pass that doesn't bring me new understanding and realisation. It is for this reason that I still find Tai Chi so fascinating and captivating. Master Huang Sheng-Shyan once said; "I could live for five life times and still wouldn't get to the bottom of Tai Chi". I promised myself if I ever understood the fundamentals of Tai Chi, I would write a book, a book that I wished I had, when I started my Tai Chi. Sharing my insights and knowledge through a series of four books on Tai Chi, it is my sincerest hope these books will save future generations time *(time is not your friend in Tai Chi)*, and energy, allowing them to elevate their Tai Chi to new heights.
This book is the first of four. They are the following;

1. Yi Chi Li Theory of Tai Chi.
2. Yi Chi Li of Opening & Closing and the Five Loosening Exercises of Tai Chi.
3. Yi Chi Li of Opening & Closing and the Five Loosening Exercises Applied to the Tai Chi Form.
4. Yi Chi Li of Push Hands.

I wish you all the best with your Tai Chi. I hope you find this first book educational, enjoyable and helpful to your Tai Chi journey.

Author's Notes

To help clarify the direction closing *(relaxation downward)* and opening *(relaxing upward)* travels, I have used colour coded arrows. Red arrows represent closing *(relaxing downward)* and green arrows represent opening *(relaxing upward)*. **Be careful not to make the common fault of mistaking the direction of relaxation with the starting point of relaxation.** A very common mistake is seeing relaxation starting at the top of the figure, moving downward to the root. When in fact downward relaxation *(closing)* and upward relaxation *(opening)* **always starts in the root and travels up to the crown of the head.** Similar to how an hour glass works, the sand drains downward causing an upward adjustment. I know this can sometimes be confusing, so I have included some diagrams below to show the sequential order relaxation takes when closing or opening.

First Stage of the Opening & Closing Exercise

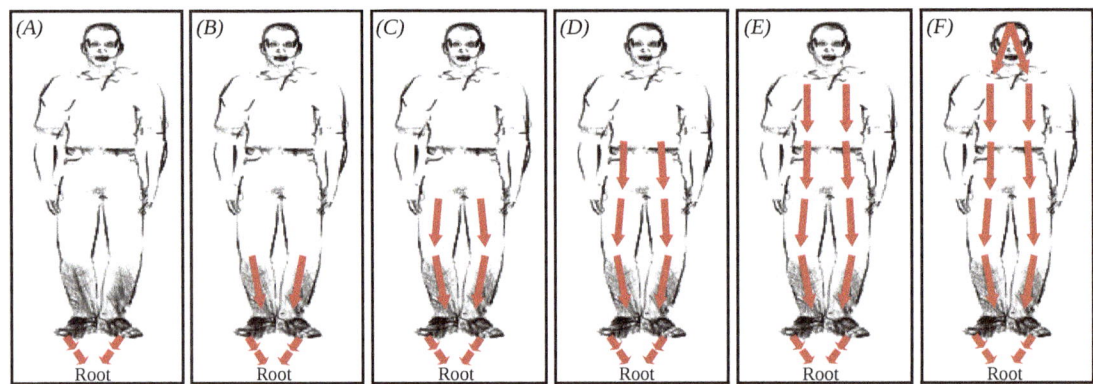

Second Stage of the Opening & Closing Exercise

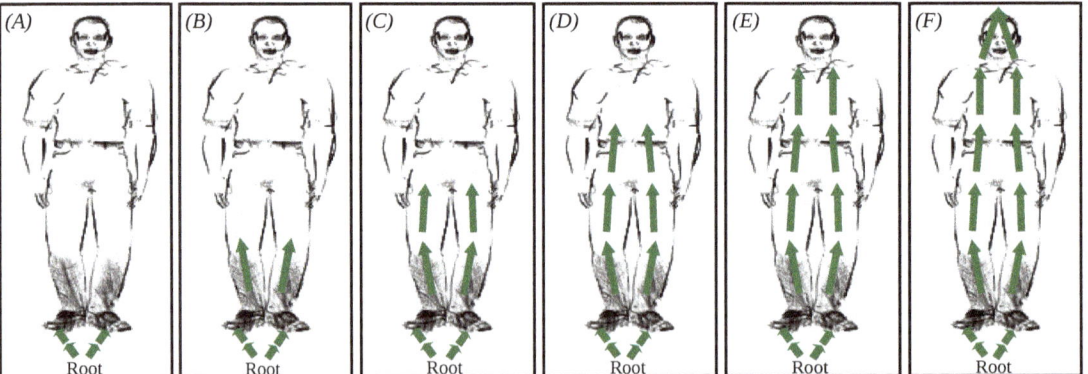

You may also notice throughout the book I have only designated one root. The reason, the substantial leg is the only leg that can access the root. It's impossible for the insubstantial leg to connect to the root directly. However, when both legs are 50/50 such as the stance used above or in the Wu Chi stance, both legs can access the one root. Throughout the book you will have noticed that I constantly interchange opening with relaxing upward and the same with closing and relaxing downward. The reason is a lot of students aren't accustomed to the term Opening and Closing and I wanted the reader to become familiar and comfortable with linking Opening and Closing to the different directions relaxation takes.

One last thing, I have also gone against tradition and moved the glossary from the back to the front of the book. It makes sense to me, for the reader to become familiar and acquainted with the definition of a word before reading the book.

Glossary

Adhere / *Jamming* / *Neutralise*
To stick to your opponent's root so they can't release.

Alignment / *Posture* / *Technique*
Allowing the joints of the entire body to align with each other in various poses so as to encourage the free flow of Gravity, Relaxation and Chi.

Adjustment
Adjustment is the moment between relaxation and physical movement.

Awareness / *Consciousness* / *Mindfulness*
Awareness monitors and observes the body and its place in relation to the constantly changing moment. Awareness can be likened to driving home from work. You're aware of the traffic conditions, speed and dashboard instrumentation while simultaneously maintaining your intent to lead you home. Tai Chi requires both intent and awareness, in the same moment.

Axis
The Cambridge Dictionary definition of an axis is "a real or imaginary straight line going through the centre of an object that is spinning or a line that divides a symmetrical shape into two equal halves". Therefore the physical axis in Tai Chi would be considered the vertical centre *(sagittal plane)* that is, the spine.

Bottom / *Stagnated Root* / *Double Weightedness*
A bottom is where opening & closing ceases interacting. The closing process stops in the root, which in turn causes the Relaxation, Chi, Gravity and Li to stagnate *(double weightedness)*.

Bubbling Well / *Base* / *Jing Well* / *Kidney 1* / *Yongquan* / *Gushing Spring*
The access point between your body and your root *(like a manhole cover between your body and your root or a plinth that separates the statue from the ground)*. It's located on the sole of the foot, 1/3 of the way from the base of the second toe and 2/3 of the way up from the bottom of the foot between the second and third metatarsals.

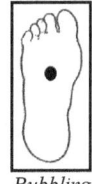
Bubbling Well

Capturing the Opponent's Root
Taking control of your opponent's root either by closing *(shearing their bubbling well)* into their root or by opening *(drawing them forward off their bubbling well)* and drawing them forward of their root.

Central Equilibrium / *Zhongzheng*
Cambridge Dictionary defines equilibrium as "a state of balance between opposing forces". The Cambridge Dictionary also defines central as "in or near the centre of something". The centre of the individual in Tai Chi, unlike the axis, is in reference to weight and not structure. Therefore when referring to Central Equilibrium in relation to Tai Chi it is in reference to the vertical median plane of the weighted leg, expanding vertically upwards from the bubbling well and not necessarily from the centre of the body *(axis)* unless weight is evenly distributed between both feet. Opening & Closing process creates substantial and insubstantial in the body and therefore maintains and promotes a stable Central Equilibrium within the body.

Chi / *Qi*
The traditional definition of Chi derives from a Chinese traditional medical word. The Ocean Dictionary defines Chi as, "vital energy or energy that circulates throughout the body". It is this Chi

that helps keep the body in optimal health. This form of Chi is in reference to Chinese medical sciences such as acupuncture, herbalism, massage and bone setting. However it is not the Chi that creates movement in Tai Chi. From a more contemporary and practical view point, Chi exists in many states of energy, depending on the context of the subject, Chi can vary accordingly. It can be a combination of relaxation and borrowing the Chi of the earth *(gravity)* which is used in the generation of movement in Tai Chi. Chi can also be considered energy from a blow or push from an opponent. Chi embraces all forms of energy such as heat, light, wind, food, architecture *(feng shui)*, thought, relaxation, intent and awareness. Chi *(energy)* is infinite.

Chi of the Earth / *Di Xin Xi Yin Li*
Gravity.

Circulating the Chi
Relaxation circulating around the body facilitates the circulation of many forms of Chi, internal and external.

Closing / *Relaxing Downward* / *Yin* / *Drawing Down* / *Substantiality Vertically*
Closing is when one relaxes muscles in combination with gravity's effect on body mass. Directed by the intent through the bubbling well into the root and applied within a circular vertical plane. Closing can only be generated through the substantial leg. The exception to this rule is when the feet are in a neutral stance such as the second movement of the form, Preparation, where weight is 50/50. Closing *(relaxing downward)* will be represented by a red downward pointing arrow.

Collapsing
When one has excessively disengaged muscle beyond relaxation causing surrounding joints and alignments to collapse or protrude.

Cross Alignment
Using the same root *(substantial leg)* from which to open and float the opponent off their bubbling well *(drawing out)* while simultaneously opening to release the opponent.

Cun / *Tsun* / *Chinese Inch*
Cun is often referred to as the Chinese inch. It's a traditional Chinese unit of length, the width of a person's thumb which is considered 1 cun long. The width of the two forefingers is 1.5 cun long and the width of four fingers side-by-side is three cun long. These unit measurements are taken in relation to the individual's own hand size.

Cutting the Opponent's Root
When you have closed *(relaxing downward)* from below into the opponent's root, causing their weight to shift slightly off their bubbling well towards their heel.

Dan Tien
Regarded in the Taoist Arts as the Elixir Field or the Sea of Chi. Located three finger width below the navel three and two finger width inward.

Double Weightedness / *Double Heaviness*
When the internal process of Opening *(relaxing upward)* & Closing *(relaxing downward)* stops interacting with each other. Opening & Closing stopping, is caused by one of three reasons; Misalignment *(physical)*, Intent *(mental)* and Awareness *(relaxation)*.

Drawing the Opponent Out / *Void*
Opening *(drawing them out by emptying)* to leading the opponent forward causing them to shift their weight slightly forward of their bubbling well.

Elongation / *Adjustments / Lengthening / Stretching*
Elongation is defined as the condition, act, or process of becoming longer. In biology, the phrase is commonly used to describe a biological process in which a biological entity is made longer. In Tai Chi the body frequently elongates, especially in relation to the spine when opening *(relaxing upward)* and closing *(relaxing downward)* are applied to the body.

Emptiness / *Insubstantiality / Weightlessness*
There are two forms of Emptiness that are relevant to Tai Chi. There is Relative Emptiness. This is when one side or part of the body is lighter in relation to its opposite side. Often used to determine or display which part of the body is the lightest. For example if the front leg has 30% weight then it would be considered the empty leg compared to the rear leg, and as long as the weight stays below 49% it remains the empty leg. Functional Emptiness is the second form of emptiness and is the one that's used in the generation of movement in Tai Chi. When weight travelling down the front leg pulls the body forward causing the rear leg to become empty to the point where weight moving down the front leg cancels the weight of the rear leg itself, acting similar to a counter weight. When this happens the functionally empty rear leg moves requiring no thought or muscle. Another example of functional emptiness in the upper body is when shoulder blades slide downward acting as a counter weight to the arms making the arms functionally empty.

Energy
Energy is in a constant state of change and movement, when left unobstructed or unopposed.

Fa-Jing / *Issuing / Releasing*
When energy is released from the root after reaching full compression. Fa Jing can only be expressed physically when in relation to an opponent *(push hands)* and cannot be demonstrated within the constrains of the form.

Following
When the opponent physically withdraws and you follow with your root and then your body.

Force
Force is the result when energy has been obstructed, resisted or opposed.

Form
Is a collection of postures brought together to create a form.

Forward Ball and Socket Rotation
When the ball and socket joints of the hips and shoulders rotate forward. Forward rotation prevents the correct circulation of relaxation *(opening & closing)* through the body.

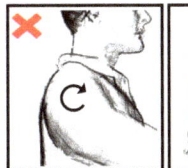 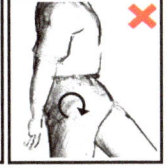

Forward Shoulder Rotation   *Forward Hip Rotation*

Full Compression / *Extreme Yin*
When relaxation in combination with sinking is led into the root by the intent to the point where it's no longer possible to continue the downward relaxation *(closing)* process without buckling, jamming joints or creating muscle tension. Full compression can only be created under the substantial leg.

Grounding
When closing *(relaxing downward)* passes into the ground without intent leading the relaxation.

Head Suspended
In most Tai Chi postures the crown of the head can be considered the extreme upper most physical point of your mass *(similar to the top of a plumb-bob)*. The exception to this is when body weight is uneven such as in Bend Low and Punch where the utmost top point of your mass and central

equilibrium would now be located between the upper shoulder blades. Suspending from the crown of the head prevents joints from jamming when applying Opening and Closing, allowing the vertebrae to adjust individually and collectively. Keeping spine, joints and root open allows the free flow of relaxation and chi helping in the prevention of double weightedness.

Horizontal Hinge Point / *Horizontal Pivot Point* / *Horizontal Axis Point*
As the name suggests a hinge allows movement along one plane. In Tai Chi the Hinge Point applied to a horizontal plane *(transverse plane)*. This horizontal plane is allowed by the insubstantial kua or empty kua to physically open and close much like a hinge does. However, only the substantial kua by opening and closing can and does create the energy that powers all horizontal movement, the empty kua only allows horizontal action. If the empty leg is touching the floor in any way the horizontal hinge point is taken from the empty kua. If however, the empty leg leaves the ground in any way the substantial kua then also acts as the horizontal hinge point.

Horizontal Circle
Horizontal Circle is generated by a vertical circle moving up and down the substantial leg, which in turn instigates the kuas to physically open and close, hence generating a horizontal circle *(action)*.

Horizontal Substantial and Insubstantial / *Rocking Forward and Backwards*
Weight moving forwards and backwards without applying opening and closing.

Internal Centre
Internal Centre is the point of most resistance within the body. Which is in constant flux due to the variable changes in your root caused by internal and external factors. The centre is not to be confused with the median plane of the body.

Intent / *Will*
Intent is considered more Yang. Intent leads the relaxation into the root which leads the chi and the chi leads the body and inner strength. Intent gives the relaxation an end point to gather so it can reach full compression. Intent doesn't move chi, relaxation helps facilitate the movement of chi, intent leads the chi.

Isolated Body Movement
Any internal and physical movement that doesn't emanate from your root.

Issuing / *True Yang Rises* / *Fa Jing* / *Releasing*
The manifestation of Opening and Closing within Extreme Yin or Extreme Yang.

Join
Capturing your opponent's root so completely as to have and share one connection to gravity through you. When you and your opponent become a single integrated 4 legged animal where you have complete control.

Kua / *Hips*
The kua is technically the area between the Greater trochanter up to the bottom of the 12th floating rib. However, the kua in Tai Chi is often referred to as the hip area.

Lead
When yielding to an opponent's push and leading them into a position that is unfavourable to them.

Li / *Strength* / *Body* / *Physical*
Strength either physical or internal *(pronounced as Lee)*.

Neutralise / *Adhering* / *Jamming*
The common definition of Neutralise is taking an opponent's energy/force into the ground is only half correct. Taking your opponent's force into the ground doesn't necessarily mean you've neutralised your opponent's force. You've only truly neutralised your opponent when you have directed their force into the ground behind them. The Cambridge dictionary correctly defines Neutralise as: "to stop something or someone from having an effect"

Opening / *Relaxing Upward* / *Sung Up* / *Insubstantiality Vertically*
Opening can only happen when one has reached full compression within the root, preceded by a deeper relaxation, causing a wave of relaxation to expand from the root in an upward direction. This in turn leads the chi upward within a circular vertical plane. Opening can be generated only through the substantial leg and only after reaching full compression *(full relaxation)*. Opening *(relaxing upward)* will be displayed as a green upward pointing arrow. ↑

Opening & Closing / *Hun Yuan Zhuang* / *Up and Down Exercise* / *Vertical Circle*
A process which is created when relaxation moves in a vertical circular plane in a never ending loop. This circulation of closing and opening creates substantial and insubstantial beyond the simple concept of moving weight horizontally, forward to back or from side to side. This circulation moves vertically with no forward, no back, no left, no right, no top, no bottom, no beginning and no end, it is created by awareness *(relaxation)* and directed by intent *(will)*.

Pivot Point / *Still Point* / *Balance Point* / *Yin & Yang Point* / *Vertical Axis Point*
The pivot point is the point where Opening *(Yang)* and Closing *(Yin)* are interchanging. Pivot Points are always generated by Opening and Closing. In Push Hands it's usually the aim of the practitioner to make it the primary point of contact with their opponent. It's the point where energies change direction where drawing out and releasing can happen simultaneously. Pivot points are usually the last physical point to move in Tai Chi.

Posture
Is created by a collection of numerous alignments brought together to create a posture.

Pull
An energy source in front of an object that generates movement *(example is a front wheel drive car)*.

Push
An energy source behind an object that generates movement *(example is a rear wheel drive car)*.

Push Hands / *Partner Work* / *Tui Shou*
Applying Tai Chi principles to a two person exercise which involves one person attacking and their partner then applies the counter technique. Roles are then reversed, the defender becomes the attacker and the attacker becomes the defender. The purpose of this exercise is to develop listening, yielding, relaxation, sticking, adhering, following, joining, intent and issuing.

Relaxation / *Letting Go* / *Sung* / *Softening*
Being physically, mentally and emotionally in balance with the immediate moment and what this moment requires. To be balanced neither excessive *(tense)* or deficient *(lifeless)*. Taoist saying "One must be in harmony *(balance)* with the universe *(the moment)*. To be fully physically relaxed in Tai Chi means to disengage as much muscle as possible, without jamming joints or collapsing alignment or structure.

Rooting / *Connecting to the Ground*
When closing *(relaxation downward)* is led through the body's alignment and bubbling well into the ground by intent.

Reverse Ball and Socket Rotation
Is when the ball and socket joints of the hips and shoulders rotate backwards. This is critical in Tai Chi for the maintenance of alignment and the redirection of relaxation through the body allowing you to create an external duality of yielding and attacking.

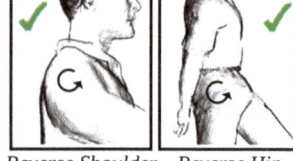
Reverse Shoulder Rotation   Reverse Hip Rotation

Sinking / *Closing / Relaxation / Drawing Down*
Gravity's effect on the body mass when muscles are relaxed, causing an internal drawing down sensation through the body.

Softening the Root
As one reaches full compression the need to soften the root is critical. This allows extreme Yin to turn to Yang. Preventing a bottom from developing, hence preventing double weightedness.

Sticking
Maintaining physical contact with your opponent.

Synchronise / *Timing / Adjustment*
When all parts of the body are moving in total relationship *(harmony)* to each other whether in solo practise or in partner work. Also when Yi Chi Li moves in perfect harmony.

Tai Chi
The physical manifestation of Taoist principles in action.

TCM / *Traditional Chinese Medicine*
Traditional Chinese Medicine covers such modalities as Acupuncture, Chinese Herbs, Bone Setting, Moxibustion, Massage, Cupping, Qi Gong and Tai Chi.

Tension / *Holding / Resistance*
Using more muscle than the physical activity *(moment)* requires.

Top / *Double Weightedness*
A top is where the opening process has been allowed to stop at the crown of the head which in turn causes the Chi and Li to stagnate *(double weightedness)*.

Two Points of Release within the Cycle of Opening & Closing *(pivots)*
There are two points of release within the form from Yin to Yang and Yang to Yin. In other words, when closing is in the process of changing to opening and opening is in the process of changing to closing *(often referred to as pivot points)*. Such as moving from yielding to attacking and attacking to yielding. I have shown the exact spot on the Yin/Yang *(refer diagram a)*. Most people tend to release at Greater Yin or Greater Yang. The correct points to release from is Extreme Yin and Extreme Yang. It's the point where you are at your most physically still.

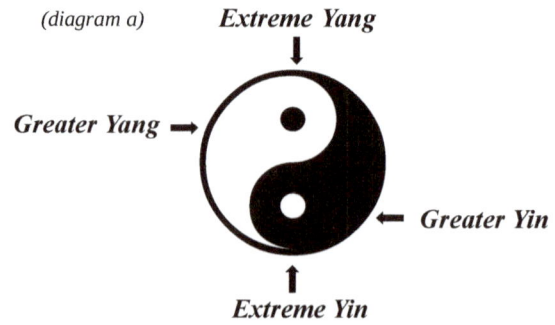

Two Thirds Rule
The two thirds rule is the point on the body when opening begins to close in the root. It is located two thirds up the body *(chest or shoulder blade height)* from the root. The two thirds rule prevents a top developing hence preventing Double Weightedness. If you were to begin the closing process only after opening had reached the crown of the head, then for a second opening and closing will have stopped, leading to double weightedness.

Unify
Another word for synchronise.

Vertebra
The spine has 33 vertebrae, nine of which fuse together, leaving only 24 with the ability to adjust.

Vertical Circle Creates a Horizontal Circle
Where a vertical *(circle)* action *(gravity)* is led through a specific alignment (Kua) creating a horizontal *(circle)* turning action.

Vertical Substantial and Insubstantial / *Vertical Circle*
Weight moving forward and back through a vertical plane by means of Opening and Closing.

When to Issue when to Yield
Dictated by your opponent. If you have captured the opponent's root then issue. If you haven't then either close to cut their root or yield and draw them off their root. Waves of relaxation moving downward is closing, waves moving upward is opening. Closing is Yin and Opening is Yang.

Wu Wei
Non Action or Non Doing. Just being in the moment and staying in relation to what the moment requires.

Yi / *Intent / Will*
Intent pronounced as *(Yee)*

Yielding / *Internally*
Allowing an energy to pass through the body for the purpose of preventing a force building on the body. Achieved by correctly applying Opening or Closing.

Yielding / *Physically / Retreating*
Physically moving backward for the purpose of preventing a force building on the body, sacrificing ground to your opponent in the process.

Yin & Yang
A Taoist concept that generically represents elements of equal opposites within the universe

Contents

1	Tai Chi Defined	2
2	Chi *(Qi) (Energy)*	4
3	Non-use of Muscle in the Creation of Movement Using Wu Wei	10
4	Tai Chi Li *(Strength)*	16
5	Relaxation	25
6	Opening and Closing	31
7	Different Qualities of Opening	44
8	Tai Chi and Speed	52
9	The Symbiotic Relationship Between Opening, Closing, Substantial, Insubstantial and Movement	57
10	Intent *(Yi)*	64
11	Push Hands *(Partner Work)*	72
12	Form	88
13	Alignments	93
14	Linear and Collective Alignments	96
15	Stepping in Tai Chi	109
16	The Classics	113
17	Following the Cause, Effect and Sequential Order From Wu Chi to Tai Chi	116
18	Opening and Closing Exercise and the Five Loosening Exercises	121

What exactly is Tai Chi? Is it a Philosophy, a Martial Art, a Meditation, an Exercise, Qi Gong or Traditional Chinese Medicine or all the above?

1. Tai Chi Defined

Ask your average Tai Chi teacher or practitioner what is Tai Chi, and you'll likely get the stock standard response; "Tai Chi is an Internal Martial Art whose origins can be traced back to ancient China. Performed at a slow pace incorporating relaxation, deep breathing, awareness, concentration and various postures, all the while being mindful of circulating the chi". While this description accurately outlines aspects of Tai Chi, and lists worthy qualities, you're still really none the wiser.

In essence, Tai Chi is based and grounded in Taoist *(Daoist)* philosophy, therefore logic dictates **Tai Chi is the physical manifestation of Taoist principles in action.** Unlike Buddhism, Confucianism, Sufism, Shintoism, Shamanism, New Ageism and especially not Capitalism, *(although you could be forgiven for thinking it was these days)*. Tai Chi roots can be traced back to the writings of Lao Tsu who wrote a Treatise around 400BC called Tao Te Ching *(Way of Virtue)*, a book based on humanity's interaction with nature. Scholars still debate if it was written by one person or a collection of authors or even the exact date of its writing. Taoism can be broken essentially into two categories. In the first there's Taoist philosophy *(Dao Jia)* which is based on the Tao Te Ching a book that I have constantly referred to, throughout my time in Tai Chi. Then there is the second category, Taoist religion *(Tao Jiao)* which became an organisation consisting of Rituals, Deities, Ceremonies, Reincarnation, Clergy and Canon. I believe the two are totally distinct to each other, with the latter incorporating past superstitions and religions of China into Taoism, therefore effectively transforming it from a philosophy to a religion. I live fifteen minutes from the largest Taoist Temple in the Southern Hemisphere. Tours are often conducted through the Temple, explaining Taoism and the various Gods and what they represent. Joining a tour once, I asked the tour leader where did all these Gods come from, as there is no mention of them in the Tao Te Ching. I was informed that many years after the Tao Te Ching was written it was enlarged to incorporate various Gods including the many rituals allowing individuals to show respect and seek favour from these Deities.

The health benefits of physical exercise in the West are explained from the view point of Western Medicine and Physiology and rightfully so. Tai Chi being a Taoist art, originating in China, you would expect the health benefits to be explained through the theory of Traditional Chinese Medicine. I understand how this came about and T.C.M does have a role to play in Tai Chi. However, it is crucial to recognise that the chi in T.C.M will sometimes differ from the chi referred to in Tai Chi. Traditional Chinese Medicine views chi as an intrinsic vital energy within the body that works harmoniously in keeping the human body alive and in optimum health. Tai Chi doesn't limit itself to this definition of chi *(vital chi)* in T.C.M, but has its own definitions of Chi. Tai Chi literature will often refer to the Chi of the Earth *(the West calls this form of chi, gravity)*. I suspect, over the years, Tai Chi teachers lacking detailed understanding how speed, movement and so called power, is created by the application of Taoist concepts have turned to Traditional Chinese Medicine or Qi Gong theory to fill the gaps in their knowledge. Being a Traditional Chinese Medicine practitioner myself, it would be very easy for me to fill this book with countless pages of T.C.M when it comes to explaining Tai Chi. T.C.M theory, though useful for explaining the many health benefits of Tai Chi, **cannot explain how power, speed and movement are generated.** That theory is a stand alone theory that clearly belongs to Tai Chi and its Taoist roots. To truly understand and train Tai Chi we need to embrace the Taoist method of Wu Wei *(Non-action)*. An old Tai Chi proverb states, "Tai Chi is the art of unlearning". Unlearning or letting go of bias preconceived ideas of power, speed and movement is **absolutely necessary** before we can take on the mental and physical attributes of Tai Chi. An old Zen proverb comes to mind; "You must first empty your cup, before it can be filled".

We have clarified and defined Tai Chi as the physical manifestation of Taoist principles in action, the next question is, which chi powers the movements of Tai Chi?

Chi, what is it, and what function does it play in Tai Chi?

2. Chi *(Qi)* *(Energy)*

The history and origins of chi, as with a lot of Chinese history, can be vague and ambiguous at times. There is mention of chi in the I Ching *(Book of Changes)*. Also Tung Chung-Shu *(179–104 BC politician, philosopher)* speaks of Earth as the controller of nothing, but being the central authority of the four seasons. He writes **"The Earth is the controller of the five elements and without the chi of the soil** *(nutrients)* **nothing can be accomplished. Everything comes from the chi of the Earth. Without the Earth's chi none of the seasons or elements would be possible"**.

The word chi, pronounced *chee,* and often spelt "qi". The first Western translation can be traced back to George Soulie' De Morant who was one of the first of numerous German, French and European scholars who encountered the word chi and attempted to write discourses on its meaning and its implications.

George Soulie' De Morant was born in Paris in 1879, and studied Traditional Chinese Medicine in Yunnan province. After many years of studying, he was the first Westerner to be awarded a Doctorate of Chinese Medicine by the Chinese, and in 1917 returned to Europe, dying in May 1955. He wrote two books on T.C.M *(Traditional Chinese Medicine)*. They were "I' Acupuncture Chinoise" and "Palmistry Chinoise." His translation of Chi is considered one of the first and most accurate translations of Chi in relation to T.C.M.

Traditional Chinese Character for Chi

The Chinese dictionary Han Yu Da Zi Dian has more than 20 distinct definitions of Chi. The everyday translation of Chi from a Chinese/English dictionary means ***vapours or gases.*** The Chinese character or ideogram for Chi is a pictogram of a cauldron on a fire with the lid half lifted by the pressure of the escaping vapour. The Chinese call cars "Chi Che". Translated it means "vapourish carriage." However, the Chinese Traditional Medical Word - Ocean Dictionary has a slightly different and specialised meaning, but the description is virtually the same as that of George Soulie' De Morant nearly a century earlier. He defines Chi as ***vital energy or energy***. This form of Chi is in reference to medical arts such as acupuncture, herbalism, massage and bone setting.

Feng Shui, the practice of Chinese Geomancy, introduces another definition of chi. Feng Shui is the method for harmonising universal energy by the placement of various items in and around a structure, in the belief it encourages the flow of chi through a building in a way that favours the occupants achieving prosperity, happiness and health. If we were to use the definition of chi from T.C.M and applied it to Feng Shui then we would assume that the Feng Shui means of harmonising chi within a building is by ripping the chi from our bodies and moving it around a building. Obviously the chi Feng Shui is referring to isn't the same chi in T.C.M or the chi that the Chinese dictionary defines as gases/vapour, or the chi that Tung Chung Shu refers to, as elemental nutrients of the soil.

Back in 1983 when I was studying Acupuncture and T.C.M in our local Chinatown, a local Chinese businessman who ran a business from a three storey building, flew a Feng Shui expert in from Hong Kong at great expense to Feng Shui his building. The businessman proceeded to knock down walls and moved windows, all under the guidance of the Feng Shui expert, so chi would move freely through the building in the hope it would improve business. The end result: the business went broke. The businessman had a reputation for dishonesty, poor service and inferior products. Feng Shui can assist up to a point. So at last count, we have four different definitions of chi and still counting.

The word chi undergoes contextual shifts, depending on the context in which it's used. When De Morant first translated the word "chi" it was in reference to T.C.M. He was alluding to the chi *(vital chi)* that travels through meridians. Meridians are "pathways of energy" that flow through the body along which acupuncture points are positioned. These meridians and the theory behind them are important if you wish to understand the process of how Tai Chi improves one's health. De Morant correctly translated this form of chi in relation to Traditional Chinese Medicine, denoting both the essential substances of the human body which maintain its vital activities, and functional activities of the Zang-Fu *(solid-hollow)* organs and tissues. From there, the chi can be divided into four distinct forms within the body. They are:

1. **Yuan chi** *(primary chi)* This chi is derived from congenital essence and constantly needs to be replenished and nourished by absorbing Ying chi *(food)*. Yuan chi is basically the chi that one inherits from one's parents and resides in the kidneys.
2. **Zong chi** *(pectoral chi)* is created by the combination of Da chi *(air)* and Gu chi *(food)* and resides in the lungs.
3. **Ying chi** *(nutrient chi)* This chi is essentially derived from the essence of food and is produced by the spleen and the stomach and is circulated through the blood.
4. **Wei chi** *(defensive chi)* This chi circulates outside the vessels and runs along the surface of the skin and protects the body from external pathogenic factors.

The chi that circulates through the body is a combination of Yuan chi, Zong chi, Ying chi and Wei chi. This chi of the meridians is referred to as True chi *(vital chi)*. We could break it down even further but it would serve no purpose. This is sufficient to give a basic understanding of chi within T.C.M. When the following schools of thought, Yin and Yang, Five Elements and theory of Chi were brought together, it formed the basis of Traditional Chinese Medicine. Translation of chi went from Chinese to French, from French to English. The T.C.M definition of chi became the standard definition used, in Tai Chi literature. It was automatically assumed it was in reference to the Chinese Traditional Medical Word Ocean Dictionary definition which is vital energy or vital force that moves through the meridians or breath, Zong chi *(pectoral chi)*. These forms of chi are considered necessary for life and optimal health. Note the different definition of chi in comparison to the English/Chinese dictionary version which refers to chi as vapours or gases. Two different meanings of chi, one medical and one used in general terms. When explaining chi in relation to Tai Chi most people default to the chi defined by De Morant. When discussing chi in Tai Chi it is crucial to clarify the context to which chi is being referred. In Tai Chi there are numerous forms of chi. Each form of chi has a purpose and function within Tai Chi. Some forms of chi are specific to the promotion of health and other forms of chi are used for generating movement, speed and so-called power. You need to be clear about which form of chi you are referring to when discussing chi in Tai Chi.

It would be the equivalent of enrolling at your State University and informing the front desk you want to study energy. I'm certain the reply from the administrator would be, to what form of energy are you referring, is it electrical, nuclear, hydro, etc. The T.C.M form of chi is perfect for explaining how the health benefits of Tai Chi are achieved. For example, when one relaxes in Tai Chi the muscles soften, encouraging blood circulation which nourishes the vital chi which in turns drives the blood. When deep breathing is incorporated, the Da chi is increased which is beneficial for Zong chi. As good as T.C.M is in explaining the health benefits of Tai Chi, it's not possible to use T.C.M definition of chi to explain how movement, power and speed is generated within Tai Chi. This is why I find it slightly curious when people discuss chi, as if there is only one form of chi in Tai Chi. There are many forms of chi at work in Tai Chi. Some forms of chi promote health, other forms of chi generate movement, speed and so called power.

Circulating the Chi *(Qi)*
Much has been written about circulating the chi in Tai Chi, a point with which I'm in total agreement. You do need to circulate the chi in Tai Chi; however we need to define which chi we're circulating and the methodology we use. Fortunately circulating the chi and the method we use in Tai Chi is quite simple, but don't confuse simple with easy. There are so many theories for circulating the chi; here are just a few examples. Some practitioners of Tai Chi focus on drawing their vital chi into their Dan Tien by means of using their consciousness. Once this vital chi is sufficiently built up to the point where the Dan Tien is full, it's then released from the Dan Tien throughout the body via the meridians for the purpose of improving one's health and to generate movement, power or strength by means of releasing this stored energy in the form of jing *(fa-jing)*. Another common method used to circulate the chi is the microcosmic orbit method. A basic explanation of the microcosmic orbit starts with deep abdominal breathing *(pectoral chi)* to help increase the vital chi which is then directed by the mind upwards through the Du meridian which runs up the centre of the spine over the middle of the skull and finishes a centimetre above the top lip. The tongue is pressed against the palate to help bridge the chi between the Du and Ren meridian. The chi then moves down the Ren meridian to the Dan Tien, from the Dan Tien to the base of spine where the process is then repeated.

This is in comparison to Western concepts of exercise, like aerobics, which requires fast physical movement, for the specific purpose of engaging the pulmonary, cardiovascular and circulatory systems, therefore improving your level of health and fitness. You don't need to know the intricate workings of the lungs, heart and circulatory systems to enjoy the health benefits of exercise. Does your personal trainer ask you to stand still and tell you to use your consciousness to move the blood around your body or to increase your heart rate? No. What they have you do is exercise, moving the body, working the body faster, harder, resulting in your lungs sucking in more air, your heart beating faster and stronger and your blood circulation improving. In other words just exercise and everything will look after itself. You don't need to know how everything works, all you need to know is what makes it work is physical movement. Similarly, I believe in Tai Chi: the focus should be on the cause of movement and not necessarily on the details of chi circulation.

When circulating the chi, you really don't need to focus on the vital chi or the meridians or what direction the chi moves *(chi managed to move okay, before you even knew anything, about chi or meridians)*. What matters is what facilitates the movement of various forms of chi in your body. Relaxation with no beginning, no end, always continuous, fits the bill perfectly. Just focus on relaxation and the chi will look after itself.

The following Classics confirms this in Explanation Of The Thirteen Postures By Wang Chung-Yueh; "The aim of the whole body is to conserve spirit *(spirit and intent are often interchanged, more on this subject in Chapter 10 Intent)* and not intrinsic energy, for if you are fixated on the energy, your movement will become sluggish. Whenever your mind is on the energy, there will be no power, whereas if you ignore the energy it will take care of itself, there will be pure strength. Intrinsic energy is the rim of the wheel, the waist is the hub of the wheel".

The Chi that Creates Physical Movement in Tai Chi
My teacher Wee Kee Jin told me that Master Huang would often use the phrase **Di Xin Xi Yin Li** when teaching Tai Chi. Chinese language doesn't have a single word or Chinese character for gravity, their equivalent is Di Xin Xi Yin Li. Translated it means **Di**-Ground *(地面)*, **Xin**-Centre, *(中心)*, **Xi**-Absorb *(吸收)*, **Yin**-Attract *(吸引)*, **Li**-Power or Strength *(力量)*, this is the term he would often use, when referring to borrowing the chi of the Earth *(a fifth definition of chi has now been added to the list)*. When I first started learning Tai Chi, I was taught that I needed to borrow the chi of the Earth when it came to generating movement in Tai Chi. I remember thinking to myself, there's no energy coming out

of the Earth that I can borrow, that would help me to physically move. Once again my biased and preconceived ideas stood in the way of my understanding. It took me quite a few years to realise I wasn't taking chi from the Earth, but in fact I was being pulled by *(borrowing)* the chi of the Earth. When you use the term "borrow" you automatically assume your taking or acquiring something. If I was to ask you, can I borrow $5 It would involve me taking *(borrowing)* $5 from you. However, borrowing can also mean to be pulled along. For example, when driving, you'll often see push bike riders slip in behind a truck and borrow the energy of the truck by means of riding the vehicle's slipstream. Another example, in my youth I used to surf, often I would borrow the energy of a rip tide to pull myself out behind the breakers and then catch a wave back to the beach. On both occasions I have borrowed the chi/energy of the ocean by being **pulled** out by the rip tide and **pushed** back to the beach by a wave. I had been training Tai Chi for around a decade before the penny finally dropped. Energy, when borrowed, can be expressed by either pushing or pulling in nature. What's the difference between pushing and pulling? The most common answer given, if I was to extend my hand away from myself then that would be considered a push, if I bring that same hand back towards myself then it's a pull. Breaking this concept down even further, **if the energy that moves an object is behind it, then it's a push** *(surfing a wave in)*, **if the energy is in front of the object it moves, then it's a pull** *(rip tide pulling me out)*. If we agree that gravity is what generates movement in Tai Chi then we need to accept the fact that we are being pulled in Tai Chi, not pushed and this applies to push hands. This understanding requires us to change the fundamental way we view and understand movement in Tai Chi and the chi we use. Recognising the subtleties of chi, both in circulation and in its role as a source of movement, improves our comprehension of Tai Chi principles and fosters a deeper understanding of the energies in play

An Explanation Of The Thirteen Postures by Wang Ts'ung–Yueh confirms the chi of Di Xin Xi Yin Li: 發勁須沉著鬆淨，專主一方。 "To deliver strength one must remain calm and relaxed and allow the centre of gravity to sink downward. One must be able to focus *(lead with intent)* this energy in a single direction". Without this form of chi, Di Xin Xi Yin Li movement and so called power in Tai Chi just isn't possible. You can perform the movements of Tai Chi in outer space, but not the principles, due to the lack of gravity in space. Tai Chi is not a movement, it's a principle of movement based on non-action which allows the chi of the Earth to create the movement for us. I feel this form of chi has been grossly overlooked in the rush to the more widely accepted chi of T.C.M. At best Di Xin Xi Yin Li *(gravity)* is given only token acknowledgement. When discussing or referring to chi there's a real need to be clear and specific about which chi one is referring to.

The Chinese have difficulty understanding their own written language from only a few hundred years ago, because of the need to know the context of the Chinese characters that's being used. English also has a similar problem. If I were to say that the weather is quite cool today, I would be referring to the temperature of the day. But if I had said that Steve is quite a cool guy, then I would be referring to his attitude and persona. My teacher Wee Kee Jin has in his possession large volumes of notes on Tai Chi written by his teacher Master Huang. To translate these notes into English would be very laborious, because it's not as simple as hiring a translator. The Master's dialect was a mix and more importantly you have to understand the context of the words that he's used, and be familiar with his theories and approach to Tai Chi. So a person from another Tai Chi school wouldn't necessarily be able to translate the full contents accurately. It needs to be someone who is not only fluent in Chinese and English, but also a senior student who has trained under him for numerous years, who is familiar with his methods, concepts and theories. Language is a living entity that's constantly changing and evolving and nuances can be easily lost in translation. You need to be very careful, especially when using words that have multiple meanings, where context of the sentence can change the meaning of a word. This is especially true when translating from Chinese into English. Therefore a lot can and has, been mistranslated or misunderstood from old Chinese to modern Chinese, modern Chinese to English. So translating Chinese to English the translator not only has to be fluent in Chinese and English, but need to have expertise on the subject that is specific to its origin and lineage they're translating from. The creation of movement in Tai Chi is based on borrowing the chi of the Earth *(gravity)*.

In Tai Chi we forgo the use of muscle to generate movement unlike other sports and activities. Gravity is a constant, rated as 1G-force, from the time of our birth to our death. Muscle strength on the other hand increases and deteriorates with the ageing process. By linking your strength and movement to muscle you'll only become weaker and slower with age. Our own Yuan chi *(primary chi)* also deteriorates with ageing. Only one form of chi stays constant in life Di Xin Xi Yin Li *(gravity)*. By linking your movement and so called power to Di Xin Xi Yin Li *(gravity)* ensures a sustained and consistent source of strength and speed throughout one's life, there will be no decline in movement, speed and power normally associated with the ageing process. In fact, you could argue, as you age, your muscles naturally become weaker and softer, enhancing the movement of the Earth's Chi *(gravity)* through the softer and more relaxed muscle, therefore fostering qualities essential in Tai Chi.

A question I often ask my students: how do you know when a process is correct when trying to achieve an objective. This objective could be business, relationships or simply, exercising? Most people would reason that if you achieve the results that you've set for your objective, then the process must have been correct. You would be half right, but for the process to be entirely correct it also needs to be **sustainable**. I live in Australia; 150 years ago it took four to six months to travel from the UK to Australia. Now UK to Australia can be done in 22 hours. Big improvement, great result, but is it sustainable? Not really, we're heating the planet and if we continue to use fossil fuel at our current rate, it will result in catastrophic climate change. Tai Chi ticks all the boxes; it's sustainable and can be performed right up till end of life; you become stronger and more powerful as you age *(power and strength will be explained in upcoming Chapters)*. A truly amazing exercise and martial art.

I often tell students the sensation of moving weight from the back to the front leg in Tai Chi is similar in sensation to walking down a very steep driveway or hill. You can feel your body weight being pulled into the front leg. To regulate and control this forward movement you use your muscles as brakes. This is the opposite to how we normally use our muscles for everyday movement. In Tai Chi we use Di Xin Xi Yin Li *(gravity)* to move us *(not muscles)* and use muscles as the brakes to restrict our movement, and not for propulsion.

To tap into the Chi of the Earth as a source for creating movement, requires certain physical and mental attributes and specific training. These mental and physical qualities are distinct from those developed for muscle-centric activities. The first quality you'll need to learn in Tai Chi is structure *(alignment)* with which to channel and direct the Earth's chi. Secondly a philosophy that encourages and facilitates the movement of this form of chi. Thirdly a mind *(awareness and intent)* that creates and cultivates the borrowing of chi and an intent to lead this chi.

Awareness *(consciousness)* creates relaxation, intent leads this relaxation, relaxation facilitates the movement of many forms of Chi, specifically the Earth's chi *(gravity)* through the body's alignments generating physical movement, what we call Tai Chi.

The Chi of the Earth is constantly pulling on you, by relaxing muscles in various degrees, sequences and speeds, allowing this chi to create sustainable speed, movement and so called power.

We have clarified and defined Tai Chi as the physical manifestation of Taoist principles in action, having qualified the chi that powers all movement in Tai Chi, that being Di Xin Xi Yin Li (gravity). How do we gain access to this power source through the application of Taoist philosophy?

Is it possible to apply Taoist Philosophy to generate Internal and External Movement?

3. The Non-use of Muscle in the Creation of Movement Using Wu Wei *(Non-action, creating action)*

Chapter 2, third paragraph, first line of the Tao Te Ching *"This is why the Sage manages affairs of Non-action and performs wordless teaching"*.
Chapter 43, fourth line of the Tao Te Ching, *"Few in the world attain wordless teaching and the benefit of Non-action"*.
Chapter 63, first and second line of the Tao Te Ching, *"Act through Non-action, Do without doing"*.

How Wu Wei *(Non-action)* and the Chi of the Earth Makes Movement Possible
The quotes from above are from chapters of the Tao Te Ching and are in reference to Wu Wei, Non-action and the benefits of Non-Action. Philosophy of Wu Wei is often explained as giving up one's desires, where one acts spontaneously without thought or outcome of expectations or going with the flow of nature. Another definition states: Wu Wei is the embodiment of the cosmos unfolding spontaneously through the constant fluctuations of the Tao. That all things in the universe, which includes human beings, are in accord with the universe, if unimpeded leads to flourishing. One of Buddhism's most basic tenets is the belief that a major source of human suffering is attachment, *(attachment prevents change)* which is similar to Wu Wei. I could write endless pages on the intricacies and subtleties of Wu Wei for very little practical benefit. When things are all said and done, we're no closer to applying Wu Wei to the internal and physical process of Tai Chi. The Cambridge definition of philosophy is; "the use of reason in understanding such things as the nature of the real world and existence, the use and limits of knowledge and the principles of moral judgement". When a philosophy *(theory)* can be applied to the physical *(physics)* world, and is tested, measured, utilised, repeatable and proven, only then does it cross over to science. Until we can apply the philosophy of Wu Wei to the physical world then it stays just that, a high minded esoteric concept of Taoism that has very little practical connection and benefit to the physical world we live in.

In the following Chapters, you'll be repeatedly shown how Wu Wei generates Speed, Power and Movement. As stated earlier, in the very first Chapter, "Tai Chi is the physical manifestation of Taoist principles in action". For this to happen, we need to apply this key Taoist principle of Wu Wei to Opening and Closing, Five Loosening Exercises, Form and Push Hands, bringing Wu Wei into the physical world. To achieve this, we need to have in place the mechanical process with which we can apply Wu Wei. This responsibility falls to the alignments of the body, not simple alignments, like linear alignment, such as the knees staying aligned with the foot, or front knee staying behind the front foot. But by means of using collective alignments, allowing every joint of the body regardless if it's a hinge joint, ball and socket joint or the spine which is an articulated joint, all moving in relation and in harmony with each other. So when relaxation creates Wu Wei, it doesn't result in the body physically pushing against itself, the ground or your opponent. The mechanical *(alignment)* application of Wu Wei will be covered in Chapter 13 Alignments. Only when Wu Wei is correctly applied to the physical world, do we receive and understand the full benefits of Tai Chi.

How do we apply this theory of Non-Action to Tai Chi? By gently disengaging *(Non-action)* distinct muscles in a specific order, allowing you to borrow the chi of the Earth to create movement *(action)*. Tai Chi unlike other forms of movement, doesn't use muscle to generate movement, instead, Tai Chi uses the chi of the earth *(Di Xin Xi Yin Li) (gravity)* with which to generate movement. Were we to use muscle contraction to generate movement this could be considered an action creating an action, better known as the Third Law of Newtonian Physics, "For every action, there is an equal and opposite re-action" *(two, opposites, sounds like Yin and Yang a bit)*. If I were to press my rear leg against the ground to propel myself forward in Tai Chi, this would be considered a classic example of Newton's Third Law of Motion. Tai Chi tends to lean towards Newton's Law of Universal Gravitation, "that every particle attracts every other particle in the universe with a force that is proportional to the product of their masses and inversely proportional to the square of the distance between their centres. Put simply, two objects with mass will attract each other, to various degrees due to their individual mass and distance to each other. Tai Chi uses Newton's Law of Universal Gravitation to generate movement in conjunction with Wu Wei. Now in saying this, when disengaging muscle, you can't be silly, and disengage every muscle in the body during this process of movement. You still need to maintain your postural muscles to create an equilibrium with gravity while simultaneously disengaging *(relaxing, letting go of muscle you don't require allowing gravity to create movement, which can be considered a non action)* select muscles, allowing gravity to power movement, while simultaneously engaging enough muscle to maintain certain alignments so the chi of the Earth moves through these distinctive alignments which in turn generates and directs movement. A balance of harmonious interplay between structure and relaxation that's known as Tai Chi. Commonly known in the West as form governs function.

The trick in Tai Chi is getting the balance *(harmony)* right. You need to disengage enough muscle *(Wu Wei, Non-Action)* to allow gravity *(Di Xin Xi Yin Li)* to move the joints, which then moves the body. Let go of too much muscle and you collapse structure *(joints)*, engage too much muscle and the joints won't move and physical movement would not be possible. Excessively engage too much muscle and you'll create isolated body movement. This balance aligns with the Tao Te Ching's teachings of Non-Action, emphasising the art of non doing. Master Huang would often state; "Tai Chi is not important, the Tao is everything.

If I were to incorrectly use T.C.M theory to explain how movement is generated in Tai Chi, it would be explained in the following way. Ying Chi *(nutrient chi)* is used to nourish the muscles of the body. This chi is essentially derived from the essence of food and is produced by the spleen and the stomach. Ying chi in combination with Zong Chi *(pectoral chi)* nourishes the chi of the muscles, which are then used in the creation of movement. The above T.C.M theory would be a perfect fit, except for one small detail; we don't use muscle to generate movement in Tai Chi, *(we do use them to support weight, but not for movement)*. We use the gentle disengagement *(non action)* of muscle to generate movement by allowing Di Xin Xi Yin Li to pass through specific alignments to create movement. T.C.M theory is correct in explaining what nourishes and strengthens the muscles, but it can't be used to explain the physical energy that specifically creates movement in Tai Chi, which once again is Di Xin Xi Yin Li *(gravity)*. In a way, the above Western and Eastern concepts of gravity or Di Xin Xi Yin Li are both correct, it largely depends on your point of view in regards to the process. I remember in high school I was told of two scholarly experts on the American War of Independence, one from the USA and the other from the UK. They were discussing heroes of the American War of Independence. The British scholar identified Benedict Arnold as one of the great patriots of the war. The American scholar took offence to this statement and replied. "I beg your pardon sir, don't you mean the greatest traitor of the war". To which the British scholar replied "Not to the British he wasn't". I guess it depends on your point of view.

Using Lao Tsu's concept of Non-action to create action in conjunction with correct alignments gives us the ability to move in the five directions of Tai Chi. They being; forward, back, left, right and central equilibrium *(hence the reason for Master Huang creating the Five Loosening Exercises)*. **Lao Tsu's method of movement is energy efficient, gentle on the body, prevents various forms of external and internal chi *(energy/force)* becoming trapped within the body. It results in less chance of injury, improves strength by moving beyond muscle limitations and under the right conditions has the ability to generate extreme speed and isn't age or gender restricted.** When compared to the more common muscular method of movement which uses the Third Law of

Newtonian Physics, which is usually the prelude to damaged joints, muscles and tendons including diminishing strength and speed due to the natural loss of muscle mass as we age. I believe there are only two physical activities that don't require muscle to generate movement. These are walking, and Tai Chi. Both use the same energy source to generate movement *(gravity, Di Xin Xi Yin Li)*. These two activities not only use relaxation *(disengaging of unnecessary muscle)* of muscles to facilitate physical movement, but that relaxation also facilitates the movement of numerous forms of chi which promotes physical and mental health. The chi we're specifically interested in is the chi of the Earth which moves joints and hence the body, by **pulling** you physically into position, in comparison to the more common method of using muscle to **push** yourself into position *(Third Law of Newtonian Physics)*.

To prove Lao Tsu's theory of non action, creating action to beginners. I ask them to perform a few simple things on their first lesson. I ask the beginners which muscles they use to lift the rear leg when walking. The usual answer is the thigh, calf or buttocks. They don't believe me when I tell them that no muscles are used in the lifting of the rear leg. To prove it, we first need to clarify muscle function in the human body. If I were standing in front of you and asked, am I using muscle? The answer would be yes, of course you are, if I wasn't, I'd be lying on the ground. When standing upright and erect, postural muscles are activated, these are your anti-gravity muscles, these muscles contract, creating a state of equilibrium between you and the earth. These muscles are your soleus muscles, the extensors of the leg, the gluteus maximus, the quadriceps femoris and muscles of the back. Postural muscles are some of the strongest muscles you possess, the legs can push up to four times the weight than the arms can lift *(probably the reason why so many people push with their legs in Tai Chi)*.

Let's break down the act of walking. Your right foot has just stepped forward, your weight is moving into the front leg by relaxing enough muscle, allowing the weight to be pulled forward from the left side of the body to the right side. This process results in your body being pulled forward. With the increasing weight transfer to the right side, muscles in the right leg *(front leg)* begin to contract to support this increased weight, while simultaneously muscles in the left leg begin to disengage as weight leaves the left leg *(rear leg)*. This process continues to the point where the body is pulled into and over the right leg *(yin)* and the left leg is virtually empty of body weight *(yang)*. At this exact moment there's no body weight in the left leg; the left hip has let go causing the left knee to travel forward which in turn lifts the left heel. The full body weight is now directly over the right leg. The right leg is substantial and the left leg is insubstantial and empty of weight except for the weight of the left leg itself. At the very last stage of walking, the rear leg is pulled forward with the last remaining weight of the rear leg having been pulled into the front leg, effectively cancelling out even the weight of the rear leg. At this very last stage of walking, the rear leg is **functionally empty** *(not just empty of body weight, but empty of leg weight)* resulting in the rear leg being pulled forward causing you to step. (*Interesting to note, physiotherapists often refer to walking as a controlled fall, which is an accurate description of the process. When stepping you are literally falling. However, the rear leg swings forward and saves you. If you look back to the times when you've tripped over, it is due to the rear foot getting caught on something which has prevented the rear leg from throwing forward, and over you go*). When the left leg is functionally empty, how much muscle is required to move an object that has no weight? Negligible, at no point during the process of walking did you consciously lift the rear leg, it was pulled into position by a combination of gravity, weight, *(substantial and insubstantial)* joints and the interaction of your postural muscles. Postural muscles are primarily designed for weight bearing. However, viewing the above process through Taoist philosophy it could be explained in the following way. Walking is created by the interaction of yin *(substantially)* and yang *(insubstantially)*. Are they wrong? No, Yin and Yang represents opposites, people often use yin & yang without giving context which can add to the confusion; without context yin & yang quickly becomes generic. In the above case weighted is referred to as yin and weight leaving the leg is yang. It is the interaction of yin *(substantially)* and yang *(insubstantially)* that makes walking possible. Have you ever watched a toddler learning to walk? It's fascinating to watch. The look of concentration on their face. They are so focused. Because they have no muscle memory or strength for walking they have no idea which muscles are needed and which ones aren't. So they use every muscle they can get their hands on, this causes them to sway from side to side when learning to walk *(they always reminded me of those old Frankenstein movies, when he walked with his arms outstretched, swaying from side to side)*. This swaying is caused because muscles around the hips are overly engaged, preventing their hip joints from moving freely. As the toddler becomes more familiar with the walking process they begin to disengage more and more muscle, specifically muscles around their hips and knees. Resulting in their walking becoming more centred, less swaying more stable and energy efficient. Interesting to note, often the very elderly with severe arthritis in their hips and knees will also sway from side to side like a toddler. Due to the pain experienced when their hips and knees move they tend to lock their knees and hips so they don't move and use the swaying motion to move themselves along.

I can't stress enough, there's a difference between using muscle to bear weight and maintain alignment and muscle to generate movement. Like walking, Tai Chi uses the Taoist principle of Non-action creating action, allowing the use of muscle to bear weight and maintain alignment and equilibrium, but not in the creation of movement. I remember giving a workshop in Cardiff and somebody commented that letting go *(non-action)* is still an action and of course it is. However, if you keep the discussion in relation to the Third Law of Newtonian Physics that for every action, there is an equal and opposite re-action, then a non action *(relaxing muscles)* creating an action is within the principle of non-action. One of the basic tenets of Taoism is that everything is in a constant state of change. I believe the Buddhists call it impermanence. When you die, you don't stay still. We have all seen those nature films that speed up the decaying process of a dead animal. Your body is still moving as it breaks down and decays.

Reincarnation is the belief that when you die your soul or spirit will be re-born into a new body, be that human or animal. Whether you move up or down this evolution ladder is dictated by your moral behaviour in the past life. If you contain the concept of reincarnation to the physical process, then it makes perfect sense. When you die your body decomposes, returning nutrients *(chi)* to the soil and supplying nutrition to various life forms that live in the soil. In the West we believe in something similar. The law of conservation of energy claims that energy can neither be created nor destroyed only converted from one form of energy to another. Everything is in a constant state of change, the only question is the size and speed of change; some changes are extremely slow beyond our human comprehension. The rising up of mountain ranges can take many millions of years; quite a long time in comparison to our own life span. Change is a constant. The only variable is the time frame in which change happens.

To physically prove to my beginners that non-action creates action, I have them take on a bow and arrow stance that most Tai Chi practitioners are familiar with, 90% of their weight in the rear leg *(90% of their body mass is now behind their rear knee)*. I ask them to shift their weight to their front leg, without disengaging any of the muscles they are currently using in the rear leg. After a few attempts they look confused and claim it's not possible without letting go of the muscles in the rear leg. They have just taken their first step into the world of Tai Chi, by personally experiencing non-action creating action. Consider this for a second: virtually everything in the world *(except for Tai Chi and walking)* creates movement, based on the Third Newtonian's Law of Motion. A jet engine pushes hot gases out the rear of the engine which in turn pushes the plane forward, or a propeller driven plane pushes air backwards pushing the plane forward, pushing your rear leg against the ground to propel yourself forward, etc, etc. These are examples of the Third Law of Newtonian Physics in action. It's the same for nearly every form of physical and mechanical movement on this planet *(except for Earth itself, which interestingly enough is being pulled through space at 107,000 kph caused by the gravitational pull of the Sun)*. Virtually every human movement requires energy to be expanded behind us to move us forward. Except for walking and Tai Chi, the energy that propels us forward is a pulling energy *(gravity or Di Xin Xi Yin Li)* not a pushing energy *(muscular energy)*. Walking and Tai Chi applies Taoist principles of non-action to create action.

At a workshop in the UK, a participant disagreed with my theory that it's the Earth's chi that moves us in Tai Chi, asserting that it was the vital chi of the body that moved us. His argument was that without the intrinsic chi of the body we would in fact be dead and therefore not able to perform Tai Chi. I asked him if he could he do Tai Chi if his heart or liver were removed? His reply was, "no, you couldn't, because you would be dead". Using his previous logic then it was the heart or liver that causes you to move in Tai Chi. There is a clear difference between the vital chi that keeps the organism alive and in optimal health and the chi that actually creates so-called power, speed and physical movement in Tai Chi. He mistakenly used the concept of chi from T.C.M to explain movement, rather than using it to explain the health giving benefits of Tai Chi.

Another exercise I ask new students to perform is to assume the same bow and arrow stance they had previously taken, with 90% weight in the rear leg. I ask them to move 90% of their weight to their front leg, without moving their body forward. They don't even try, saying it's impossible, which it is. So what moves first, weight or the body? Weight is pulled or channelled through various alignments first, followed by the body. What moves weight is a combination of relaxation, alignment and chi *(chi of the Earth)*. Substantiality creates movement, insubstantiality allows movement. These days, students of Tai Chi tend to move their body first to create substantiality rather than through closing *(relaxation downward)* and opening *(relaxing upward)* which creates substantial and insubstantial which in turns creates external movement *(more in Chapter 9 on the relationship between substantial and insubstantial and opening and closing)*. In Western physics there are four energies that make up the universe. These energies are Gravity, Electromagnetic Force, Strong Nuclear Force and Weak Nuclear Force. Tai Chi uses one of these energies to generate movement using Taoist principal of Wu Wei, Non-action creating action.

Relaxing certain muscles in the body while maintaining other muscles creates certain alignments within the body which then channels gravity through the body resulting in specific directions of movement. Looking at how certain Martial Arts move tells you a lot about their movement, technique and power source. You only have to look at Bagua *(Baguazhang)* which is also considered an internal martial art when performed correctly, you can visibly see the body being pulled forward, through the back leg. When the front leg becomes substantial it smoothly takes over from the rear leg and continues the gravity feed unbroken pulling of the now rear empty leg forward. Another martial art considered an internal martial art is Hsing I *(Xing Yi Quan)*. Once again if you watch a capable Hsing I practitioner you'll witness the pulling of the back foot forward with very little use of muscle. If you were standing in the Begin posture of Tai Chi with weight 50/50, feet are level with each other, feet hip width apart and you wanted to turn to the right. Using Non-action to create movement you would need to relax the muscles of the left foot, moving this relaxation up *(opening)* the left leg and under the left buttock in a sequential order so the left knee moves forward causing the left hip *(kua)* to physically open and the right hip *(kua)* to close. This results in the upper body turning to the right. It is for this reason, that it's critical to learn Opening and Closing and the Five Loosening Exercise of Tai Chi, these Five Loosening Exercises help you to understand, and give you the means to create the Five Directions of Tai Chi by means of Non-action. The Opening and Closing Exercise teaches and trains you how to create the passive power that is used to generate movement in the Five Loosening Exercises, Form and Push Hands.

We have clarified and defined Tai Chi as the physical manifestation of Taoist principles in action, having qualified the chi that powers all movement in Tai Chi, that being Di Xin Xi Yin Li (gravity). We can now access this power source by applying Taoist principle of Wu Wei, Non-action to create action. For Tai Chi to be used as a martial art, it will need strength and power. How is it possible to create power without using muscle?

Taoist Internal Strength and Muscular Strength. Are they the same, and if not, what differentiates them?

4. Tai Chi Li *(Strength)*

The source of Tai Chi strength is without question the most misunderstood concept in Tai Chi today. Tai Chi has the reputation for possessing nearly super human strength. How is it possible for an elderly Tai Chi Master to throw around relatively strong young men like rag dolls. I understand how people would view it as fake, I truly do. Hopefully after reading the following Chapter you'll begin to understand a little better the physics and principles behind these feats of strength. These feats of strength and power need to be viewed within a quantitative and relative frame work. Before proceeding any further I really need to define and clarify these different types of strength.

Cambridge dictionary defines strength as, "the ability to do things that demand physical or mental effort, or the degree to which something is strong and powerful". Strength is quantitative and relative in nature. For strength to be considered strength it needs to be in a relationship with something other than itself. The quantitative aspect of muscular strength is pretty much black and white and is easy to explain. For example, let us say you are lifting dumbbells with two 25 kilo weights on each end, you're lifting a combined weight of 100 kilos. A week later you add an extra 5 kilos on each side, and your now lifting 110 kilos. There is no question that you have demonstrated an increase in strength. It is measurable. Muscular strength is the most common method used in measuring an individual's strength, the stronger the muscle or muscles are, the stronger you are, fairly straight forward. Is muscular strength the only method to which power can be measured? Or are there other forms of strength that are as real as muscle but harder to define, measure and acquire? Most martial and pugilistic arts tend to see strength through the more popular muscular approach, which without question is practical and effective. Making yourself physically stronger than your opponent allows you to use your strength advantage to overpower one's opponent. However, there are pros and cons to muscular based strength.

Pros
1. Progress is made in a relative short time frame, and is measurable and is relatively easily achieved.

Cons
1. Age restricted, the peak of an adult male is in their late 20s to early 30s. For an adult female it's a little later in their late 20s to mid 30s. Once these ages are passed, muscular strength steadily declines due to natural loss of muscle mass known in Western Medicine as Sarcopenia, leading to a gradual decline in strength in conjunction with the ageing process.

2. Muscular strength has its limitations; there will be a point where physically you'll reach your utmost limit of muscular strength, dictated by your physical size, gender and genetics.

External or Harder Martial Arts correctly promote themselves as a great way to learn how to defend oneself. Generally you're told you needn't be big or strong to be able to defend oneself against a larger and stronger aggressor, because you'll be taught how to defend yourself through the application of technique, timing, focus, intent, breath using the opponent's own force against them. All worthy attributes, hence the reason why you can defeat a larger and stronger aggressor *(something I have always found curious, if the above is true, then why is there such a heavy emphasis on strength training, such as knuckle push ups. If self defence doesn't rely on muscular strength then why train it)*. You pay for the first month's tuition, membership fees and uniform. You are then started on a fitness and strengthening regime, followed by forms, patterns and applications. As practical as this method is, it will have built in limitation due to your size, gender, age and limited muscle strength. However, there are assorted sports and martial arts which use gravity in conjunction with muscle to various degrees. Below are just a few of them;

Judo
Uses leverage when throwing the opponent. The hip is used as a fulcrum when performing O Goshi-Major Hip Throw, resulting in the opponent being flipped effortlessly. Would it be possible to throw someone in Judo without first breaking their physical connection to gravity?

Jiu-Jitsu
Can and does use pain to control the opponent's centre of gravity. Joint locks can be incredibly painful, so painful that a person will literally throw themselves in the direction of the joint lock to mitigate the pain.

Greco-Roman Wrestling
Usually starts in a low stance with upper body bent forward from the hips, arms extended outward. They generally lock on to each other and proceed to pull and push feeling for weaknesses in each other's defences. The moment one of the wrestlers feels the slightest break in their opponents connection to gravity they make their move, either by taking them to the mat or to move into a more advantageous position.

Aikido
Similar to Tai Chi, Aikido also believes in softness overcoming hardness. They use a Naga-Waza throwing technique. Aikido's signature method of leading an attackers arm to over extended, resulting in the opponent's connection to gravity to weaken is well known. Taking control of their opponent's centre of gravity allows them to dictate the direction, speed and final destination of their opponent.

I find most people involved in martial arts tend to over-emphasie muscular strength and overlook the connection between gravity and strength. Maybe it's because we are born into gravity, and like air it's just taken for granted. Strength and gravity are inter-connected and are nearly indistinguishable. Below are some examples of muscular strength in relation to gravity.

Muscular Strength in a Harness
If you placed the strongest man in the world in front of me and asked him to push or throw me across the room, I have little doubt he would not have any trouble moving my 100 kilo frame. If I was to ask him to repeat this action again, but this time around, I placed him in a harness, tied a rope to the harness, threw the other end over a beam and pulled on the rope so his feet left the ground, the outcome would be completely different. I seriously doubt he'd be able to move me, in fact I would wager that when he pushed me, it would be him that moved, not me. But surely if muscle is the sole measurement of strength shouldn't I have been the one who moved. By losing his physical connection to gravity his muscular effectiveness was greatly reduced to virtually nothing. **Without a physical connection to gravity** *(the ground)*, **muscle loses most of its effectiveness in relation to another object.**

Muscular Strength in a Pool *(weightless environment)*
This is another example of how size and muscle doesn't always win the day. Let us say you are treading water in a pool, not touching the bottom or sides *(this is the closest you'll get to being in a weightless environment without going into space)*. You're having fun with your seven year old son who decides to splash water in your face. You grab him by the leg, pulling him towards you so you can dunk him a few times. He knows what is coming his way, so he grabs onto the pool's ladder that's bolted to the side of the pool. When pulling on his leg, you soon discover he doesn't come to you, but

in fact you go to him. All that muscle and strength you supposedly possessed outside the pool is useless without a physical connection to gravity. A seven year old has more strength than an adult when they have a connection to gravity and the adult doesn't. Just another reminder of the need to be and stay physically connected to gravity when using muscle.

Dan Tien as a Means to Create Power and Movement?

When writing or commenting on a subject, I always try to stay in my field of expertise. In the following, I'm quick to admit, I have very limited personal experience on the Dan Tien. If I was to write about my personal experiences on the Dan Tien, it would literally fit on the back of a postage stamp. Now in saying this, we still need to investigate the Dan Tien as a power source as it's often referenced in Tai Chi as the source of energy that powers Tai Chi movements and internal strength. Often referred to as the Elixir Field or the Sea of Chi, it goes by many names. It is positioned three finger width below the navel in line with the perineum. A large amount of material has been written on the Dan Tien. There being three Dan Tiens, we're going to focus on the lower one. Taoist and Buddhist believes that the lower Dan Tien is the reservoir for vital chi within the body. This is particular true for practitioners of Qi Gong who place a heavy emphasis on energising the Dan Tien. It's interesting to note, in T.C.M theory, energy starts in Lung 1 *(Zhong Fu)*, in Tai Chi the energy starts in Kidney 1 *(Yongquan)* and in Qi Gong and various meditational disciplines the vital energy often starts in the Dan Tien. Much has been written in Tai Chi literature about the need to fill the Dan Tien with chi before releasing it. Believing that the Dan Tien acts like a large cauldron filling with chi until it over flows which at that point is released to the outer limbs of the body supplying power and movement to Tai Chi.

The following statement I'm about to make could be considered a form of heresy in Tai Chi. I personally don't subscribe to the theory of the Dan Tien's method of creating energy in Tai Chi, which is then used to generate movement and power *(fa-jing)*. I question the very application of how it creates movement and power within Tai Chi. I have a few reasons for this; firstly, there is no mention of building energy up, in the Tao Te Ching. In the Tao Te Ching it states in Chapter Four line one, "Tao is an empty vessel; it is used, but never filled". Chapter Nine, first line, "Better stop short than fill to the brim". Chapter Sixteen first line, "Empty yourself of everything". There is constant reference in the Tao Te Ching to the negative affects of acquiring excessive wealth, power and strength or the chasing and hoarding of these qualities. Often in Tai Chi you're actively encouraged to build the chi within the Dan Tien and release it in an explosion of energy referred to as fa-jing. The problem with this concept of building or storing any form of energy whether it's in the Dan Tien or in your root is clearly in breach of core Taoist beliefs. This energy that's stored is more dangerous to yourself than your opponent. If this stored energy is contained or re-directed back to its origins, be it the Dan Tien or your root at the moment of release, it will cause a backfire of energy, resulting in you experiencing the full effect of your own energy being re-directed back to you, causing you to be thrown out.

There are countless mentions in Tai Chi literature of returning energy from a push or a blow back to your opponent. To which I'm in total agreement, but this process must follow Taoist principles of energy movement *(more on this in Chapter 11 Push Hands)*. This buildup of energy is more dangerous to the person who builds up this energy than the person who is about to receive it. Like nuclear weapons, countries that possess these weapons of mass destruction need to keep them well maintained so not to leak or malfunction. They also need a large amount of security to prevent these weapons from falling into the wrong hands, all extremely expensive and labour intensive. If you look into the history of nuclear weapons, you'll find incident after incident of fires in missile silos that nearly resulted in nuclear detonation. And the loss of numerous nuclear bombs by accident from military planes. And this is just from the USA! I imagine Russia would have had similar incidents. All this power and it's of more danger to the people on whose lands these weapons are stationed. The second reason is that the Tao Te Ching constantly stresses that we are all connected to the Tao. When focusing on building your chi within the Dan Tien for the purpose of releasing energy in a push or a blow, you're overly focusing on yourself, seeing yourself separate from the Tao, separate from your opponent. There is this constant belief in Tai Chi that strength can be developed in isolation, when in fact isolation is weakness, integration is strength. Letting go of strength *(muscular strength)* is the beginning of integration that leads to true strength. Using the Dan Tien as a method for increasing the chi levels within the body for the promotion of one's physical and mental health is to be encouraged. Circulating this vital chi within your body within a self contained circulatory system can do no harm and can only improve one's overall health. But to use this energy for an external purpose, in my opinion, is in breach of Taoist principles.

Relaxing muscle *(non-action)* allows you to move the chi from a push or blow through the body by means of using the chi of the Earth *(Di Xin Xi Yin Li, gravity)* to draw this energy/force through your alignments, led by your intent to be re-directed under the root of your opponent's feet.

Having returned their energy to a compromised root, having affected their central equilibrium with gravity means your opponent can no longer physically or internally adjust their body to diffuse this build up of returned energy/force/chi. In push hands, most practitioners of Tai Chi will incorrectly try to push their opponent off their centre of gravity, instead of leaving their opponent's body where it is, and moving their opponent's centre of gravity. Breaking your opponent's connection to gravity causes them to become isolated *(gravity is part of the Tao)*. Without this ability to adjust and change *(which is critical in keeping yourself in harmony with the Tao)*, their returning energy becomes blocked, resulting in their returned energy changing to a force in their root. This causes the opponent to be thrown outward, confirming the Taoist proverb, "The longer you resist change the more violent the change will be". Another Taoist proverb, "The essence of true power is the power you give *(return)* to your opponent". The Dan Tien is mentioned in Tai Chi literature by many reputable Tai Chi teachers, including from my own lineage. Master Huang mentions the Dan Tien in his Thirteen Questions. When I first started with my teacher Wee Kee Jin I asked him about the Dan Tien. He told me not to overly focus on the Dan Tien, otherwise I would end up with bloated chi in the abdomen. Thirty years later I asked him if Master Huang mention the Dan Tien when he was training under him. He said Master Huang would say that you need to be aware of the Dan Tien, but no more than any other part of your body.

Taoist Physics in Comparison to Western Physics
Taoist Physics looks at gravity slightly differently, compared to Western Physics. As an example, lets say I weigh 100 kilos and I lift up a coffee table weighing 50 kilos. In Western physics I still weigh 100 kilos and the coffee table still weighs 50 kilos, they may say you have a combined weight of 150 kilos, but they view you and the coffee table as separate. However, in Taoist physics they would say I now weigh 150 kilos and the coffee table weighs nothing. The Taoist rationale is that the coffee table is now part of me; I am one with the coffee table. When you hear the old martial art proverb, "That you must become one with your opponent", they weren't being esoteric, or that you should mirror your opponent's every movement. What was meant is that you need to sever your opponent's connection to gravity, so your opponent now relies on you for their relationship with gravity. In Tai Chi the term to **join**, means that you and your opponent have joined as one. You and your opponent share one connection to gravity; you have it and they don't. In other words you have become one with your opponent, and you must stay as one *(which is mind-numbingly difficult)*. As stated earlier, Judo achieves this mainly through leverage. Jiu-Jitsu can do it by pain and Aikido uses momentum and re-direction. Tai Chi does it in a very subtle manner, so subtle that when performed correctly the opponent doesn't realise they've lost their connection to gravity *(Di Xin Xi Yin Lii)* until they try to initiate movement.

Relative and subjective strength is a grey area and this is where Tai Chi strength resides. An example of relative strength would be a 7 year old child who would view an adult as extremely strong in comparison to himself, but that same adult would be considered weak in comparison to a full grown water buffalo *(this reminds of an old proverb; "animals don't know their own strength, humans don't know their own faults).* The same concept can be applied to speed: a tortoise would be considered very fast from the view point of a snail, However, in relation to a rabbit, the tortoise is painfully slow everything is relative by nature. Both quantitative and relative strength needs to be measured similarly in relation to an external source for it to be deemed as strength. Quantitative strength doesn't change. Fifty kilos will always be 50 kilos while on Earth. Relative strength is different and can shift and move around and is more pliable, never static due to the constant changes of external factors. The adult to child relationship mentioned earlier changes over time. The adult's strength will diminish with age, in comparison to the child, whose strength will only grow and increase as they transition to adulthood. Strength also needs to be experienced or felt for it to be truly appreciated. If I were to flex my arm muscle by holding an isometric pose, as often seen in body building competitions, this does not demonstrate strength. It shows muscle size, which a person with a biased view point may equate with strength. Interesting to note, you'll never see a body builder competing in a weight lifting event. If muscle is the true measure of strength, body builders would dominate all weight lifting events. But they can't, and don't.

If muscle is physically connected to gravity then you are able to contract and create resistance by pushing against the Earth *(gravity)*, commonly known as free weight strength training. Sadly, we are seeing this more and more often in push hands these days. Where one person leans into their opponent, relying on their opponent returning the favour by also leaning in against them. Both parties are actively pushing against gravity, actively engaging their muscular strength, it tends to look more like a sumo wrestling match than Tai Chi *(can you envision these same people engaging in push hands in the same manner at the age of 70 or 80, I seriously doubt it)*. The big problem with a lot of Tai Chi practitioners, is they still see themselves as the source of all strength either through muscle or chi. Tai Chi practitioners wrongly believe that it is still okay to use small amounts of muscle to lift an empty leg when stepping in Tai Chi. Or when moving forward and back it's acceptable to engage muscle to press their feet against the ground to achieve this forward and backward motion. Because they see themselves as the sole originator of all strength, be it muscle or building chi. One of the main goals of Tai Chi is the letting go of one's ego, *(ego is seeing yourself as the centre of everything)*. While ego exist you will always see yourself as the source of all strength. The sooner you let go of strength *(muscular strength)* the quicker you'll enter the world of Tai Chi.

We have a rule in Master Huang lineage: what you train in the Opening and Closing Exercise, you train in the Five Loosening Exercises. What you train in the Five Loosening Exercises you bring into the Form, and what you train in the Form you then apply in Push Hands, consistently applying the same principles to all four levels of your Tai Chi. If you believe muscle is permitted in the creation of movement when performing the Tai Chi form it's not such a big jump of logic to believe it's okay to use muscle when practising push hands. Allowing muscle to be used during the form is the thin edge of the wedge as this use of muscle will only grow and infiltrate your push hands. Going down this path of thinking, it's not such a big jump to lean into the push by pushing against the ground to help balance any incoming force. If muscle becomes physically isolated from gravity at any time, it then becomes localised strength. Which means strength which is confined or restricted to a location. An example of localised strength would be when using a bow and arrow. One hand grips the bow pushing outward, while the opposite arm pulls on the bow string in the opposite direction. This strength doesn't receive its resistance from gravity, in fact gravity plays no part. It obtains its resistance from opposing muscle groups in the two arms from pulling and pushing in opposite directions, creating localised strength. In Tai Chi during push hands we don't use gravity the same way as most sports or martial arts do, such as pressing our feet against the ground to create localised strength which is used against our opponent. Using muscle goes against the prime directive of Tai Chi. Tai Chi uses softness to overcome strength, the weak overcoming the strong, no-action creating action, non-action creating so called power.

Tai Chi Strength

Tai Chi strength is a bit of a misnomer, you may have noticed that I often refer to strength as so-called power. **A Tai Chi practitioner does not try to make themselves stronger than their opponent, they make their opponent weaker, which gives the false appearance the Tai Chi practitioner has increased their physical strength.** Recalling what I said earlier, muscle strength is relative to its physical connection to gravity. If you sever your opponent's connection to gravity, then your opponent who has based their entire muscular strength on their resistance to gravity, loses all power and strength. As stated earlier some sports and martial arts do use muscle in conjunction with gravity to various degrees. Tai Chi practitioners achieve this, not by leverage or pain, **but from allowing the opponent's force to pass through their body,** leading *(returning)* it back under their opponent's feet resulting in their root *(gravity)* being severed. *(I often use the term energy/force because technically it only becomes a force if energy is allowed to settle or becomes blocked. The very purpose of Tai Chi is to keep energy in a state of energy, therefore preventing it from converting to a force).* I have a video of Master Huang, one of the last videos taken just months before his death. He was on a stage giving a speech, and after the speech he walked to a chair on stage. You could see by the way he moved he was very frail. He gingerly shuffled to the chair. Gently sitting himself down he proceeded to push hands with various people. His issuing of relaxed force was the best that I had ever seen, each person being launched across the stage with such force. Another example of a Tai Chi practitioner sitting down and doing push hands is a video of Grandmaster Wang who also is very elderly and frail sitting in a wheel chair, also issuing and sending various people back 2 to 3 metres.

How is this possible? Men of such advanced years able to send people out with such force. It can't be their leg strength. They can barely walk and besides, they're sitting in a chair. It can't be arm strength as their arms barely move. Their own vital chi is so weakened that both men were visibly unsteady on their feet and passed away relatively soon after these videos were taken. However, both men were extremely relaxed and soft, allowing energy placed on them to instantly pass through their bodies and led *(I personally don't like the word direct or directed, I much prefer the word lead, the reason for this will be covered in Chapter 10 Intent)* by their intent back into their opponent's root. Resulting in their opponent being compressed within their own root *(similar to a loaded spring)*. At this point the slightest pressure *(less than 4 ounces)* will tip them over the edge, resulting in their throwing themselves out. It often looks fake, because it looks as though these people are throwing themselves out. And they are, but not by choice. To be fair these days it's more often exaggerated by overly co-operative students, but when pushed out by an experienced and reputable teacher, the sensation is unquestionably real.

Fa-Jing

In Tai Chi there is a belief and heavy emphasis on training to release explosive power *(fa-jing)* during form work. We really need to qualify and define what is fa-jing and how it's created. I'm going to go against popular belief of what is fa-jing. Starting with the form, you can't really display or express fa-jing in the form. I know in some styles, mainly Chen style and in some Wu styles they still express fast movements within their forms, which is fine and totally legitimate as long as this speed is in keeping with the principles of Tai Chi. I think an assumption has crept into Tai Chi, that any posture performed with speed is automatically considered fa-jing *(power)*. This is not true, you can generate speed simply by contracting muscle and passing it off as fa-jing. Even if speed is generated by applying the principles of opening and closing *(this will be covered in Chapter 8 Tai Chi and Speed)* it doesn't mean you've necessarily generated fa-jing. In the general field of pugilism and martial arts speed is closely associated with power, which is correct when using muscular strength under normal conditions. This is explained in physics as Power = Force × Velocity. However, this rule can't be applied to Tai Chi, due to its Taoist links to Wu Wei. To understand fa-jing, we really need to separate speed and power and view them separately. As explained earlier in this Chapter, Tai Chi's power works on a completely different model from that of muscle generating speed and power. Tai Chi so called power begins with cutting your opponent's root by means of intent, relaxation and alignment. By cutting your opponent's root, you create an imbalance in their equilibrium and their relation to the Chi of the Earth, *(Di Xin Xi Yin Li, gravity)*.

Put simply, you've caused your opponent to lose balance, not enough for them to fall over, or even enough for them to realise their balance has been compromised, but enough so they can't bring their muscles into play. Returning your opponent's energy/force back to their root, results in them becoming isolated and weakened. When this imbalance reaches an extreme point, your opponent literally releases themself *(throw themselves out)*. This so-called power *(if you can call it that, making your opponent weaker, in comparison to making yourself stronger)*, isn't created by speed, in fact, the exact opposite is true. Fa-jing is at its strongest when you're physically still, when you're **not physically moving.** In reality there is no release or exchange of explosive energy/force from yourself to your opponent in the regular sense, within the form or in push hands. The source of power *(fa-jing)* in Tai Chi is by making your opponent weaker by means of cutting their root. With this process continuing to its natural conclusion of compressing your opponent's root, creating such an imbalance in your opponent, that they inevitably discharge themselves. **This then raises the question, how is it possible to create fa-jing in a form where there's no opponent's root for you to redirect their energy/force with which to create the conditions for fa-jing.** Without an opponent's root, there can be no fa-jing. Fa-jing release has nothing to do with speed or muscle. It's about leading your opponent's own force back into their own root, creating an imbalance. Therefore claiming speed in the form as the source of fa-jing is incorrect.

Try to look at fa-jing like an epoxy glue. Epoxy glue consists of two compounds; one is a resin and the other is the hardener. To create glue you need to mix both compounds together in equal amounts and thoroughly for it to transition into glue. If you applied only one of the compounds to the object you are trying to repair, this would result in a gooey mess. To generate fa-jing, to state the obvious, you first need yourself of course *(you're the resin)*, generating an intent forward of yourself by two metres, just under the ground. Then relaxing from your intent's location, to move energy/force by means of relaxation through your body. Having done everything correctly you've created the condition where fa-jing is at least now possible. However, there is still one thing missing to complete the fa-jing process - **your opponent** *(the other compound, the hardener)*. Without an opponent, more specifically the opponent's root, the energy/force has nowhere to compress and cause your opponent to throw themselves out. It's for this reason you can't display fa-jing in the form or solo work - you don't have the other half of the equation which is required for the process to generate fa-jing. You can train your part of the process by training the form work and other solo work, but you still need the other half *(your opponent)* to generate fa-jing.

We not only apply the philosophy of Wu Wei to generate movement in Tai Chi, we also apply Wu Wei to generate so called power/fa-jing. Letting go of muscle *(non action)* in Tai Chi allows your opponent's energy/force to pass through these relaxed muscles. Led by your intent back under and behind your opponent's root, resulting in your opponent being thrown out. This is in comparison to the traditionally accepted method of contracting muscle to generate power. When muscle is contracted to create power and speed, energy from your opponent's push becomes caught within these newly contracted muscles and converts to a force. By giving up *(letting go)* our traditional concept of what power is, **only then can we access nearly unlimited power *(the soft overcomes the hard and powerful)*, by making our opponent weaker and not by making ourselves stronger.**

Because form work is a solo exercise, you don't have an opponent's root to feed and return their energy/force back to. Without an opponent's root, it's just not possible to generate fa-jing in solo work. Fa-jing can only be expressed and demonstrated in push hands. I remember being told by my original Chow Ga Tong Long teacher over 45 years ago, power *(fa-jing)* can't be seen, it can only be felt *(experienced)*. It took me decades to understand this statement. It's similar to looking at an exposed electrical wire. Can you tell by looking at it if it's alive with electricity? No, you can't, until you touch it. Then you'll know if it's alive or dead. You can't see gravity, but you can feel the effects of gravity. Internal martial arts essentially means unseen energies are at work. **You literally can't see fa-jing, it can only be felt.** When practising the form you're training and cultivating all the necessities needed on your part for fa-jing, such as opening, closing, relaxation, timing, alignment, sticking, following, yielding, intent, awareness, joining, etc, etc. You still can't create fa-jing, because you lack the root of your opponent to apply the above qualities for the purpose of redirecting their energy/force, which is needed to generate an imbalance. How far the opponent is released is largely dictated by how much the opponent resists change. As stated earlier, "The longer you put off change, the more violent the change will be". This belief that speed is the source of fa-jing is the mistaken assumption that you generate power in isolation to your opponent. The Tao doesn't operate in this way. When speed is applied to the form by means of opening and closing, has the effect of speeding up the above process. When the process is sped up in push hands, the opponent who is having their energy/force returned to their root at a much faster rate will be thrown out much more violently.

There are also pros and cons to Di Xin Xi Yin Li *(gravity)* based strength.

Pros
1. It's not age restricted.
2. No natural limitations in making your opponent weaker, restricted only by your ability to relax and soften. Therefore no limitations to ones power *(if you can call it power)*.
3. Strength is not limited by size or gender.
4. Not prone to the same injuries in comparison to muscle based strength.
5. Improves ones vital chi and general health.
6. Due to its meditational qualities it improves concentration, awareness and cognitive process.
7. Increases and maintains joint mobility.

Cons
1. Tai Chi done correctly is neither physically nor mentally easy.

Master Huang once remarked, "Tai Chi is physically very difficult, mentally nearly impossible". My teacher Wee Kee Jin told me Master Huang was once admitted to hospital for surgery, I think it may have been to have his gallbladder removed, I can't be certain. Wee Kee Jin when visiting him in hospital was asked by Master Huang, to touch his arm. The second he touched, he was gently uprooted and thrown out. Master Huang remarked, "What a great art Tai Chi is! What art do you know of that would allow you to do this so soon after surgery?

We have clarified and defined Tai Chi as the physical manifestation of Taoist principles in action, having qualified the chi that powers all movement in Tai Chi, that being Di Xin Xi Yin Li (gravity). We can now access this power source by applying Taoist principle of Wu Wei, Non-action to create action. By re-directing our opponent's energy/force (chi) through relaxation back into their own root, causing them to become isolated and weak, giving the false appearance of you've becoming physically stronger. What is the internal process that allows us to return this energy/force in a way that creates movement and power?

Relaxation: do we Physically Switch On, Switch Off, become Mindful or Mindless and what function does it play in Tai Chi?

5. Relaxation

What is relaxation? It's literally the first question I ask new students. If we're going to train relaxation, achieve relaxation we had better qualify what relaxation is, it's far to important to leave it undefined. Everyone knows what relaxation is, until they have to explain it. I believe it was Saint Augustine who said "What then is time? If no one asks me, I know what it is. If I wish to explain it to him who asks, I do not know." After all, we may have totally different ideas and concepts of what relaxation is. We need to be all on the same page when it comes to relaxation. Students often claim they know, what relaxation is, however, when trying to verbalise it, the subject tends to turn pear shape pretty quickly. New students tend to say things like, "it's when you're not tense" a bit vague and you still haven't told me what relaxation is. You've told me what it isn't. When pressed further on the subject some claim relaxation is when you let go of every muscle in your body, often referring to relaxation classes they've taken in the past. Where they lie on their back and told to tighten the muscles in their feet and then disengage their feet muscles, they then move onto the calf muscles which again they tighten and also let go of, repeating this process, all the way up the body. As proof of their deep physical relaxation, they tell you, were you to lift their arm up by their fingers and let go, their hand would flop to the floor, as proof of their total relaxation. If complete physical relaxation is demonstrated by going limp, then following that logic, if I was to go to the local hospital and entered an ICU *(intensive care unit)* and lifted up a patient's arm and let go of it, their arm would also drop limply on to the bed. Are they relaxed? I doubt it, they're unconscious, they're not even aware I'm there. If you believe relaxation is lifeless energy then go to the morgue, usually located in the basement, it's full of relaxed people, lifeless energy is not relaxation.

Socrates once said, "Always question common assumptions, what you know to be true, under closer examination it falls apart" - great advice. If you can't verbalise a concept or a thought then you really don't have such a clear understanding of what you think you know. Albert Einstein was credited with having said; "If you can't explain your theory to a six-year-old, then you don't understand it yourself". So once again, what is relaxation? I prefer the Taoist definition. There is a Taoist proverb that states, "One should be in harmony with the universe". What does this statement mean? Breaking down the above meaning of the words used in context of Taoist philosophy, the word *harmony* is interchangeable with *balance*, they mean the same thing. Taoist philosophy places a very heavy emphasis on the moment; they strongly believe that everything is in relation to the moment; all their action and thoughts relate to the moment. So when they say the universe, it doesn't always mean the universe where all matter and energy reside in space. The term *universe* is often in reference to the moment you are currently in. So rereading the above proverb with this new definition gives clarity to the meaning of this proverb. Reviewing the above statement: One *(you)* should be in harmony *(balance)* with the universe *(the immediate moment you're in)*.

Relating the above proverb back to you and your everyday life and the moment you're currently in, I know for a fact that at this exact moment you're reading my book, maybe you're sitting in a chair at your desk. I would be correct in assuming you're currently using certain muscles and energy to maintain yourself in this chair while reading. Were you not to use enough muscle strength, you would be lying on the floor and not sitting in the chair. Lets us say you added more muscle to the act of sitting than you're currently using. Your back would straighten even more lifting your back off the chair, making yourself more erect. You're still sitting, reading this book, however, you're now using excessive muscle and energy for the act of sitting. The first example is muscle that is energy deficient *(Yin)* where you've let go *(disengaged)* of too much muscle and energy, resulting in your sliding off the chair. The other example is excessive use of muscle and energy, where you're still sitting in the chair, but you are now sitting ram rod straight. This is considered excessive use of *(Yang)* muscle and energy *(tension)* for the act of sitting. If you're using the exact amount of muscle to maintain yourself in a comfortable sitting position, in the chair, then you are relaxed *(in harmony)* for what the universe *(the moment)* requires from you, which is the act of sitting, no more, no less *(balanced)*.

Another Taoist proverb that helps explain relaxation is "The Tao holds no position, but holds every position, for this is the nature of the Tao". Just one of the many Taoist proverbs that uses riddles and double meanings to explain what should be a fairly elementary concept. Actually the above statement is quite simple and straightforward when the underlying principle is understood. We have come to the conclusion that relaxation is in a constant state of flux, always changing, depending on the physical requirements of the moment. Let's say the above proverb is in relation to relaxation *(it could be applied to a number of things though)*. Referring back to the above proverb, the Tao holds no static position *(like relaxation)* and because it holds no static position and is always changing and in a constant state of flux *(like the Tao)* it's then capable of changing *(dynamic)* its position and therefore is able to hold every position, depending on the requirements of the moment.

We are told that a state of softness is the preferred state of being, compared to a state of hardness or rigidity. The Tao Te Ching is always referencing the superiority of softness. People are always quoting examples of the pre-eminence of softness, often stating the softness of water will wear down the hardness of rock or the softness of a tongue will outlast the hardness of teeth: I'm sure you've heard all this before. Students love to tell me how water is an amazing force of nature, which it is. However, I know another form of energy that makes water look insignificant. That would have to be gravity. Gravity moves water, water doesn't move gravity. Gravity in some cases, doesn't even allow light to escape. The Tao Te Ching is trying to convey that when something is soft, be it government, business, institutions, society or families it has the ability to change depending on the situation *(moment)*. Things that are soft are flexible and can change, things that have the ability to change tend to last longer, than things that refuse or don't have the ability to change. Winston Churchill once said, "Democracy is the second best form of government". When asked, what's the best form of government? His answer: "It hasn't been invented yet". Why is democracy considered the best means with which to govern? Because it follows Taoist principles, it allows change. You can vote the party or people *(government)* out of power, you can strike, or if you feel strongly enough you can protest. This allows the release of pressures that can at times build up within a society. Democracy has stood the test of time and lasted thousands of years, spread throughout the world, because it follows the Tao. Democracy like the Tao itself is in a constant state of change. The ancient Greeks, specifically the Athenians who invented democracy only allowed men over the age of 18 who had completed their military service and whose both parents were citizens of Athens to vote. Females, slaves and free non citizens weren't allowed to vote; this meant only 30% of the population of Athens was allowed to vote *(that doesn't sound very democratic)*. Closer to modern times, women were only given the vote in the early twentieth century. In my own country, Australia, the indigenous population were only given the right to vote in 1967. For conditions to stay in balance *(harmony)* it needs to have the ability to change to the constantly changing environment; softness allows change to happen. Don't make the mistake of thinking change is good. Change is neither good or bad. It's just change. If you change when it's not required then your out of relation *(balance)* to the moment *(the Tao)*.

Balance is generally the key to a successful and happy life. Wee Kee Jin told me that Master Huang once said; "There are only two types of people who can't do Tai Chi, the first are the extremely rich and the second are the extremely poor". Because their thoughts are constantly occupied by money. The problem is, no sooner do you get the balance right *(and this could be work/life balance)* and your situation *(moment)* changes. You have an unexpected expense and you may need to work overtime to cover this sudden expense. Or you've become unemployed and now you have too much leisure time on your hands. Balance could be the relationship between a parent and a child *(one of the hardest things to do, is getting the balance right as a parent)*. A classic example: anyone who has been a parent knows of the constant supervision a three to five years old requires. You're at a party or BBQ with your partner. You have turns following your three year old around, making sure they don't pull a scalding hot coffee on to themselves. Or they climb up on something dangerous, like a book case or pull that ridiculously large TV onto themselves. After half an hour, you swap places with your partner, and you now get to socialise and your partner is the new chaperone. You've got the balance right; you and partner have some social time and your child is safe. Now lets us jump 13 years forward, and once again the three of you are at a party or BBQ. You start following your now, 16 year old around. Your 16 year old asks, "why are you following me?" You answer, "to stop you doing something stupid and hurting yourself". Well, that's going to go down well! What was right and balanced when the child was 3 is not appropriate or balanced when the child is 16. To get the balance right requires an understanding of the variables. The mental and emotional maturity of a 16 year old must be considered. Some mature slower or faster due to their gender, genetics and environment. These are variables that need to be considered when getting the balance right when deciding how much freedom a 16 year old is given. The freedom requirements of a 3 year old is different to that of a 16 year old. Get the balance right and everything goes relatively smoothly *(as smoothly as things can go with a teenager)*. Too much freedom could lead to poor decisions and actions being made by the 16 year old, not enough freedom you stunt their transition into a well balanced adult. Change is a constant, what worked 13 years ago, doesn't necessarily mean it won't or will work now, you need to look at the moment you are in, including all the variables that exist in this moment. Get the balance right for what the moment requires and the situation will resolve itself with a positive outcome.

Relaxation brings many qualities to Tai Chi other than just giving the body the ability to change and adjust. One of many applications of relaxation is allowing movement to be created through the application of Wu Wei in the use of muscle which we covered in Chapter 3. Relaxed muscle is the perfect conductor for energy *(chi)* to pass through the body, this energy could be gravity, Di Xin Xi Yin Li, kinetic energy from a push or a blow or your own vital chi. A relaxed, centred and well aligned body is an ideal vehicle to facilitate the movement of the many forms of chi, passing through the body. Often when teaching a new student I ask them to take on the starting Posture of Tai Chi. Begin where their feet are shoulder width apart with the front of the feet parallel to each other, weight is 50/50. I then have them tighten their muscles in their body to about 90% capacity. I ask them if their body feels heavy. The most common reply is negative, that no, they don't feel heavy. I then ask them to relax from the ground up *(opening)*, to start softening and relaxing their muscles all the way to the crown of the head, not so much that they start to physically lower, but to minimise their muscle usage to an absolute bare minimum without creating movement. This generally takes about fifteen seconds to achieve this relaxed state. I ask them again do they feel any heavier than before relaxing the muscles? The usual reply is yes, they do feel heavier. Have you ever nursed a baby in your arms, trying to nurse the baby to sleep? You know when they've fallen asleep, when they suddenly feel heavier. So what just happened? Gravity didn't increase, it's still 1G. By letting go of muscle through relaxation students become more aware of the pulling effects of gravity.

When muscles are allowed to relax through the entire body it gives the body the ability to move as an integrated homogeneous collective unit. The chi of the Earth pulls other forms of chi or energy/forces that contact the body into the root. This chi is led by intent into the ground *(root)* in the direction of the practitioner's choosing.

Not only does relaxation allow physical movement, it also transports various forms of chi internally through the body. Relaxation is not technically chi, per se, however relaxation facilitates the movement of many forms of chi through the body. Try to view relaxation like that of water in a river, with fish and various fauna representing chi moving freely through and over the surface of water. The bank of the river acts like the alignments of the body, it contains the movement of water *(relaxation)*. Movement of the fauna *(chi)* is increased exponentially when you factor in that the river is itself moving downstream taking the fauna *(chi)* with it. Relaxation in conjunction with correct alignment allows gravity to move the physical body and the direction it takes. More importantly it pulls other forms of chi through the body before there is even the slightest physical movement. It is this adjustment inside the relaxation before any physical movement is generated that gives push hands its devastating effect. Imagine the following analogy, a river totally frozen, from the river bed to the surface, does the river move? No, now likening the frozen state of the river to tension in the body, everything becomes rigid and loses the ability to change or move. As soon as the weather becomes warm enough, the ice begins to melt and the river begins to move again. When relaxing, the body's internals *(Vital Chi, Di Xin Xi Yin Li, Kinetic Chi, Blood, Breath, etc, etc)* all begin to move. Relaxation *(figuratively)* liquefies the internal movement of the body. This movement of chi also has a beneficial effect on ones health, with the added benefit that it can be used as an exercise and a martial art.

Awareness creates relaxation, intent leads relaxation, gravity moves relaxation, relaxation facilitates the movement of chi and chi creates li *(strength)* **by means of returning the chi** *(energies such as gravity and kinetic)* **into the opponent's root causing them to become isolated, weakened and imbalanced.**

This gives the false appearance and sensation that you've become stronger, which you haven't. You've made your opponent weaker which gives them the confusing and misleading sensation that you've become stronger and more powerful than them. Don't fall into the trap of chasing *(muscular)* strength, instead let go of short term perceived strength *(muscular)* and soften *(relax)* and access limitless strength, *(the means with which to weaken your opponent is limited only by your softness)* as the Classics state, "Only when one becomes truly soft, can one be truly hard". I feel a better wording of this Classic should have read, "Only when one is truly soft, can one seem to be truly hard to one's opponent.". When the root of your opponent is so totally cut and isolated, your opponent senses that you are like this immovable object, like a mountain. You're not an immovable object, however, everything is relative, in the opponent's weakened state you do feel immovable. In T.C.M this situation would be considered as false Yang, because I've made you weaker, which gives you the false sense of me becoming stronger.

<u>**I firmly believe that this incorrect interpretation of a sensation has caused students to chase and train muscular strength in Tai Chi.**</u>

I have taught my students to always question and challenge what they think and doubly so, with what they feel. In this excellent book, There Are No Secrets written by Wolfe Lowenthal, he talks about Cheng Man-Ching trying ten pin bowling while in New York. Cheng Man-Ching was asked the next day how he found it. He said he wasn't going to continue with it, as the ball was far too heavy. Yet he had no problems throwing a 100 kilo man across the room. Yang Lu-ch'an once stated that there were only three kinds of people he couldn't defeat: men made of brass, men made of iron and men made of wood. This tells you he couldn't influence inanimate objects, because they don't move under their own volition or chi. In other words he had nothing to feed off and draw out and re-direct. Relaxation brings a softness to the body that facilitates the internal movement of chi and the physical movement of the body by means of substantial and insubstantial *(more on this in Chapter 9)*.

How Is Relaxation Created?
The prelude to relaxation is awareness *(consciousness)*. To physically relax you first need to become aware. You can't relax a muscle or muscles if you can't feel them. Awareness or consciousness, starts by gently bringing the mind into the body to discern between tension and relaxation. This awareness is constantly moving up and down the body *(opening and closing)*, like an elevator, constantly feeling for tension. Creating a state of relaxation where the body isn't moving, such as lying on the floor or

sitting in a chair, isn't all that difficult to achieve. However, in Tai Chi where you're in constant state of motion internally and externally, it becomes extremely hard to maintain this state of awareness which in turn creates relaxation. This is due to the nature of movement in Tai Chi where one is required to continuously disengage muscle to generate movement and contract muscle to bear shifting weight and maintain structure *(equilibrium)*. Without constant awareness to discern which muscles are required to let go *(Wu Wei)* so that Di Xin Xi Yin Li is allowed to create movement and which muscles need to be engaged, to maintain equilibrium *(structure)* with gravity. Tai Chi wouldn't be possible.

Muscle contraction to bear weight is permissible, but not enough to create movement. The process of moving weight from one leg to the other smoothly *(substantial and insubstantial)* to create movement is very similar to running a relay race. As you hand over the baton to your team mate, should you let go of the baton too soon, it will drop to the ground, forcing your team mate to double back to retrieve the baton. Let us say, this time when handing the baton to your team mate, you hold on to the baton for too long, resulting in your team mate dragging you up the track. To correctly pass the baton to your team mate requires perfect timing. Tai Chi is similar, moving from one posture to the next requires constant letting go of muscle and simultaneously engaging muscle *(contraction to bear weight, not to create movement)* with perfect timing. If you don't let go of various muscles you don't create movement. Let go too much muscle and you collapse structure and alignment. Use too much muscle and you create movement. All these muscles need to contract and let go in relation to each other to have the ability to generate substantial and insubstantial, which in turn generates movement through non-action. This requires a lot of awareness *(consciousness)* to keep this process harmonised.

If muscle contraction is insufficient around the joints of the body, you will collapse structure and fall to the ground. If muscle contraction around the joints is in perfect equilibrium with gravity, no movement is possible. If excessive muscle is engaged, isolated movement will be the result. Letting go of just the right amount of muscle to allow movement is the sweet spot.

Taoist philosophy often states, "that one should be child like". What's the meaning of this proverb? Should we play like children, be as innocent as a child? As adults we have responsibilities, we need to earn an income, keep a roof over our head and food on the table. All children, regardless of race, culture or gender share one thing in common *(other than toilet humour)*. They all live in the moment. Young children will happily chase a ball onto the road, giving little care to the traffic. When babies cry they are easily distracted when their favourite toy is shown to them. As adults, we are too easily taken out of the moment and can sometimes overly focus on the past or future. You can't be silly; as adults we have responsibilities. We need to engage the future and the past. It becomes a problem when we excessively focus on the past or future. To be child-like means to be in the moment. As we say in the West, "stop and take time to smell the roses". This brings to mind an old proverb: "Everything in life is designed to enhance your life, not control it".

The Tao Te Ching places a heavy emphasis on change. Relaxation is not static, but like the Tao is in constant state of change in relation to your immediate environment *(moment or universe)*. Balance is the product of change, change maintains balance. **Physical relaxation uses only the energy and muscle that's required for the moment, with demands of the moment in constant change, as is the Tao.**

We have clarified and defined Tai Chi as the physical manifestation of Taoist principles in action, having qualified the chi that powers all movement in Tai Chi, that being Di Xin Xi Yin Li (gravity). We can now access this power source by applying Taoist principle of Wu Wei, Non-action to create action. By re-directing our opponent's energy/force (chi) through relaxation back into their own root causing them to become isolated and weak, giving the false perception of you becoming physically stronger. Relaxation is the means with which we move many forms of chi/energy/force around and through the body. What method of relaxation is used, that allows us to maintain a continuous state of relaxation?

Does Relaxation have a Yin & Yang Element?

6. Opening and Closing

If there is a secret to Tai Chi it would have to be Opening *(relaxing upward)* and Closing *(relaxing downward)*. A secret that hides in plain sight. Master Huang often said, "there are no secrets in Tai Chi, just infinite small detail that students don't see". Relaxation in Tai Chi can be broken into two separate, but interconnected processes known as Opening *(relaxation upward, Yang)* and Closing *((relaxation downward, Yin)*. This opening and closing creates an enclosed internal circulatory process within the body. *(Figure 1)* Opening and closing behaves similarly to a pulley. Pulling down on one side of the rope causes the other side of the rope to rise. Using the pulley analogy, relaxation travels up and down the body in a continuous and never-ending process. Were you to stop pulling down on the rope, likewise the other side would also stop rising. When Tai Chi practitioners press their foot/feet against the ground this results in relaxation upward *(opening)* and relaxation downward *(closing)* to instantly cease. Were you to continue the closing process *(relax downward)* to the point *(pivot point)* of reaching full compression in the root, relaxation upward *(opening)* would travel unimpeded up the body. Pressing the foot/feet against the ground disrupts this cycle of Opening and Closing results in your pushing *(resisting)* against any incoming energy/forces, leading to double weightedness or double heaviness *(Figure 2)*. This cyclic opening and closing is critical in allowing various energy/forces *(chi)* to pass through the body into your root *(closing)* and back up *(opening)*. Relaxation is the fuel that generates all movement in Tai Chi, whether it's moving forward, backward, turning left or right. Even when physically still when between postures, relaxation must remain a constant. Opening and closing serves two functions. The first is supplying the body with a constant, endless, uninterrupted source of relaxation allowing the internal movement of chi *(gravity, vital chi and external forces)* to move unopposed in the body. Secondly, Opening and Closing creates a dynamic interplay between substantial and insubstantial, which in turns generates all physical movement in Tai Chi *(more on this is in Chapter 9, The Symbiotic Relationship Between Opening, Closing, Substantial, Insubstantial and Movement)*.

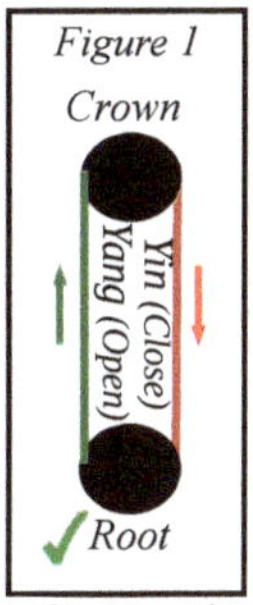

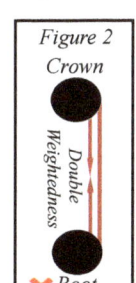

Figure 1
Crown
Yin (Close)
Yang (Open)
Root
Opening & Closing is an enclosed circulatory process.

Figure 2
Crown
Double Weightedness
Root
Pressing your foot against the ground results in double weightedness.

Opening and Closing not only creates internal movement, thus preventing energy/forces from settling on the body, but simultaneously generates substantial and insubstantial which create physical movement *(internal moves external)*.

These two movements, internal and external, are interconnected in Tai Chi. All relaxation regardless whether it's Opening or Closing, originates in the root. **This rule is unbreakable**. Closing can be considered downward relaxation, starting in the root, more commonly known as sinking. Closing always precedes Opening, it's not possible to Open without first Closing. Closing and Opening always pass through the substantial leg; the only exception to this rule is when you're in a neutral stance where weight distribution is 50/50, the same stance that is used in the starting posture of Begin. Only after closing has been achieved *(closing is concluded when one achieves full compression. Refer to the glossary for definition of full compression)*. Can one begin to Open *(relax upward)*. Opening is a secondary wave of relaxation, a more refined relaxation, commonly known as jing, moving from the root up through the body. In some of the older Tai Chi literature opening is sometimes referred to as song up *(relax upward)*. When closing is performed correctly it terminates in the root. Upon reaching full compression in the root, relaxation goes through a qualitative change, becoming more refined or less coarse. This relaxation changes to a form of jing, which is commonly known in Tai Chi as fa-jing. I'm not a big fan of calling this refined relaxation *fa-jing*, I will give the reasons later in the section covering Opening. In Tai Chi there is constant reference to circulating the chi. Vital chi needs to circulate continuously throughout the body to achieve optimal health. Relaxation also needs to continuously circulate throughout the body without interruption. Even a momentary pause in relaxation leads to double weightedness. When closing *(relaxing downward)* reaches full compression in the root it needs to transition to opening *(relaxing upward)*. Without this transition to opening, relaxation will cease, resulting once again in double weightedness. Closing *(relaxation downward)* always starts in the root, instigated by gravity *(chi of the Earth) (Di Xin Xi Yin Li)* which travels to the crown of the head. To explain this process I like to use the analogy of an hour glass. **(Figure 3)** The only reason why sand from the top compartment *(consider the upper compartment of the hourglass as your whole body)* is allowed to move downward is because the bottom compartment *(the lower compartment representing your root)* is filling up with sand. Sand falling downward *(represents closing)* into the bottom compartment, creates an upward space *(yang)* between the grains of sand, allowing the sand to pass through the neck of the hour glass *(bubbling well)* and fall to the bottom compartment *(the root)*. This ripple effect continues upward till all the sand resides in the lower compartment *(full compression)*. Most Tai Chi practitioners tend to start their relaxation in the upper body rather than in the root. This akin to the sand positioned at the very top of the hourglass moving first, rather than the lower sand in the top compartment initiating movement as it falls into the bottom compartment.

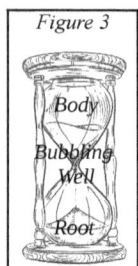

Often opening and closing is referenced in Tai Chi literature to the joints of the body opening and closing when in movement, which they do. I don't subscribe to this theory even though the joints do open and close during Tai Chi. However, the joints also open and close in the external martial arts. Closing in Tai Chi is referenced to closing *(relaxation downward)* into the root and opening *(relaxation upward)* expanding from the root. Opening and closing terminology is also used in T.C.M theory; an acupuncturist will often close an acupuncture point which means to gather the vital chi and other times they'll open the acupuncture point and disperse the vital chi. Closing can also be considered as gathering and opening as dispersing.

When Opening and Closing interact with each other, they can produce substantial and insubstantial. It's this substantially and insubstantially which make every millimetre of physical movement possible in Tai Chi without using muscle. Master Huang Sheng-Shyan clearly understood and appreciated the importance of Opening and Closing in Tai Chi. So much so, he formulated an exercise called Opening and Closing Exercise to cultivate and encourage this process. This is the first exercise and easily the most important exercise you'll learn in Master Huang's lineage, specific for the development and training of Opening and Closing *(continuous relaxation)* within the body. In this Chapter, I'll explain Opening and Closing and how it generates substantial and insubstantial which in turn makes all physical movement possible by means of non-action.

Where Does Relaxation Originate?
True relaxation starts in your root, not the crown of the head, not the centre of your body *(Dan Tien)*, **in the root.** However, before the relaxation process can start in the root, you will need to first eliminate tension by bringing your awareness into the whole body to soften and disengage muscles not required *(eliminate tension)*. You need to minimise muscle usage to a bare minimum, allowing the joints of the body to be pulled into alignment with each other, allowing the body to take on the necessary physical alignments for cultivating relaxation. Then gently connect your awareness to your intent that you have established 20 centimetres under the bubbling well. You should have now established a relaxed connection from your root *(earth)*, up through your entire body *(man)* to the crown of the head *(heaven)*. Now, imagine your intent is pulling deeper into the ground *(closing, relaxing downward)* while keeping your head suspended, this will elongate the whole body. This elongation of the body opens all the joints, making it conducive to moving relaxation through your body, which in turn moves many forms of chi. It's important to keep a light consciousness to the

crown of head when training Tai Chi. When teaching students this principle, I often pull a coin from my pocket showing the student the coin. I place the coin on the crown of their head, and tell them to do the form, not allowing the coin to slide off their head. After the student has finished the form, I ask for my coin back, they start patting the top of their head with their hand looking for the coin. What they didn't realise, when placing the coin on top of their head, I palmed it and slipped it back into my pocket. The student swears they could feel the coin on the crown of their head even though it wasn't there. If you're having trouble keeping your head suspended in Tai Chi it sometimes helps to place something light on the crown of your head, it helps maintain a light awareness there.

Starting relaxing *(closing)* from the root, *(intent)* the second you begin to draw down from the root through the back of the substantial leg *(an old Tai Chi proverb states; the flesh from the buttock to the heel should be soft to the touch)* you'll need to soften *(relax)* from the root, through the substantial leg, to the crown of the head *(just like the hour glass)*. Try to visualise relaxation being pulled from the root through the core of the median line of the body to the crown of the head; this establishes a relaxed connection to your root *(intent)*. With relaxation being pulled from where the intent is, through the core of the body in a downward direction *(closing)*, it also simultaneously expands outward from the centre of the body *(like the hour glass, as the sands falls through the neck, the sand movement expands outward as it drains upward, yin creates yang)*. Performed in this way, relaxation moving downwards will also expand upward and outward, so if an external force is placed on the body it's immediately pulled into the root. A very common mistake I see students make is the tendency to start their relaxation in the upper body first and relax downward resulting in collapsing or physically dropping into the root. Where at best you can hope for is becoming more grounded before the opponent's force slams into you. This results in your becoming compressed and lodged within your own root, resulting in you and your muscles becoming jammed. Another common fault when it comes to relaxation is that students tend to relax from the extremities and move inward, this becomes more obvious during push hands. Students tend to relax the area of their body that's being pushed first. This causes the outside of the body to collapse onto the inner part of the body that hasn't yet relaxed, resulting in forces settling on the body. Master Huang would often say, "these people are like a half cooked potato, soft on the outside, rock hard on the inside". Tai Chi is an internal art moving upward and outward, not from top to bottom or outward to inward. **The definition of isolated body movement can be considered as any movement that doesn't emanate from the root.**

When relaxation is achieved and starts to move, it needs to be led by intent to a point under the ground of the Tai Chi practitioner's choosing. Without intent relaxation is still achievable by means of awareness, but you won't have the ability to position it. Without intent the best you can hope for is some physical yielding and grounding. Grounding is when you relax from above without intent, into the ground, whereas rooting, is relaxation led by intent that's already in the ground. The Classics state, "The Yi leads the Chi and the Chi leads the Li". Another Classic: "Ultimately everything depends on one's Will *(intent)*". Yi is first; without Yi, relaxation *(chi)* has no direction. So before relaxing, make sure intent is established first: Once intent has been established keep your head suspended so the intent by means of relaxation can connect from the ground *(root)* through the body to the crown of the head. So when relaxation is pulled through the body by the chi of the Earth *(gravity)* it's led by intent to a point of the practitioner's choosing. Creating movement is easy *(movement in stillness is hard)*, all you need to do is relax enough muscle to start the relaxation process of opening and closing. As opening and closing moves up and down the body, body weight shifts. This in turn creates substantial and insubstantial, resulting in the joints of the body moving forward, backwards, left and right *(this method of joint movement generated by relaxation will be explained in Chapter 13 Alignments)*. It is this interplay of substantial and insubstantial which causes you to physically move in the direction of your alignment and intent. To physically stop movement, simply engage enough muscle to stop the internal movement *(relaxation)* of opening and closing.

This will also terminate the interplay of substantial and insubstantial, bringing the body *(joints)* to a standstill.

Stop for a second to consider this. **All your life you have been taught, correctly so, that if you want to create movement, engage muscle. If you want stop movement, disengage muscle, and all movement ceases. The Taoist's concept of movement teaches that we do the exact opposite. If you want to create movement, we disengage muscle *(non-action)*. To stop movement, we engage muscle.** Both are correct, the problem is, it's impossible to apply both methods simultaneously, they'll cancel each other out. You need to choose your method of movement. Either muscular version of an action creating an equal and opposite action, or the Taoist version of non-action, creating action. These days the majority of Tai Chi practitioners tend to press their feet against the ground to move their body which then moves their weight which then creates substantial and insubstantial, instead of relaxing *(opening and closing)* through the body which moves weight, creating substantial and insubstantial, which then moves the body. When students press their feet against the ground, they have effectively put the cart before the horse. There is also a fine balancing *(harmony)* point when doing the form, that's in constant change between using too much muscle and too little muscle. Too little muscle to support weight and your structure *(alignment or posture)* collapses. Too much muscle and you won't be able to move *(like having the hand brake engaged when driving a car)*. And extreme muscle use generates movement, which you don't want.

Closing *(First Stage)*

In Master Huang's lineage we introduce the student to the concept of opening *(relaxing upward)* and closing *(relaxing downward)* early on, by teaching an exercise called Opening and Closing Exercise. Master Huang introduced this exercise into his schools in the early 1980s. It's the very first exercise learnt in the Huang's lineage, before the Five Loosening Exercises, Form and Push Hands. The Opening and Closing Exercise teaches the student how to relax their entire muscular system, allowing the muscles of the body to integrate with each other in ways that isolated muscle just can't match. The common thread that literally connects these relaxed muscles is the chi of the Earth *(gravity)*. Di Xin Xi Yin Li, when applied under the right conditions of alignment, relaxation *(opening and closing)*, substantial and insubstantial and intent, can generate movement, speed and power. In comparison, muscle-based movement which is compartmentalised and isolated will work against gravity and each other.

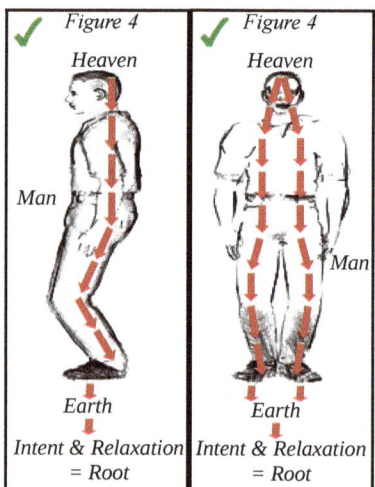

First place your intent into the ground, then connect to the crown of the head. Start closing from the root to the crown of the head.

First of all we need to take on the correct alignment *(structure)* that allows and encourages opening and closing *(relaxation)* to move freely up and down the body. For the student to experience these subtle sensations of opening and closing, I need the student take on the alignment of the Opening and Closing Exercise. Placing their heels together with feet turned out from the centre, 45 degrees, which means the feet are 90 degrees to each other. Knees bent just enough so the pelvis is relaxed under in a slight sitting position, head suspended, spine straight, middle fingers touching the seam of the pants, weight 50% in each leg, weight moving through the bubbling well **(Figure 4)**. I ask them to place their intent 20cm directly under the bubbling well *(when first learning the Opening and Closing Exercise you don't need to send your intent outward, just straight down is sufficient for now)*. With the student's intent directly under the bubbling well, I ask them to bring a light awareness to the crown of the head and connect these two points *(heaven and earth and what* *connects these two points, is man)*. Having established your intent in the ground, connect to a light consciousness to the crown of the head. Once these two points are connected, I tell the student to slowly relax downward *(closing)* starting from the root *(intent & relaxation)* allowing the closing *(relaxing downward)* to move up through the whole body *(like the hourglass analogy, the sands draining downwards causes an adjustment upwards)*. During this stage, I tell the student not to physically move at first, but to keep the head suspended, allowing the body to adjust and elongate. The purpose of this is that students learn intent moves before relaxation and relaxation moves before body *(Yi Chi Li)*. The student learns and realises that the body can be physically still in Tai Chi when in transition between postures, which it is, however, the intent and relaxation is always moving. The classics confirm this in the Explanation Of The Thirteen Postures By Wang Chung-Yueh; 似鬆非鬆，將展未展，勁斷意不斷。"The inner strength may seem slack, but it is not. It may seem stretched but it is not. The physical force may break but the intent does not".

I instruct the student to continue relaxing downward *(closing)* until they reach a point, where it requires more effort to hold this static position, than it does to allow movement. At that moment, I tell them to let go from the crown of the head allowing the body to physically lower caused by relaxing muscles and the chi of the Earth. How low the student physically lowers, is entirely up to them, as long as they don't lose alignment, collapse or jam joints. When they physically stop, it is **absolutely critical to continue closing with their intent and relaxation** until they find it physically and mentally *(intent)* impossible to keep relaxing and letting go. Why is this so important? The students need to understand and realise, just because the body has physically stopped, the process hasn't. It is at this very moment the student reaches the second stage of opening and closing... **full compression.**

Root is created when you have both intent and relaxation. Relaxation without intent can be considered grounding. Intent without relaxation is just thought. It is important to understand the difference between grounding and rooting: grounding is similar to having dug a hole 60 centimetres deep, dropping a pine log into the hole, and filling the hole back up. Come back in 30 years, the log will still be there, nothing will have changed. That's grounding. Now imagine you've planted an oak sapling, that's 30 centimetres high. Come back in 30 years and you'll find a very large oak tree-that's relaxation with intent *(rooting)*. Before a tree grows upward, it first grows its roots downward and outwards, expanding its root system. These new roots give stability and structure to any new growth above ground and supply nutrients for the new growth to happen. This is probably the reason why trees are so often used in Tai Chi analogies. Interesting note, trees do have intent, it has been proven the roots of a tree move in the direction of running water or where soil moisture is at its highest. Intent is extremely important in the later years of your training. It will grow your internal strength by making your opponent increasingly weaker. *(your internal strength will be reflected in your ability to affect your opponent's connection to the chi of the Earth, weakening your opponent's physical strength, and giving them the false appearance that your stronger)*.

Over time, training your relaxation, whether it's opening or closing to connect to your intent will result in the developing of your root. When root has been established and you've become comfortable with the process of opening and closing from your intent, under the bubbling well, the next step is to move the intent from directly under your bubbling well forward by a metre. Make sure to maintain your connection of opening and closing to your forward intent, so when an opponent touches any part of your body, while you're closing *(the intent leads the relaxation to a point under the ground, forward of yourself)* it will lead your opponent's energy/force to where your intent is positioned. Which is under and behind your opponent's root, resulting in your opponent's energy/force being returned to their root, causing their root to be instantly severed. A little bit of advice: don't wait for the opponent to touch you before starting the process of closing from your root. If you do, you'll be too late and the energy/force will have already settled on you and more importantly you will have started your relaxation from above. The process of closing from the root must be established before any physical contact is made with your opponent. Most Tai Chi practitioners mistakenly press their feet against the ground when moving or pushing in Tai Chi. This is the equivalent of pushing against a tree while standing on top of the tree's roots. *(Figure 5)* The force of the push is returned to the tree's roots which is positioned under their feet, making the tree stronger.

While we're on the subject of trees students often ask me the meaning of the following Tai Chi proverb; "If you don't move, I don't move, if you move, I move first" or "You leave first, I arrive first". Like a lot of the Classics, the above proverb at first appears contradictory, until the underlying context is understood. Intent in conjunction with relaxation behaves like the roots of a tree. Any force placed on the tree such as a strong wind is instantly transferred to the tree's roots, resulting in the roots absorbing a large amount of the wind's energy. This is the exact process used in Tai Chi.

Figure 5

As in Tai Chi, when pushing against a tree your force is fed back into the root system under your own feet, making the tree more stable.

Continuing with the tree concept, one of my senior students Marcello Abbate came up with a great analogy that I use when teaching. At one of the halls where I teach is a large poinciana tree. I often take students to this tree to physically demonstrate the above proverbs; 'If you don't move, I don't move, If you move, I move first". Another similar proverb; "You leave first, I arrive first". I ask one of my students to stand next to the tree, while I stand around three metres from the same tree, I make the claim, that I can touch the tree before they can. So the race is on, the student's hand is only centimetres from the tree, I say; "GO" the student's hand is on the tree in a heartbeat. I haven't moved, the student proudly proclaims they're the winner. I declare that's not so... I'm the winner, they protest, you can't be, you haven't even moved. I tell them to look at my foot, looking down, they see my foot is resting on top of a large root running along the ground from the tree they're now touching. I was touching the tree with my foot before the student had even moved. The Classics, often refer to sensations, and are not to be taken literally. As stated earlier in this Chapter, I have already started the closing process, using my intent before my opponent touches me. All I need to do is wait for my opponent's physical touch to complete the circuit of energy/force by means of relaxation. Your opponent's sensation of the process is that they are instigating the push. However, the second that contact is made, your opponent feels as though you were there first in their root. The reason for this sensation, is that you are there first... with your intent and relaxation.

Your intent leads the relaxation outward and under the ground *(like the roots of a tree)*. When an opponent touches you, this completes a circuit which instantly transfers any energy/force through your body, returning it to your opponent's root *(the source of their strength)*. In the more advanced stages of your training you need to train your intent as much if not more than your relaxation and alignment when practising the Opening and Closing Exercise, The Five Loosening Exercises, Form and Push Hands.

Over time and with correct training, your form and push hands will start to merge and become literally inseparable. It doesn't matter whether it's your own relaxed energy being pulled by gravity and led by intent, or a greater energy/force from your opponent, it slowly becomes irrelevant. Like a moving river, whether it's a leaf or a large ship being carried downstream, size doesn't matter *(water is relaxation, intent is the current)*. In the form you're always opening and closing with intent leading the process. It is irrelevant whether someone is touching you or not, everything is drawn into the root that you've placed in front of yourself, which is behind and under your opponent *(more on this in Chapter 12 Form)*. The second someone touches you, they're taken to where your intent is, by means of relaxation acting in conjunction with the chi of the Earth. Hence Master Huang's statement; "when practising the form, practise so if someone was to touch you they would be thrown out instantly".

When first starting your training in Tai Chi your primary focus should be on generating relaxation *(internal movement)*, and correct alignments *(postures)*; the least important aspect in the early stages of your training is intent. However, it is necessary to have a light intent so you become comfortable and familiar with placing your intent under the ground even if it's only minimal. In the later years of your training intent takes on a more dominant role in your Tai Chi. I'm often asked, what comes first relaxation or intent? It's a little like the chicken and the egg conundrum. I would have to say both are equally important, however, I would have to say intent is ever so slightly first. Like a missile, you need the engine to propel it, but without a guidance system it's useless. Guidance systems without an engine are also useless. Intent *(guidance system)* leads relaxation *(fuel)*, relaxation allows Di Xin Xi Yin *(engine)* to propel the rocket. One of the primary functions of intent is to lead relaxation after it's been created by awareness *(remember relaxation helps facilitate the movement of many forms of chi)*.

Full Compression *(Second Stage)*
Having reached the point where it's not possible to continue the closing *(relaxing downward)* process, you're now at the point of full compression, sometimes referred to as reaching extreme Yin, which is a pivot point. Be careful not to excessively disengage muscle, otherwise your structural integrity will distort, causing your joints to collapse and buckle. You may also feel the joints of the body starting to jam and compress into each other. these are signs that you have closed too much. Keeping your head suspended will prevent this from happening. This is where most students of Tai Chi tend to start pushing against the ground in the mistaken belief that they're opening or releasing the force from the ground, having reached full compression in their root. The sensation should be continuing the relaxation process, but is not physically possible. You have used up *(closed up)* every bit of space within the body. Where you choose to place your intent, whether it is in the ground directly under the substantial leg like when in a bow and arrow stance or if both legs are weighted 50/50 *(Figure 6)* is where you will start your opening process from. Where you start your opening from largely depends on your level of Tai Chi. If you're fairly new to Tai Chi I strongly recommend you start your opening 20 centimetres directly below your bubbling well. If you've been practising Tai Chi correctly for the last four to five years, and you've started training push hands then you should consider placing your intent under the ground a metre in front of you.

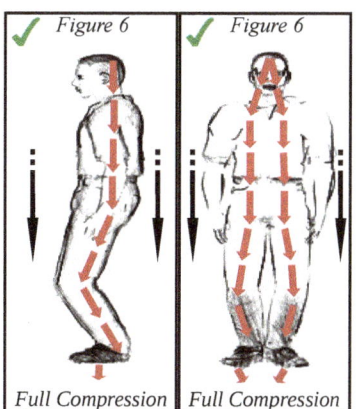
Reaching full compression in the Opening & Closing Exercise.

Placing yourself in full compression directly under your own bubbling well, though good when starting off in Tai Chi, is not fit for purpose when applied in push hands. Reaching full compression directly under your bubbling well is fine when first learning relaxation and alignment *(form)*. However, in push hands directly under your bubbling well is not a good place to be, because your root is directly under your own bubbling well, placing the source of movement back in front of your opponent *(which they can now block)*. When you position your root a couple of metres in front of you under and behind your opponent, your opponent can't block you because your force is already behind them *(refer to the glossary the difference between a push and a pull)*. Reaching full compression under your own bubbling well when training push hands will lead to the sensation of you being compressed and not your opponent.

Students often mistakenly believe this is root *(strength)*. You've effectively loaded *(compressed)* the spring and guess whose the spring is? *(And it's not your opponent)* This situation is fine if you believe movement and strength being achieved in Tai Chi by pushing/pressing your feet against the ground as a means of delivering force, then you're in the ideal position. Compressing yourself into your own substantial foot means your opponent still has control over their own root *(the old Tai Chi proverb "if you're not in control of your opponent's root, then they are")* therefore you haven't neutralised your opponent. You on the other hand having compressed yourself into your own root *(double weighted)* are vulnerable to becoming jammed or worse. When attempting to release your force onto your opponent, this results in your force being re-directed *(similar to a car back firing)* back into your own root, resulting in you, not your opponent, being thrown out. If however, you've managed to compress behind and under your opponent's root, you will have succeeded in cutting their root causing them to become isolated and restricted in how and what direction they can move, if they can move at all. The sensation your opponent will experience is similar to standing on top of a brick wall and you're wobbling forward and back with arms outstretched, going around in circles desperately trying to maintain your balance. A touch from either side will send you off the wall.

In Tai Chi, the following example is often used to explain how an ounce can move a thousand pounds. Like a nose ring through an ox's nose, a few ounces of pressure on the ring causes a thousand pound ox to move. The cause of the ox moving is the pain the animal experiences if it doesn't follow the direction the ring is pulled in. What the above proverb is trying to convey, by placing four ounces of pressure in the right place, which is your opponent's root after the root has been cut, you can move a thousand pounds. **An ounce at the right moment, in the right place, which is in your opponent's root, will have more of an effect than a 100 kilos of force being placed on your opponent's body.** You create the moment and conditions in Tai Chi. From experience when closing is performed properly and is concluded correctly in your root *(under and behind your opponent during push hands)* it results in your opponent experiencing the sensation of being compressed, **effectively making them a spring.** The sensation your opponent will feel is that of being trapped within their own body, it's as if their body; is being physically compressed, but they don't feel any force on their body *(a very confusing sensation, when experienced for the first time)*. The person who is causing the compression feels no pressure in their root or at the contact point with their opponent. The Classics often state; 發勁如放箭。 "releasing the energy in issuing is similar to releasing an arrow from a bow". The arrow is loaded *(compressed)*, not by pulling the string back, but by holding the arrow still *(this is similar to the form, where often the hands stay still and the body moves forward and back)* and moving the bow forward *(intent & relaxation moving forward)* all you need to do is let go of the string and the arrow *(opponent)* is released. The arrow is pulled forward, not pushed forward. The energy is stored in the bow, not in the bow string, the bow string is merely the conductor for stored energy, therefore the energy propelling the arrow is in front of the arrow.

Upon reaching full compression in the root under the ground, the relaxation undergoes a qualitative change and becomes more refined. I believe it's at this point relaxation changes to a form of jing, often referred to as fa-jing in Tai Chi. It is at this moment you're ready to start the third part of the relaxation process...*opening*.

Opening *(Third Stage)*

Opening in the context of Tai Chi is upward relaxation from the root once full compression is attained. This opening *(relaxing upward)* can be used for dual purposes of issuing or yielding depending on the direction the opening process takes. The details will be covered in Chapter 7, Different Qualities of Opening. To instigate opening after reaching full compression you'll need to soften in the root *(under the ground where your intent is ultimately, all closing and opening starts in the mind, specifically your intent)*. To tell the truth, with over 45 years of Tai Chi training, teaching on average 6 to 12 hours a day for the last 40 years, I still don't understand why it works. I know opening comes from closing, I know how to create opening by softening the root after full compression, I know the qualities of opening when it comes to yielding or issuing, but I still don't understand fully why it works, the actual softening of the root. When teaching the opening process to students, I try to have the student experience these incredibly subtle sensation within their root and body, so they can reproduce, cultivate and grow these refined sensations. Master Huang would often say "cultivate the awareness". I believe he was referencing growing these subtle sensations. By their nature, they are extremely challenging to explain and verbalise and are ineffable.

Creating Opening *(True Yang Rises / Emptiness / Void)*

I rarely ask students to take what I say on faith, I always encourage them to question everything, regardless of the source, the only exception to this rule, is when it comes to the creation of opening *(upward relaxation)*. I ask students to suspend reason and logic, because what I'm about to explain is neither rational, nor logical. When first performing Tai Chi we spend the vast majority of our time moving our consciousness up and down the body, literally thousands of times, cultivating relaxation by means of heightened awareness. Not only is it logical, but necessary to bring awareness into our body, to bring about a state of physical relaxation. However, to create opening we need to move beyond our body and move to where our intent *(mind)* is located. *(intent and relaxation combined create root)*. For the first three to four years of your training, intent needs to be positioned 20 centimetres under the bubbling well of the substantial leg as previously mentioned. There is no hard rule for how many years you need to stay directly under your bubbling well, some may need longer than four years, others less. There are too many variables at play, such as the student's natural ability, time spent training and the quality of their training to give an exact time frame.

Where you open *(relax upward)* from, is fully controlled by where you've closed *(relaxed downward)* to and reached full compression all led by your intent. In push hands and eventually in the form where you open *(relax up)* from, is ideally behind your real opponent in push hands or behind your imaginary opponent during the form. The process is identical regardless if it's solo work, form or push hands. For teaching purposes we'll start the opening process from directly under the bubbling well. Having reached full compression in the root, 20 centimetres directly under your bubbling well, the next step involves an unconventional concept. **You now need to soften the ground.** You've read it correctly; soften the ground. This is where a large leap of faith becomes absolutely necessary. Teaching students how to open *(relaxing upward)* is usually undertaken when the student is learning the Opening and Closing Exercise that Master Huang developed. This is the first and without question the most important exercise in Master Huang's lineage that you'll ever learn. This exercise is the cornerstone of Tai Chi and is applied to every millimetre of movement in every posture in Tai Chi. The only variable is the alignment that opening and closing takes, but the process always remains the same.

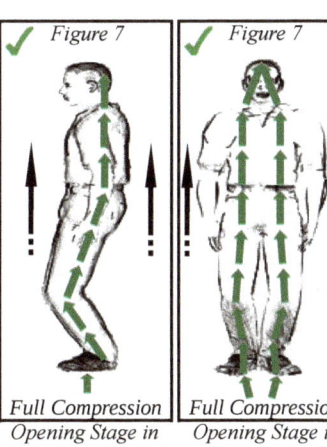

Figure 7

Figure 7

Full Compression | *Full Compression*
Opening Stage in the Opening & Closing Exercise. | *Opening Stage in the Opening & Closing Exercise.*

The student having reached full compression, is then instructed to keep their head suspended at all times throughout the following process. I then tell them to go to where their intent is, 20cm under the ground, directly below their bubbling well. At this stage of the process I usually stand directly in front of the student with my palms lightly touching both shoulders *(deltoids)*. The purpose for this is to help lead the student through the following process by means of using my awareness. Asking them to visualise the dirt under their feet being very hard and firm. Now, imagine I'm pouring water over the ground they're standing on, slowly they feel the hard and firm dirt turning to soft mud under their feet. The student needs to focus only on the ground becoming softer and softer, and their head remaining suspended and nothing else. After a few seconds, they can actually sense the imaginary mud softening under their feet, seeping up between their toes. While focusing on the mud softening, the student becomes aware of their body starting to make subtle adjustment again. It's as if their body has found more space within which to continue their adjustments and their chest area starts to soften and let go again. Visualising the softness of the mud moving up from the root through the back of the legs and the upper body to the crown of the head, causing the body to physically rise *(similar to a back pressure moving upwards through the body)* without pushing. *(Figure 7)* The strangest part of the whole opening process is the second you soften your root *(not the body, the root)*. This instantly results in the body re-relaxing and softening again. It is this part of the process that I just don't understand. How does the relaxation of the root create space in the body, so the relaxation process can be continued. It is a total mystery to me, all I know is it works.

When opening reaches the crown of the head the closing stage starts in the root, and the process is repeated once again. When students become comfortable with the opening process from the root, I then have them start closing *(relaxing downward)* in the root the moment when opening reaches chest or shoulder blade height. This is known as the two thirds rule, which is extremely hard to apply, and shouldn't be attempted until you are proficient with the opening and closing process. The purpose of the two thirds rule is to prevent a top developing. If you wait until the opening *(relaxing upward)* reaches the crown of the head before starting to close in the root, the opening and closing process will have stopped *(this is a dead spot or a hollow)*. There is a Tai Chi proverb that I constantly quote, "In Tai Chi there is no left, there is no right, *(when opening or closing moves through the kuas, causing the kuas to either physically open or close, creating left and right turns without the use of muscle or thought)* there is no forward, there is no backward *(reference to relaxation regardless whether it's opening or closing moving through the front or back leg resulting in the body moving forward and back without the use of thought and muscle)*, there is only up and down, *(the up and down is in reference to closing, relaxing downward and opening, relaxing upward which are vertical actions,* with no top and no bottom *(the no top is in reference to the application of the two thirds rule, and no bottom is in relation to opening at full compression)*, no beginning and no end *(is in reference once again to the two thirds rule and opening from the root after reaching full compression resulting in the process never having to stop, no beginning and no end)*".

The above proverb is a typical Taoist riddle that is so ambiguous it renders the proverb almost useless. However, understanding the underlying principles behind Opening and Closing, the proverb's deeper meaning becomes obvious. When opening *(relaxing upward)* and closing *(relaxing downward)* stops, the result is double weightedness. Double weightedness is distinct from the common belief of having your weight 50/50. Double weightedness is when relaxation stops at any point during the opening and closing process, especially when opening and closing are in transition with each other *(pivot points)*. When relaxation stops, double weightedness is the result. Relaxation prevents energy/forces from settling on the body. The second that relaxation stops you have created the conditions internally for double weightedness. This creates internal resistance *(force against force or double heaviness)*. To become double weighted, you only need to momentarily stop opening and closing. In other words you don't need to do something wrong to become double weighted, you just need to stop doing something right *(relaxing)* for a millisecond to become double weighted.

Timing of Opening and Closing
Learning to Close *(relax downward)* and Open *(relax upward)* is critical to your Tai Chi development. However, it's the interaction of internal movements of closing *(yin)* and opening *(yang)* moving in relation to each other that generates so called power, movement and speed. Similar to the process of generating electricity, a magnet rotates inside a coil of copper wire will generate an electrical current. If the magnet is stationary and doesn't move, no electrical current is possible. Opening and closing

need to move in relation to each other to create movement, substantial and insubstantial and so called power. Try to view opening *(relaxation upward)* and closing *(relaxation downward)* like a car engine. Hundreds of parts are brought together to build an engine with the vast majority of these parts moving. What makes the car engine work is all the different parts moving together in relation with each other. The pistons need to move up and down at different times to each other, the valves open and close at different times in relation to the movement of the pistons. Exhaust is taken away and fuel is then added. Spark from the spark plug needs to spark at the right time to ignite the right mix of air and fuel. All these parts not only have to exist, but these various parts need to move in timing with each other, otherwise the engine doesn't work. This is the same process for opening and closing inside your body. When first training opening and closing it's best to just focus on alignment *(structure)*, followed then by training the downward relaxation *(closing)* process, starting in your root just under your bubbling well. Upon reaching full compression, you'll need to train yourself to open *(relax upward)* from the root *(opening is a lot harder to develop and train than closing)*, through the bubbling well to the crown of the head. I can't stress enough the importance of establishing root. Root can only exist when intent and relaxation are brought together. When intent and relaxation are combined, only then do you have the beginnings of root. Root having been established, the direction relaxation takes whether it's opening or closing from the root in conjunction with your alignment will dictate the direction your physical movement will take. Whether it's turning left, right, moving forward, moving backward and central equilibrium *(central equilibrium means the outside is still but the inside is still opening and closing)*. This is all dictated by alignments, powered by opening *(relaxing upward)* and closing *(relaxing downward)* creating substantial and insubstantial all from the root.

When you can close and open from the root this channels the relaxation through your alignments, you possess the basic qualities required to be able to generate physical and internal movement. The only thing left now to do is to create the timing of opening and closing so everything works. When training opening *(relaxing upward)* and closing *(relaxing downward)*, **there can be no point where these two opposites** *(yin, closing and yang, opening)* **stop interacting with each other** if opening and closing should stop or pause even for a millisecond, then internally everything shuts down, resulting in double weightedness. However, if your timing of opening and closing is correct, the two will seamlessly flow and interact without break, Hence the saying; "The ending of one move is the beginning of the next move". This is not in reference to physical movement of one posture to the next. It's in relation to closing that's coming to an end *(full compression)* that starts the opening process and when opening reaches chest height *(two thirds rule)* the closing process starts in the root with the opening process continuing and concluding at the crown of the head. Opening and closing create the internal movement that travels through the alignments, which creates movement we call postures. It's the timing and interaction of relaxation upward *(opening)* and relaxation downward *(closing)* that makes opening and closing work in Tai Chi. To explain this timing I need to go back to two points *(pivot points)* in the opening and closing process, specifically, the two thirds rule and full compression in the root. The first point, when closing *(relaxing downward)* in the root has reached full compression, full compression is created when you have physically reached the limit of your closing *(downward relaxation)*. It undergoes a smooth transition from closing *(relaxation downward)* to opening *(relaxation upward)*, this process needs to be smooth and seamless without hollows, holdings or protrusions. This change from closing to opening is often referred to in Tai Chi as releasing the Jing.

This timing from closing *(relaxing downward)* to opening *(relaxing upward)* is not easy and takes time to achieve. How long? I was told when I first started training in Master Huang's lineage, with proper training and practise, four to five years. When I asked what was this mysterious force that came out of the ground, I was told I would know it when I felt it. What do you have to do to cause this force to come out of the ground? Once again I was told to just keep relaxing into the ground, and have faith and eventually it will happen. I now realise what comes out of the ground was a more refined and subtle relaxation called opening sometimes referred to as jing. It is this same relaxation that is so incredibly soft when used for yielding, or alternatively can feel as hard as rock *(to your opponent)* when used for issuing. At the risk of repeating myself, this transition from closing to opening **must be seamless** otherwise the closing will all be for nothing. The second part where you also need to be seamless is in the last third of the opening stage. In Master Huang's lineage we're taught the two thirds rule; this rule is applied when opening has reached two thirds of your body height, *(which is chest height or shoulder blade height)*. Upon reaching two thirds you start the closing process in the root. Don't make the mistake I made. For years I started the closing process in the chest and upper body, rather than in the root. Chest height is the timing point; the closing starts in the root, not your chest. If you follow the two thirds rule you'll prevent a top developing, so the changeover from opening to closing will be smooth and seamless with no hollows or protrusions. It's at these two points *(pivot points)* where issuing is made possible *(refer to glossary Two Points of Release, Extreme Yin and Extreme Yang within the Cycle of Opening & Closing)* for closing it's at full compression **(extreme yin)**, remember the old Tai Chi saying; "Only after reaching extreme yin, does true yang rise" and for opening it can be at the crown of the head **(extreme yang)** when the release happens. It is at these two extreme points *(pivot points)* when the energy of Opening *(Yang)* and Closing *(Yin)* transition from opening to closing or closing to opening that creates movement, so called power and speed. These two points of extreme yin and yang have no relation to your physical position in the form. You can be 100% in the rear leg and be at extreme yin *(full compression)*, about to open and release, or alternatively you could be at extreme yang *(opening)* with 100% of the weight in the rear leg and about to finish the opening process and move into closing and release.

Using the following analogy of flicking a tea towel *(dish towels)* at your brother or sister when drying the dishes, when you were kids. You spin the tea towel around a few times to get the tea towel nice and tight, you pinch the towel between your two hands. You throw the front hand forward, letting go of the towel with the rear hand, the towel is pulled forward, consider this action as closing, when your hand is at its full reach you quickly pull your hand back towards you, consider that as opening. Now you need both actions, forward hand movement *(closing)* and backward hand movement *(opening)* to make the tea towel snap and release its energy. The releasing of energy is caused by the timing of the change from closing to opening. If you were to throw your hand forward then stopped and waited for the end of the tea towel to catch up and then pulled your hand back, nothing would happen. It's the same with opening and closing in Tai Chi, if you were to stop relaxation at the bottom of closing before opening, you would have nothing. And if you stopped relaxation at the end of opening before closing, once again you would have nothing. It's the timing of opening and closing interacting with each other that creates these two extremes points of Yin *(closing)* and Yang *(opening)* that releases energy.

We have clarified and defined Tai Chi as the physical manifestation of Taoist principles in action, having qualified the chi that powers all movement in Tai Chi, that being Di Xin Xi Yin Li (gravity). We can now access this power source by applying the Taoist principle of Wu Wei, Non-action to create action. By re-directing your opponent's energy/force (chi) through relaxation back into their own root causing them to become isolated and weak, giving the false appearance of you becoming stronger. Relaxation is the means with which we move the many forms of chi/force around and through the body. Dividing relaxation into two categories, closing (Yin) and opening (Yang) gives us access to a continuous source of relaxation. Both opening and closing emanates from your intent. When opening & closing emanates from intent, root is generated. How is it possible for opening to yield, (soft) and yet issue (hard).

Opening (upward relaxation) is it Soft, Hard or Both?

7. Different Qualities of Opening

Opening *(relaxing upward)* can express itself physically either by yielding or issuing *(fa-jing)*. Depending on the direction in which opening is directed changes the quality of the opening. Master Huang once said; "there are times to be an egg and times to be a rock, but they're the same thing". The above statement sounds rather confusing and contradictory at first, however, after this Chapter hopefully this concept will become a little clearer. Master Huang's statement is in relation to the duality of opening. Like a scalpel it can save someone's life if used correctly during a medical procedure or it can take a life if used maliciously. It's the application of opening that changes the nature and the outcome. The classics state; "Only when one is truly soft can one be truly hard". This goes to the heart and nature of opening. In this chapter, I'll break down how two seemingly opposite actions *(yielding and issuing)* can be generated from the same process of opening. First let's break down the definition of yielding.

Definition and Purpose of Physical and Internal Yielding

What is yielding and its function? Do you remember when you first started learning push hands, learning to physically yield when being gently pushed by your partner. Learning to yield backwards, in the direction of the push. Even the most basic and simplest form of yielding, achieved by incorrectly pressing the front foot against the ground to rock backwards achieves its primary aim of preventing force from settling on the body. **One of the most central and primary tenets of Tai Chi is to not allow a force or forces to settle or build on and within the body. Without question, the primary function of physical yielding *(rocking backwards)* is the prevention of a force settling on the body.** Sure, yielding has other functions, but its primary purpose is the prevention of forces building on the body. Rocking backwards in relation to the push does prevent a force from settling on the body. The first and most basic method of yielding learnt in push hands is rocking backwards in relation to the push/force being applied to your body by your partner. You quickly learn: Yield too slowly in relation to the incoming push, and force begins to build on your body. Too fast and you physically break from your opponent, therefore losing any hope of controlling their root. In Tai Chi, it's absolutely critical to understand cause and effect. When you hear the word yielding, you automatically think of rocking backwards, which is only one method of yielding. If you physically yield to a force by pushing the front foot against the ground, *(even if it breaches the Taoist principles of non-action)* it will still achieve the intended result you want for a second or two. Until you run out of space *(room)* in which to continue the yielding process

Does this scenario sound familiar to you? Feeling a push on your body, you pull yourself into your back leg, rocking backwards and yielding, keeping the force from settling on you. It's all going fine until you run out of physical room and you've backed yourself into a corner, causing you to become jammed within your own root. Having run out of room you have no real alternative other than to dig in and push back, hoping to catch your partner off balance. The first half of the encounter went reasonably well, you

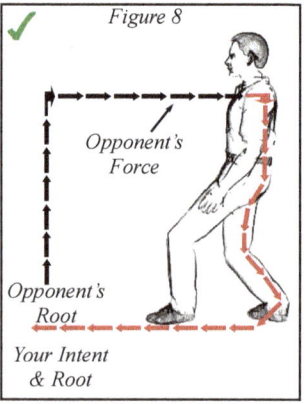

Redirecting the opponent's force back into their own root by means of closing, led by your intent. Results in your opponent's root being neutralised (cut).

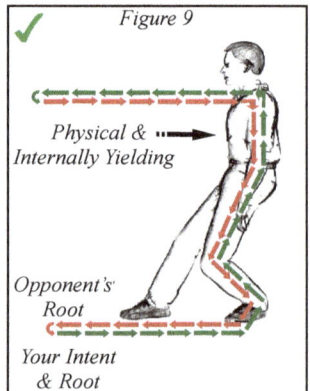

After neutralising your opponent's root, you open towards yourself causing you to physically and internally yield, while maintaining control over your opponent's root.

followed the basic premise of Tai Chi, preventing a force from settling on the body, by yielding. The second half sounds more like a commentary from a college wrestling match, rather than a Taoist Art. Most Tai Chi practitioners mistakenly believe the only means of yielding to a force is to physically move backwards. Physically yielding is only one means of preventing a force from settling on you, usually the first method learnt in push hands. As usual in Tai Chi it's not the result that's wrong it's the process that brings the result. We have established that the primary purpose for yielding is to prevent forces from building on our body, but when relaxation stops, *(specifically opening and closing)* the result will be double weightedness. The method of relaxing downward *(closing)* or sinking into the back leg, only buys you time, it doesn't solve the problem of what to do with the incoming force. You can't run away from the force indefinitely. It always ends with the inevitable, with you becoming jammed in your own root under your back foot.

There is an old Tai Chi proverb. "you open to yield and close to follow". This proverb cuts straight to the process we need to apply, **"open to yield".** To physically yield correctly requires you to open *(relaxing upward)*, so we need to understand and apply the opening process *(relaxing upward)* to the act of physically yielding. Before starting the process of opening, we need to create the conditions from which yielding *(opening)* is first possible. The precursor to opening *(relaxing upward)*, yielding, is closing *(relaxing downward)*. When closing, your intent needs to be positioned under the ground, behind your opponent. When your partner starts to push, your downward relaxation *(closing)* pulls your partner's force through your body, led by your intent, returning it back under and behind your partner's substantial foot. No physical movement is even required for this. Cutting your opponent's root results in their inability to create a muscular force, effectively making your opponent null and void. You have effectively neutralised your opponent. The dictionary definition of Neutralise: **"to stop something or someone from having an effect making them inconsequential"** *(generally speaking, if you've neutralised your opponent you wouldn't bother yielding, you would open to issue rather than opening to yield)*. Upon reaching full compression under and behind your opponent **(Figure 8)** you're ready now to open and generate physical yielding **(Figure 9)**. When opening *(relaxing upward)* from behind your opponent the relaxation upward *(opening)* **moves towards you**, from under the ground, originating from where your intent is *(a term I use when teaching the relationship with intent and awareness,"awareness starts where your intent finishes")*.

When starting the opening process from under your partner's root, the opening *(relaxing upward)* moves towards you, resulting in the muscles letting go in a controlled, sequenced process resulting in your yielding and moving backwards, caused by Di Xin Xi Yin Li. Using an analogy of termites to help explain how the opening *(relaxation upward)* process works when physically yielding: Termites always enter the building from under the ground and eat their way upwards through the building. Opening can also be likened slightly to fainting. If you've ever seen someone faint from a standing position, you witnessed their ankles collapse, knees, hips, spine collapse, ending with the person lying unconscious on the ground. As their consciousness shuts down, so did the messages from the brain which normally tell the muscles to stay contracted to support body weight. Thus, the person collapsed from the ground up. Opening to yield is slightly similar, but not as extreme. During the yielding process we also soften *(disengage or Wu Wei)* the muscles from the ground up, enough to allow movement not enough to collapse structure.

This requires a very fine balancing point, demanding a large amount of awareness and intent. As relaxation moves up from the root, muscles in the foot soften. This allows the ankle to adjust, and the opening *(relaxation upward)* to travel up the leg, causing the muscles around the knee to release. Resulting in the knee bending allowing you to move backwards. Opening continues up the back of the leg to the buttocks *(gluteal fold)*, allowing the hips to reverse rotate causing you to rock back. Opening continues up the spine to the crown of the head, with the result that each vertebra adjusts upwards *(elongating the spine)*. This is the opposite of the more popular method of closing *(relaxing downward)* from above, into the back foot. The two actions are chalk and cheese in comparison. On the outside they look the same; internally they couldn't be further apart. If you close *(relax downward)* into your back foot, you will effectively paint yourself into a corner and jam yourself. But with opening from where your intent is *(relaxing upward)*, you have much more space internally and physically.

Advantages of Opening to Yield over Closing to Yield

Opening to yield gives you more options than closing to yield. When you open from your intent *(under and behind your opponent)* the opening creates an emptiness or a void as it travels up your body. You **must never** bring your intent back when relaxing upward *(opening)* towards yourself otherwise you'll lose connection and control over your opponent's root when yielding. When opening, emptiness moves up through your body towards the push *(energy/force)* of your opponent, so when you're rocking back and physically yielding, the relaxation and emptiness moves **towards the push and not away from the push.** I was always told early in my training never to run away from a push, but soften towards the energy/force of the push. I was told the last thing to move in push hands was the part of the body that was being pushed. I was taught upon feeling the slightest pressure anywhere on the body, you were to take it into your root. You then open *(relax upward)* through the body to the point from where you are being pushed, causing you to physically rock back and lastly yielding from the point of contact. I would change this process only slightly. These days, my preferred method is to place my intent behind and under my opponent and start the closing process from this point before they even touch me. This way your opponent is pulled into their own root the second they touch, before they can even apply pressure. The original method was okay, but I found you were still relaxing from above and the force from your opponent was already beginning to settle on you. In comparison to the more common method of closing to yield, *(Figure 10)* where you're effectively running away from the push, leading your opponent into your root while simultaneously giving control of your opponent's root back to your opponent *(remember the Tai Chi proverb, "if your are not in control of your opponent's root, then they are")*. With opening to yield, the emptiness from your root moves towards your opponent's push; when the two meet the push falls harmlessly into emptiness *(void)*. Master Huang said; "Yielding should be similar to a banister that's been eaten away by termites, it looks as if it can support your weight, but the second you place your weight on the banister it gives way". In Tai Chi you need to learn how to yield *(relaxing upward)* towards the push, not away *(relaxing downward)* from the push. When yielding is created by opening, the person pushing will be lured into believing everything is going well, they're making good headway, until everything literally disappears from under their hands. Another positive experience you will have when opening *(relaxing upward)* to yield, is that you will soon discover that you have an excess of physical and internal room with which to move. You won't have the sensation of your body becoming more and more restricted as your yielding progresses, in comparison to closing *(relaxing downward)* to yield.

Another very important advantage of relaxing upward *(opening)* to yield in comparison to relaxing downward *(closing)* to yield. When opening to yield, should your opponent insist on pushing regardless, even if they're breaking the principles of Tai Chi? Either by using muscle or over reaching, maintaining your intent under and behind your opponent during the whole

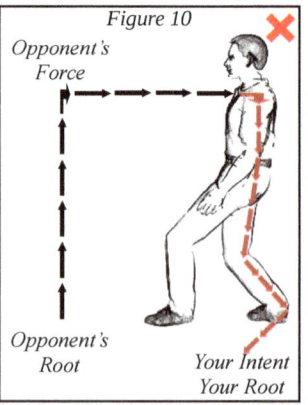

Closing to yield by directing the opponent's force into the ground under the substantial foot.

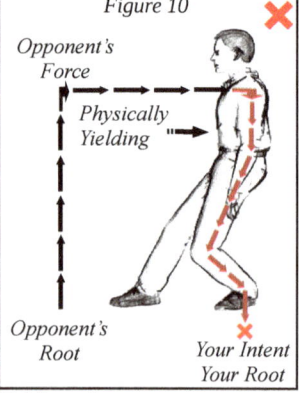

Yielding into your own root becomes problematic. Results in you becoming jammed in the root.

opening *(physical yielding)* process gives you the ability to close in your root should you begin to physically run out of space. Because your root has remained connected to your opponent's root throughout the opening *(relaxing upward)* process which is behind and under your opponent, you're still connected and in control of your opponent's root. The second you close in your root, your opponent is physically, internally and abruptly shut down. It reminds me of a vicious junk yard dog running at you full speed, until it reaches the full length of its chain where it is stopped in its tracks, quite suddenly and violently.

I understand why relaxing *(sinking)* into your back foot **(Figure 10)** is so popular. It does feel strong and powerful. The relative ease in achieving results is nearly instantaneous; it seems logical and it's also **wrong**. Opening to yield is counter intuitive, it feels weak, it is not easy and results take time to achieve, however it is correct. When you experience the benefits of opening to yield, you'll never go back to closing to yield *(the process is to important and needs repeating)*. The second you feel the slightest pressure anywhere on your body, you need to begin the opening *(relaxing upward)* process from your root *(which, hopefully is under your opponent's root)*. As the push progresses from your partner, the relaxation moves upwards *(opening)*, towards the pressure and **not downward and away from the pressure.** I can't stress this enough: opening moves towards the energy/force, not away from the energy/force. As the relaxation moves towards the force from your partner's push, your partner will feel as if they're pushing on something that feels quite substantial at first. What they don't realise is that the emptiness from your root is moving towards their push *(their substantiality)*. When your upward relaxation meets the energy/force from your partner's push, your partner, who a second ago thought they were onto a sure thing, suddenly finds themself falling into an empty hole. What we call in Tai Chi, the emptiness or void. Referring back to the banister analogy, Master Huang would often say; "In push hands you should be like a banister that looks solid, firm and sturdy, however, the second you place your weight on the banister, it collapses, causing you to fall forward".

One of the most difficult military manoeuvres is an organised and structured retreat. Here in Australia we celebrate the Gallipoli landings during Anzac day *(basically our remembrance day)*. Gallipoli is located on the Turkish Peninsula. During World War One, the Australian and New Zealand forces launched an assault on Gallipoli in the hope of moving up the peninsula and knocking Turkey out of the war. The assault was a complete failure. The Australians and New Zealanders were stuck there for 8 months and only managed to move 900 metres inland from the beachhead. However, the retreat from Gallipoli was held up as a text book example on how to retreat correctly and was taught for many years in military colleges as the perfect retreat. When eventually the Australian and New Zealand armies did retreat, they did so during the cover of night, withdrawing their rear troops first and evacuating their front-line troops last, to the point where there was only a handful of men holding the line, until they too were taken off Gallipoli. The Turkish forces didn't realise the Anzacs *(Australian New Zealand Army Corps)* had gone until the morning.

Physical yielding in Tai Chi is essentially retreating. If you yield from the point of contact by pulling into your root under your back foot, you'll end up being rolled up by your opponent. Militarily when retreating you have to be careful not to collapse the front line onto your rear, it will end in total chaos with the whole army being thrown into disarray. With Tai Chi, like Gallipoli, opening from the root, retreating *(yield)* by relaxing upwards, hollowing out towards the incoming force will cause the force to fall into emptiness. If you retreat *(yield)* from where you feel the force by pulling into your root, you will cause the force from your opponent to crash into your root *(rear)* resulting in you becoming jammed and double weighted within your own root.

Opening to Issue *(Fa-Jing)*
Opening to issue is basically the same as yielding. The only difference is the direction opening is channelled and led. As stated in earlier chapters strength and power does not originate from you in

the traditional sense of strength. Most Tai Chi practitioners tend to be egocentric when it comes to strength and power. You are not building strength by loading the legs up like coiled springs or building energy *(chi)* up in the dan tien and exploding it outwards at the right moment. *(I think I've made it clear; my view point on localised muscle strength)*. You often see Tai Chi practitioners displaying bursts of speed in their form, claiming it as fa-jing; maybe it is, maybe it's not. Fa-jing can be fast, it can be slow, but it must always be generated from your root *(under and behind your opponent)* using relaxation, not muscle. The easiest way to know if you're issuing correctly if you feel any muscles contracting during the issuing process, then it's wrong. Most times in Tai Chi, muscle is mistakenly used in the creation of speed. However, in Tai Chi speed is generated as a by-product of opening and closing. Generally speaking, fa-jing usually happens with the smallest of movement. The old Tai Chi proverb confirms this. "Always issue from stillness", meaning the body is quite still when issuing. *(When the body moves the hands are still. When the body is still the arms adjust).*

Fa-jing, similar to opening to yield, you first need to close from the root, your root being behind and under your opponent. **The only means with which to achieve this is by using your intent to lead the relaxation to the point under and behind your opponent, anything else will result in pushing.** Redirecting your opponent's force by means of relaxing downward *(closing)* behind your opponent's root results in their root being cut causing your opponent to become isolated. *(Figure 11)* The sensation of having your root cut in this fashion is like standing in a large bucket and trying to lift yourself up by the handle. The harder you pull on the handle the more you push your feet downward, each action cancelling the effect of the other. Another sensation is similar to standing in a very stable bow and arrow stance feeling relaxed and grounded, when suddenly from nowhere, the ground under each foot suddenly shrinks to the size of a matchbox. After closing in the root you need to reach full compression before relaxing upward *(opening)*. Closing through the back leg will cause you to move forward and reach full compression. *(Figure 12)* As in opening *(relaxing upward)* to yield, the relaxation travels upwards from under the ground where your intent is. The only difference between yielding and issuing is that with issuing, the relaxation is directed **upward and forward** of your intent. This results in the uprooting of your opponent *(Figure 13)* causing them to be

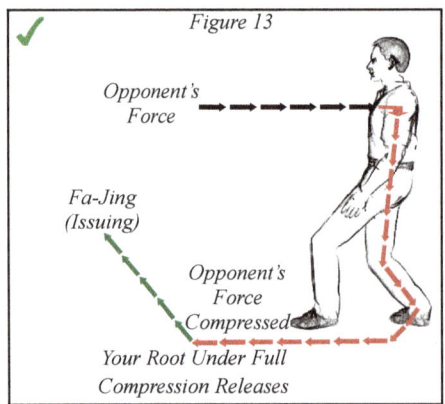
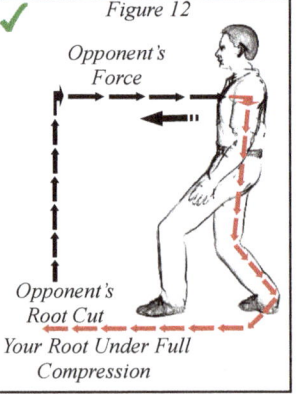
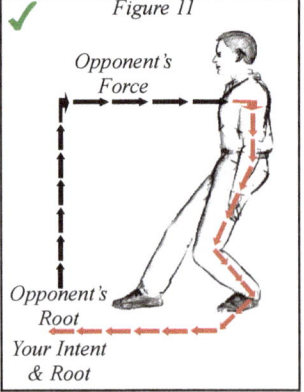

Upon reaching full compression from closing (relaxing downward) in your root, results in your opponent becoming isolated and weak. You then open, (relaxing upward) and forward resulting in your opponent, throwing themselves out (issuing).

Closing down the rear leg results in you moving forward cutting your opponent's root and reaching full compression in your root, behind and under your opponent.

Initiating closing (relaxing downward) from your root, led by your intent. This causes you to start to move forward.

discharged, throwing themselves out.
I recall being told this story many years ago by either Tony Ward or Wee Kee Jin: When Master Huang was teaching the more advanced students, one of the seniors would occasionally bring their

young children to class. Master Huang would often call the child over, place his hand on one of his senior students and then ask the seven year old to gently push the student that Master Huang was lightly touching. The child complied, ever so gently pushing the senior student, resulting in the senior student being thrown out. Master Huang was making a point. It is was not the hand pushing that causes the fa-jing, but the opposite hand lightly touching the student, creating the conditions so the hand gently pushing had such a devastating effect. When Master Huang touched the student, he effectively cut the senior student's root so thoroughly that when a mere four ounces of pressure was placed on the senior student from the seven year old this resulted in the student being thrown out. Unless you believe a seven year old can produce the sort of fa-jing that can throw a full grown adult a couple of metres.

It has come to the point in my teaching that I have become adverse to referring to the so called pushing hand as the issuing hand. When a small child can supposedly issue, it makes you question the whole concept of issuing *(fa-jing)*, when you realise the hand lightly touching is doing all the hard work and the purported issuing hand gets all the attention and fame. In Cheng Man-Ching and Robert Smith book *Tai Chi The "Supreme Ultimate" Exercise for Health, Sport and Self Defence* on page 89 section 4. Cheng Man-Ching says; "When attacking, don't use force with both hands. The Tai Chi Chuan Classics say "that in an attack it is necessary to aim in one direction of your opponent. To use force with both hands is technically known as "double weighting" and contradicts the principles of Tai Chi. The correct way is to attack with one hand while the other hand simply touches the body lightly". The hand touching lightly, really... I think a little more information could have been forthcoming. The hand lightly touching was in fact doing all the hard work. Effectively closed *(relaxing downward)* into the opponent's root causing it to be compressed and cut. This is followed by using the same hand to open *(relaxing upward)*, drawing them out of their root. While simultaneously opening *(relaxing upward)* from behind their root with the other hand, the so called pushing *(issuing hand)* hand causes them to be thrown out.

In Master Huang's Five Loosening Exercises the Third Loosening Exercise specifically trains cross alignment. Cross alignment is used extensively in push hands. Most students tend to believe cross alignment is when the weight is in the front left leg, like in Brush Knee and you issue with the right hand, which is correct, however, one important part of the process has been left out. The left hand next to the left leg is doing all the hard work, opening up from the front substantial leg causing the left hand to draw the opponent out of their root, while simultaneously the right hand issues from the same opening *(relaxation upward)*. This relaxation moving up *(opening)* the substantial left leg, through the spine, upon reaching the shoulder blades the relaxation process then splits. The left hand draws out and the right hand issues simultaneously. This whole process is known as cross alignment in Tai Chi. Cross alignment requires a large amount of skill and should only be trained when you're completely familiar in how opening can be used for both issuing and yielding. I remember teaching a student cross alignment who was a diplomat employed at a foreign embassy. He commented, "Cross alignment is a lot like diplomacy. They have a joke in foreign affairs. The definition of diplomacy is patting the dog with one hand, while the other hand is looking for a rock". A little brutal, but basically true. The whole process is like a magician's trick - sleight of hand. Everyone is watching the hand that is issuing, while no one is paying attention to the hand lightly touching the opponent.

The general rule in Master Huang's school was never to use more than 4 ounces of pressure when pushing in push hands. The purpose of this rule may seem obvious at first, preventing your pushes from becoming physical. If more than 4 ounces of pressure is used, it's a sign that you are moving back to using muscular force. If your push has become more physical, more than likely the problem is not the hand pushing, but rather the opposite hand, the one controlling the opponent's root which is keeping the opponent light and disconnected from gravity *(remember the concept of Taoist Physics)*. The most likely cause of the increase in pressure is the loss of your connection to your opponent's root. The causes of these are numerous. You may have allowed a hollow *(disconnection)* to develop/occur in one of the following; intent, relaxation or physical. Or there could be a protrusion *(holding)* also with either intent, relaxation or physical. Interesting to note, when I started training in Master Huang School I was constantly told in push hands to control the opponent's root with one hand while the opposite hand issued. Funny how you don't hear this anymore.

When opening to issue, the release begins forward from where your intent is, not from your hand or hands. If you instigate the push from your hands you'll only succeed in pushing your opponent back into their root. However, if you relax *(open)* upwards from your root while at the same time physically relaxing upwards *(opening)* through the body this results in the opponent gently being uprooted. The hardest part throughout the process of issuing is maintaining your intent while opening *(relaxing upward)*; the second you focus on the push your intent is broken and so is control over your opponent's root. Intent is by far the hardest quality to teach a student. The beneficial effect of intent won't be first experienced in the Opening and Closing Exercise, Five Loosening Exercises or the Tai Chi Form because you don't have a partner. Intent can only be first experienced through the touch of push hands. Only then can you hope to replicate the sensation in your Opening and Closing Exercise, Five Loosening Exercises and Tai Chi Form. It's not possible to explain or visibly demonstrate intent, intent needs to be experienced, it needs to be felt, there is no other way. By looking into a glass room can you tell if there is oxygen in the room? Not until you enter the room. Can you tell if an electrical cable is alive with electricity just by looking at it? No, you need to touch it, it's the same with intent. You only sense the effect of intent when you touch someone who has trained it.

I had an interesting experience when I was in a shop once. I was looking through a shop killing time between classes when I suddenly had a strong sensation that I was being watched. Everyone has this sensation now and then. I looked up and couldn't see anyone looking at me. However, I did hear a light tapping behind me. I noticed a woman with a white stick with a ball at the end of the stick tapping the ground in front of her. Being visually impaired with no visual process to rely on, out of necessity she had to place her awareness and intent at the end of the stick. I believe it was her intent and awareness that I had felt and became aware of. A little side story, when she walked past me, I noticed the word "pride" written in permanent marker along the side of her stick. It took me a few days to work out why pride was written on her stick. I realised, she had named her stick Pride, because as the old saying goes; "Pride comes before a fall".

The only analogy that I can think of that demonstrates the difference between opening to yield and opening to issue is a push bike pump. If you place your thumb over the outlet end of a push bike pump and start pumping *(closing)*, a few quick pumps and the air pressure has built up within the pump *(full compression)*. If you were to take your hand off the handle, the handle would shoot backwards, consider that as opening to yield. If you were to take your thumb off the outlet, air pressure would be released outward and forward, opening to issue, the pump is your root under your opponent's root under full compression.

We have clarified and defined Tai Chi as the physical manifestation of Taoist principles in action, having qualified the chi that powers all movement in Tai Chi, that being Di Xin Xi Yin Li (gravity). We can now access this power source by applying the Taoist principle of Wu Wei, Non-action to create action. By re-directing your opponent's energy/force (chi) through relaxation back into their own root causing them to become isolated and weak, giving the false appearance of you becoming stronger. Relaxation is the means with which we move the many forms of chi/force around and through the body. Dividing relaxation into two categories, closing (Yin) and opening (Yang) gives us access to a continuous source of relaxation. Both opening and closing emanates from intent. When opening & closing emanates from your intent, root is generated. Having established that opening possesses two different qualities, opening for yielding and opening for issuing what changes these two qualities, is the direction opening moves in. How is it possible to generate speed without using muscle?

Is it Possible for Tai Chi to Generate Speed without using Muscle and if it can, then How?

8. Tai Chi and Speed

For Tai Chi to be an effective Martial Art, it will need to have the ability to produce speed at a moment's notice. Anyone who has trained martial arts or any form of pugilism knows the importance of speed. Most people tend to associate Tai Chi with slow graceful movements often seen in parks throughout the world, but Tai Chi can be extremely fast, this is often demonstrated in Chen style Tai Chi. If you've ever watched an exponent of Chen style Tai Chi, it looks like a cross between Tai Chi and Kung Fu. Chen style is made up of a combination of slow movements, punctuated with very fast explosive strikes and punches.

Speed doesn't breach Tai Chi or Taoist principles in any way, providing muscle isn't used in the creation of this speed. Most people are accustomed to using muscle for speed in everyday life and martial arts are no different. The reliance on fast-twitch muscle fibres to generate quick movements is ingrained into our pattern of movement. When starting Tai Chi, the challenge is to shift this paradigm to create speed without the use of muscle. If muscle isn't allowed, then how is speed created? I've been training Chow Ga Tong Long *(Southern Praying Mantis)* slightly longer than I've been training Tai Chi. I'm 63 years of age, my hands move faster, much faster than when I was 18. I'm well past my physical prime and I should be moving slower, not faster. I remember being told by my Kung Fu teacher, that Kung Fu is like your weekly wage, it's what you're going to use today in a physical conflict. Tai Chi is similar to your superannuation, you don't receive a return on your superannuation for 30 to 40 years, but when it kicks in it really lifts your income. It's the same with Tai Chi, as your Tai Chi matures it will naturally permeate through your harder and more semi external martial arts. Master Huang originally trained in White Crane Kung Fu. It wasn't until many years later, that he started his Tai Chi training with Cheng Man-Ching. Master Huang's contemporaries would often say he was so good in his Tai Chi because of his White Crane. His White Crane contemporaries would often say the reason for his high standard in White Crane was due to his Tai Chi.

There are only two methods of creating speed. The first is the commonly accepted method of contracting muscle to move a weighted limb; how fast you move the limb is dictated by how fast these muscles contract. The second method, uses Taoist principles of movement, by first creating **the conditions** where muscle isn't required for generating speed or movement. Therefore taking the need to use muscle out of the equation is critical. Emptying areas of the body of weight before moving them eliminates the need to use muscle, allowing the body to move freely and quickly without relying on the typical muscle-driven speed. This is achieved in Tai Chi by creating states of substantiality *(weighted)* and insubstantiality *(weightlessness)* by means of relaxation, using the process of opening and closing which was explained in Chapter 6 Opening and Closing. When an object has no weight, how much muscle is required to move an object that weighs nothing? Literally none. We've all moved house; when it came to moving the wardrobe, you first empty the wardrobe before moving it. An empty wardrobe is a lot easier to move than one full of clothes. You move the wardrobe to its new location and refill it. Also how fast can you move something that has no weight; Extremely fast. An added benefit, if something is empty of weight it has no centre of gravity, nothing for your opponent to lock on to. The hardest part of creating speed in Tai Chi is creating the conditions so muscle isn't required.

I often ask students when teaching push hands, why is it Tai Chi practitioners often use muscular force in their push hands when they know they shouldn't? I'm not talking about the occasional bumping into each other; we all do that in push hands. I'm talking about the push hands you frequently see in competitions. They start with good intentions, but quickly regress to where both parties start shoving and leaning on each other, trying to push their opponent off their centre of gravity. Keeping this question restricted to the physical process, why do these participants use muscle, when they clearly know it's in breach of Tai Chi principles? Students often give esoteric answers, such as the ego's need to win. Or they can't lose face. However, the answer is quite simple, they need to use muscle because they really don't have a choice. If an object possesses weight, the only means with which to move it is by engaging muscle. So you are left with only two options, when encountering a weighted object. The first option is to go down the road of using muscle to try to move the weighted object or the second option, make the object lighter, and therefore easier to move, hence the need to use muscle is greatly reduced. **In a nutshell, the simple reason why students use so much muscle in push hands is because the person they're trying to move is still fully weighted** *(grounded)*, **fully connected to gravity so they're left with no other option other than to use ever increasing muscle**. Breaking your opponent's root results in your opponent losing their connection to gravity, causing them to float which makes them so much lighter and easier to move. This takes away the need to use muscle, or at the very minimum greatly reduces the need for muscle.

By emptying various areas of your body you'll achieve the following five objectives;

1. The area which is empty of weight requires virtually no physical strength to move.
2. When an area of the body is empty it moves extremely fast, beyond what a contracting and disengaging muscle can possible produce.
3. Your endurance increases because no muscle or so little is used when generating speed and movement, thus negates the demand for oxygen in comparison to using muscle, which burns oxygen at an alarming rate.
4. The fact that there is no weight in the limb you are moving means that there is no weight in the joints. Therefore, the chances of joint injury is nil.
5. The area that's empty has no centre of gravity with which your opponent can control.

All the above allow you to move faster, easier and for longer periods with little chance of injury and with none of the usual age or gender restrictions.

I was taught very early that the very first person in Tai Chi you are going to float is yourself. If you can't empty *(float)* one side of your body when stepping, then how are you going to float an opponent. Only after many years of focused and correct training by means of Opening and Closing Exercise, Five Loosening Exercises and Form can you hope to bring this process beyond your body by means of intent into push hands. Intent allows you to take this process beyond your body allowing you to not only empty parts of your body, but in time, to extend to your opponent. How far can you throw someone who is nearly empty of weight? Quite a distance. How much physical and muscular effort is required? Negligible. How fast can you move something that has no weight? Extremely fast. Emptiness doesn't create speed, movement or so called power, it's the prelude to speed, movement and power. Opening and closing is what creates emptiness *(under the right conditions)* which is the prelude to speed and so called power in Tai Chi. Closing *(relaxing downward)* from your root has a pulling like sensation through your body. Closing not only empties the areas of your body you wish to move, but also creates a vacuum-like effect on the empty part of the body causing it to be literally pulled into position with extreme speed.

Yang Cheng Fu's Legacy

There is a bit of a controversy within Tai Chi circles when it comes to Yang Cheng Fu *(1883-1936)*. He was the grandson of Yang Lu Chan *(1799-1872)*, the founder of the Yang style, making Yang Cheng Fu the head of the Yang style in the earlier part of the 20th Century. Yang Cheng Fu was the first person to teach Tai Chi to the public in Shanghai in the late 1920s. It was around this time he removed all the fast aspects from the Yang form leaving only the slow continuous form that Yang style is so well known for today. A lot of Tai Chi enthusiasts believe when Yang Cheng Fu removed the fast aspects from the Yang form he did the Yang style a great disservice. By removing the fast aspects from the form some Tai Chi practitioners believe he also removed the martial component from the Yang form. *(Writing the above reminded me of a story my teacher Wee Kee Jin told me many years ago. A student once asked Master Huang in class "How can you use Tai Chi as a martial art, when it's so slow? "Master Huang told him to do the form and he would show him. As the student started playing the form, Master Huang suddenly started lightly slapping the student across the face repeatedly. Saying, are you so stupid to do your movements this slow when you're being attacked).* This belief is misplaced when you assume anything fast in the Tai Chi form, is automatically linked to the martial art aspect of Tai Chi. It is my opinion Yang Cheng Fu didn't remove or sacrifice the martial aspect of the Yang style. He did the opposite and saved it. Yang style during the Yang Cheng Fu era had fast aspects within the Yang form. This is confirmed by Master Ma Yeuh Liang whose teacher was his future father in-law Wu Jianquan, the founder of Wu style. Yang Cheng Fu and Wu Jianquan would train with each other at Yang Cheng Fu's home. Patrick Kelly told me many years ago that Master Ma Yeuh Liang once told him that he would often wait for his teacher to finish training with Yang Cheng Fu. While watching he watched both Yang Cheng Fu and Wu Jianquan train together. Master Ma Yeuh Liang stated he saw Yang Cheng Fu perform the fast Yang form on many occasions. Yang Cheng Fu was also accompanied by a student who waited for him to finish training. That person was Professor Cheng Man Ching. Patrick asked Master Ma if the two ever trained Push Hands while waiting for their teachers. Master Ma said; "No, they only played chess while waiting" *(Hard to believe they only played chess, we'll never know)*.

Wu style kept the fast aspect of the Wu form, and Yang Cheng Fu removed them from the Yang form. Now, before everyone says that this is proof that Yang Cheng Fu removed the martial aspect from Yang style, leaving Yang Tai Chi nothing more than a dance for health, let us go back a few years, before Yang Cheng Fu decided to openly teach Tai Chi to the public. Before Yang Cheng Fu opened his classes to the general public, Tai Chi had only been taught privately to a limited clientele, such as wealthy individuals, nobility, royalty and their family members. Tai Chi was considered a treasure and the internal workings a secret.

Yang Cheng Fu was a renowned pugilist in his day, famed in the martial arts world and throughout China for his martial prowess. Opening his School for the first time to the public in Shanghai would have attracted any person who ever had an interest in studying Tai Chi. Seeing an opportunity to expand their martial abilities and learn from the best, they would not have hesitated to join. Especially the first to join, would have been martial artists from various styles, ranging from internal to external, hoping to advance their martial skills. It would be the equivalent of hearing that your nation's top tennis player had decided to personally teach the general public in your area. Everyone and anyone who had a serious interest in tennis would be signing up for tennis lessons. I am guessing, the same happened with Yang Cheng Fu's school. Now I just want to be clear, the next part is pure speculation on what may have happened next. I imagine that when Yang Cheng Fu taught, it would have been to large classes, ranging from beginners to advanced to external and internal martial artists and everything in between. When it came to the fast movements of the Yang form, I am guessing everyone would have used muscle to generate this speed. Yang Cheng Fu may have realised that the size of these classes limited his time to go to every student, constantly correcting them to the subtle differences between speed created by muscle and speed created by opening and closing. Knowing students would inevitably revert to using muscle when it came to the fast aspects of the form, he chose the lesser of two evils and changed the form and removed the fast movements. This was done in the hope students would first learn how to generate opening and closing, and then eventually apply opening and closing rather than muscle to generate speed and movement. Only by understanding opening and closing, will you understand speed, movement and the so called power of Tai Chi.

From my personal experience the difference between teaching a class of 10 to 15 students and a private lesson of one on one, is that you can make very small and exact corrections, due to the nature of the personal interaction between teacher and student. For instance, the quality of movement generated by the relaxation being applied to opening and closing. These sensations need to be fed to the student over time, so they can discern these subtle and refined sensations. With a public class you just don't have the opportunity or time to make these fine corrections. In the larger public classes these finer correction are given over a longer time frame. Teaching form work is different to teaching push hands. You can teach a fairly large class the form, due to the visual nature of it. When it comes to push hands, you can only teach one student at a time. I am not talking about learning the sequence of moves that make up the pattern of a push hand set; that is relatively easy. It is the teaching of subtle sensations of intent, the application of opening and closing, sensitivity of cutting and maintaining control of the opponent's root while moving forward and back, and the changing of hands. It's the imparting of the internal process that requires one on one training of push hands.

We have clarified and defined Tai Chi as the physical manifestation of Taoist principles in action, having qualified the chi that powers all movement in Tai Chi, that being Di Xin Xi Yin Li (gravity). We can now access this power source by applying the Taoist principle of Wu Wei, Non-action to create action. By re-directing your opponent's energy/force (chi) through relaxation back into their own root causing them to become isolated and weak, giving the false appearance of you becoming stronger. Relaxation is the means with which we move the many forms of chi/force around and through the body. Dividing relaxation into two categories, closing (Yin) and opening (Yang) gives us access to a continuous source of relaxation. Both opening and closing emanates from intent, When opening & closing emanates from your intent, root is generated. Having established opening possesses two different qualities, opening for yielding and opening for issuing, what changes these two qualities, is the direction opening moves in. One of the many byproducts of opening and closing is its ability to generate speed without the need for muscle. So what part does substantial and insubstantial play in relation to relaxation and movement?

Does a Relationship Exist between Relaxation, Substantial and Insubstantial and Movement?

9. The Symbiotic Relationship Between Opening, Closing, Substantial, Insubstantial and Movement

There is such a heavy emphasis on weight positioning in Tai Chi, more so than probably any other martial art, external or internal. I feel weight movement in Tai Chi is now taken for granted, no longer questioned, just assumed to be part and parcel of Tai Chi. The question needs to be asked, why is there so much forward and backward movement in Tai Chi? The answer to this question starts to become more apparent when we begin to understand the function of weight movement in Tai Chi and how weight movement is then generated. In Tai Chi, weight can be broken into two categories, substantial *(Yin)* and insubstantial *(Yang)*. Substantial is when weight on one side of the body is between 51% to 100% causing the opposite side to become insubstantial from 49% to 1% of weight. Don't mistake insubstantial with empty, empty is when one part of the body has zero weight just for a millisecond before the limb moves. One of the many purposes of rocking forward and backward in Tai Chi is to avoid blows and to shorten the distance between you and your opponent when counter-attacking. This action is not unique to Tai Chi; it is also common in the harder/external martial arts. Another purpose of rocking backwards is to destabilise your opponent's root, allowing you to take control of it. Where Tai Chi differs from external martial arts is how we move forward, backward, left or right. Weight movement in Tai Chi is important, however, what is far more important is how the movement of weight is created, without the need for muscle.

The Three Methods Used in Tai Chi to Create Substantial and Insubstantial

There are three methods with which to create substantial and insubstantial in Tai Chi, but only one method follows Taoist principles. The Taoist method applies Taoist philosophy and principles when it comes to generating substantial and insubstantial, the other two methods don't. Most Tai Chi practitioners tend to view substantial and insubstantial as the result of moving the body forward and back and not the source of the body moving forward, backward, left and right.

Forward Movement *(Rocking Forward)*

1. The most common and incorrect method of moving forward in Tai Chi involves pressing the rear substantial leg against the ground to generate a forward movement, resulting in the body moving forward along with weight. This weight moving forward is clearly a by-product of the body moving forward caused by the pressing of the substantial leg against the ground. This method is constantly repeated throughout the form and push hands. Having covered extensively in previous Chapters the many faults of using muscle in the creation of movement, I don't feel the need to revisit the subject on muscle use in Tai Chi to generate movement.

2. The second method is when relaxation is used to generate substantial and insubstantial. However, this relaxation downward *(closing)* doesn't start in the root, but in the upper body and travels down into the root. *(Figure 14)* Even though the body movement is correctly derived from the inter action of substantial and insubstantial and is based in relaxation, it can be still considered an isolated body movement, due to the fact that it is not generated from the root. Relaxing from above will result in you generating substantiality and insubstantiality which in turn will generate physical movement in the form. Unfortunately it's not fit for purpose, and can't be successfully applied in push hands, due to the fact the relaxation didn't begin in the root, but finished in the root. This means, you have no connection to your root when creating substantial and insubstantial. Dropping your weight from the upper body into your root would be the second most common method of generating substantial and insubstantial in Tai Chi.

3. The third and correct method of creating substantial and insubstantial is by means of opening *(relaxing upward)* and closing *(relaxing downward)*. This is achieved by initiating opening and closing from your root in a vertical direction. Closing from the root of the substantial leg *(Figure 15)* will cause the body to be pulled forward. Because closing pulls you forward through the rear leg, it will result in an increase of weight in the insubstantial front leg. Should this increase of weight continue to the point where the weight of the front leg reaches 51%, this will now make the front leg the newly substantial leg resulting in the opening and closing process to automatically transfer to the front leg *(white arrows represent the opening and closing disconnecting from the rear leg)*. Once opening and closing accesses the newly substantial front leg, the root is automatically transferred to the newly substantial front leg. This requires you to now open *(relax up)* from the front substantial leg, resulting in the seamless continuation of the body being pulled forward *(Figure 16)* by the upward relaxation *(opening)*. This opening or closing process will not only move you forward and backward, but when applied to different alignments can be used to generate left or right turns. **Opening and closing, substantial and insubstantial mutually create each other and share a symbiotic relationship that can't be separated without destroying the process that generates all movement in Tai Chi.**

We've established in previous Chapters that relaxation comes in two vertical waves from the root. Downward relaxation is referred to as closing *(sometimes cited as contracting or gathering)* and upward relaxation, referred to as opening *(occasionally referred to as expanding or dispersing)*.

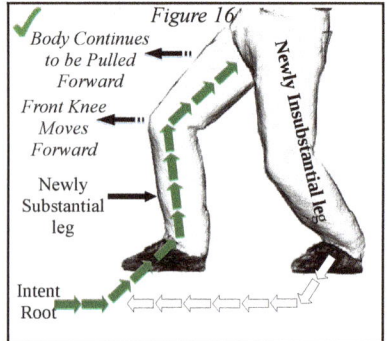

The front leg reaches 51%, making it the substantial leg. Opening and Closing transfers to the front leg. Opening up the front leg allows you to perpetually and seamlessly be pulled forward.

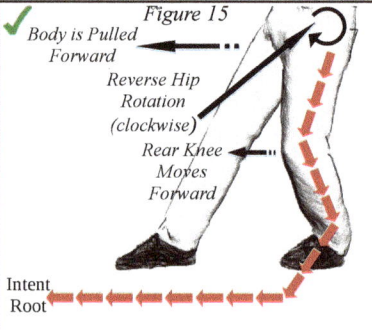

Closing down the substantial rear leg, will cause the rear knee to move forward, causing the hip to reverse rotate which in turn pulls the body forward. Increasing the weight of the insubstantial front leg.

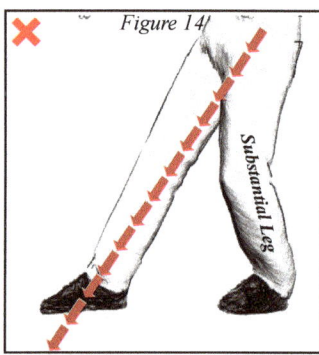

It's not possible to close from the substantial leg straight into the insubstantial leg. It will result in disconnection from your root.

Regardless whether they are opening or closing, these waves of relaxation can move up and down only from the intent/root, moving vertically through the substantial side of the body in a never-ending circular action. *(Figure 1, page 31)*

If you try to close down *(relax downward)* both the substantial and insubstantial legs simultaneously, *(Figure 17)* even if closing is started in the root, it will only confuse your intent and your closing. You only have one closing, one root, one intent, not two. If you try to relax through both legs it will result in your breaking from your own root. The opening and closing process runs through only the substantial leg that is connected to your root.

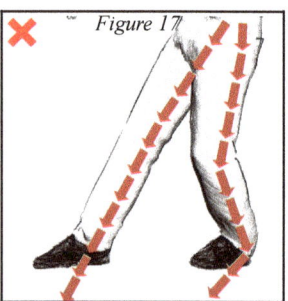

You can't close through both the substantial & insubstantial legs at the same time, as it scatters the intent. No intent, no root.

Opening & Closing, Substantial & Insubstantial Changes Alignments

It's imperative the opening and closing works in with substantial and insubstantial to create the correct alignments which in turn generate the correct movement. For example, if we re-examined Figure 16 at the moment when the front leg became substantial and we wrongly continued to close down the back leg even though it was no longer the substantial leg. It would result in the rear knee pushing into the rear foot, causing the back foot to push against the ground. Applying the wrong cycle of relaxation to the wrong insubstantial leg creates incorrect alignment *(the rear hip would forward rotate resulting in pushing against incoming energy/force)*. Referring again to Figure 16, if instead of relaxing upward *(opening)* if we incorrectly closed *(relax downward)*, *(correct leg to apply opening and closing cycle, but wrong cycle of relaxation)*. Closing down the front substantial leg will cause the front knee to push against the ground causing the front hip to forward rotate, resulting in your alignment pushing against any incoming energy/force. Correct substantial leg wrong cycle of relaxation creates wrong alignment. The front hip needs to reverse rotate, so as to allow energy/force to pass through into the root

While we are speaking about opening and closing moving up and down the legs, let me ask you this question. Does relaxation move through the front of the legs *(thighs)* or the back of the legs *(calf and hamstrings)*? This old Tai Chi proverb gives a big hint; "The muscles from the buttocks to the heel, should be soft to the touch". Opening and closing must always move through the back of the legs. The next question would have to be… why? Because if you opened and closed through the front of the leg it would destroy your collective alignments. Which means one of your joints would be moving in the wrong direction and out of relation to your other joints, effectively creating disharmony. If you relaxed up *(opening)* from the root and if opening travelled up the front of the leg *(Figure 18)* it would result in the knee dropping into the foot. This will cause the front hip to forward rotate, resulting in you pushing against the ground, causing you to push against any incoming force *(double heaviness)*. However, if you opened up from the root, through the back of the front leg *(Figure 19)* this would cause the front hip to reverse rotate allowing energy/force to be fed into the root.

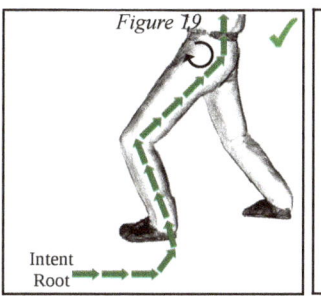
Upward relaxation moving up the back of the substantial front leg, will cause the hip to reverse rotate.

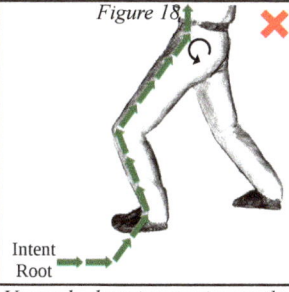
Upward relaxation moving up the front of the substantial leg, will cause the hip to forward rotate

Were you to close down the front of the rear leg, *(Figure 20)* it would once again result in the knee pressing against the ground, resulting in the rear hip forward rotating and push against any incoming energy/force *(double heaviness)*. On the other hand if you closed from the root through the calf up through the hamstrings and gluteal fold *(behind and under the hip)* *(Figure 21)* it would have the opposite effect. The hip would reverse rotate allowing energy/force to feed into the root. If you have the opening and

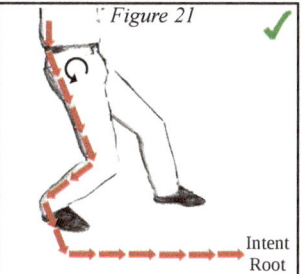
Downward relaxation moving up the back of the substantial leg, causes the hip to reverse rotate

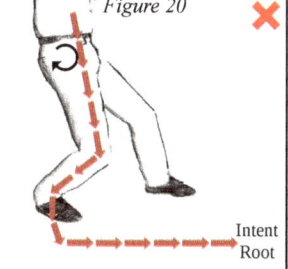
Downward relaxation moving up the front of the substantial leg, causes the hip to forward rotate

closing process moving through the correct leg *(which is always the substantial leg)*, and you open *(relax upward)* and close *(relax downward)* correctly through the back of the leg, the hip will automatically reverse rotate, which will correct a lot of your alignment issues.

It is this very interplay of substantial and insubstantial caused by opening and closing that generates physical movement, while simultaneously allowing any external forces to pass through the body harmlessly to where your intent *(root)* is positioned. A perfect symbiotic relationship between the internal movement of Opening and Closing and the interplay of substantial and insubstantial creating correct alignment, generating physical movement.

This above process is so vital and critical to all movement in Tai Chi. I feel the need to revisit the process of how substantial and insubstantial are generated in relation to opening and closing resulting in movement. With 90% of weight in the rear leg, you begin to close down the rear substantial leg. **(Figure 22)** This results in the substantial leg moving you forward until the front insubstantial leg takes over and has now become the substantial leg. The second the front leg becomes substantial, opening and closing transfers to the front substantial leg and starts to open *(relaxing upward)* from the root of the newly substantial front leg. The rear leg now becomes the insubstantial leg and has now disconnected *(represented by the transparent arrows)* from the intent and root. **(Figure 23)**

Figure 22

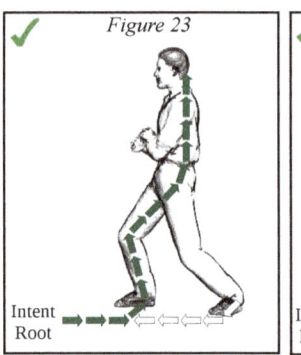

Figure 23

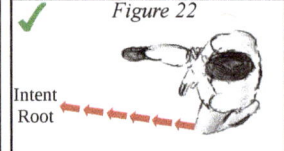

Figure 22

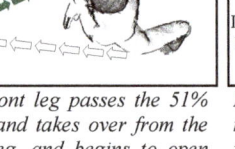

Figure 23

The front leg passes the 51% mark and takes over from the rear leg, and begins to open from the root, causing the body to be pulled forward as substantiality increases.

Relaxing down (closing) the rear substantial leg moves you forward, causing the front leg to slowly take on more weight in the process.

It's absolutely critical that the change from insubstantial *(Yang)* to substantial *(Yin)* is performed smoothly and without breaks *(hollows)* or interruptions *(protrusions)*. Otherwise your opening and closing will disconnect from your root, and with it your ability to move the internals, which moves the physical and to maintain control of your opponent's root during push hands. Opening and closing, substantial and insubstantial are all achieved without losing connection to your root *(intent)*. Opening *(relaxing upward)* up the substantial front leg causes an increase of substantiality in the front leg, which has taken over from the rear leg and continues to pull the body forward. **(Figure 23)**

Intent

Intent is always connected to the opening and closing process through the substantial leg. Opening and closing through the substantial leg is the source of constant interplay between substantial and insubstantial which in turn creates all physical movement in Tai Chi. It is for this exact reason that transition between substantial and insubstantial needs to be seamless, regardless if you're rocking forward backwards, turning left or right. If substantial and insubstantial aren't clearly defined, opening *(upward relaxation)* and closing *(downward relaxation)* also become incoherent. When opening and closing becomes incoherent, the root becomes scattered. The moment the insubstantial leg becomes 51%, it's no longer the insubstantial leg, but the substantial leg, and opening and closing must smoothly be transferred to the newly substantial leg *(the old Tai Chi saying confirms this:* *("When moving to the front leg you must first go through the back leg.* **(Figure 22 & 23)** *If you want to move to the back leg you must first go through the front leg")*.

Horizontal Turning of Left and Right

As the opening and closing moves up and down the body in a vertical action, created from the root.

 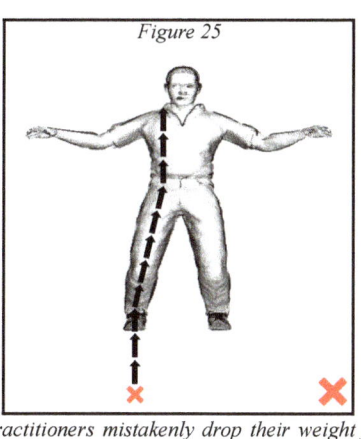 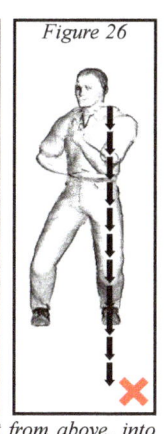

The opening and closing process, disengages muscles as it moves through the ankles, knees, hips and buttocks, especially the gluteal folds *(The Classics: "droop the buttocks")* are disengaged. The kuas *(hips joints)* then physically open or close, creating horizontal turns of left and right through the vertical process of opening and closing. Opening and Closing can only travel up and down the body through the substantial leg. The following Classics confirms this; "虛實宜分清楚。一處有一處虛實，處處總此一虛實 " Substantial & insubstantial should be clearly differentiated. In every part there is both substantial and insubstantial. The principle of substantial and insubstantial applies to every situation". 意氣須換得靈。乃有圓活之趣。所謂轉變虛實也. "There should be agility in the interaction of the yi and chi, only then can it achieve a smooth and lively quality. This is what is meant by alternating between substantial and insubstantial".

Often Tai Chi practitioners mistakenly drop their weight from above, into the insubstantial leg. (figure 24) They then press their foot against the ground to move back into the centre. (figure 25) Then repeating the process of dropping their weight into the insubstantial leg (figure 26).

It is for this exact reason that transition between substantial and insubstantial needs to be seamless, regardless if you're rocking forward, backwards, turning left or right. If the mind *(intent)* isn't clear where you are, whether substantial and insubstantial, then opening and closing becomes confused. When opening and closing is confused, relaxation is confused, and the chi will be scattered. The moment the insubstantial leg becomes 51% it's no longer the insubstantial leg, but the substantial leg, and opening and closing is smoothly transferred to the newly substantial leg.

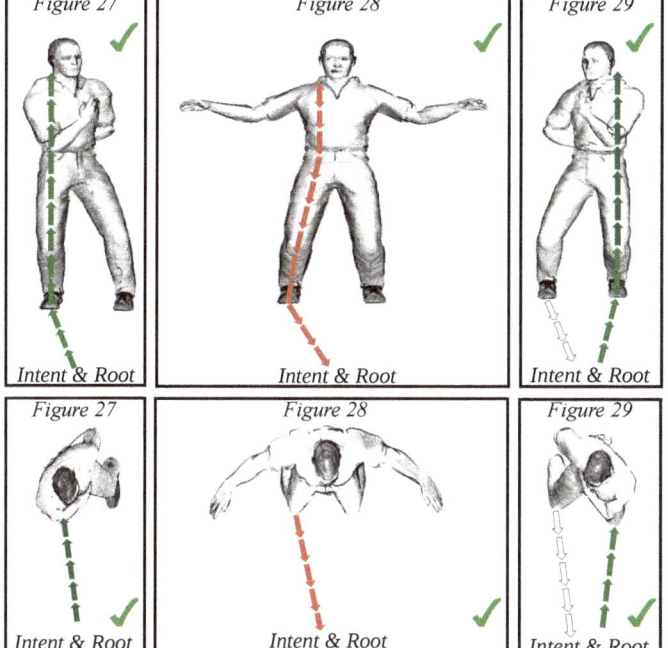

As the opening travels up the right leg, it pulls the body to the right side, causing the right kua to physically open and turn the body to the left. (figure 27) After opening has finished, closing starts in the root down the right side pulling the body back into the centre. (figure 28) When the left leg reaches 51% and smoothly takes over from the former substantial leg (represented by the transparent arrows) it now becomes substantial, opening from the root, moves up the left leg, pulls the body to the left side, causing the left kua to physically open and turn the body to the right. (figure 29)

Tai Chi practitioners often believe that the substantial leg itself is the root, which is incorrect. The substantial leg only accesses the root from which the opening and closing processes begin. When performing the First Loosening Exercise it's common for students to press the substantial foot against the ground **(Figure 25)** to move themselves back to a central position, then relax from above, down into the opposite leg. **(Figure 26)** The problem with this method is that every time you start to develop some sort of coherent root you then disconnect from it by pressing your foot against the ground and dropping your weight from above down the opposite leg. Repeating this process continuously, you then wonder why your root hasn't grown stronger or expanded. This is the equivalent of planting a sapling tree, then next month digging it up and moving it to a new location. The next month you dig it up again and move it to another location, and you do this every month. Then you wonder why the sapling hasn't grown. It's just not possible to grow your root when every time you move from one leg to the other, you press against the ground and then drop from above into the insubstantial leg.

The correct method for generating horizontal movement or any other form of movement is when the right leg becomes substantial *(51%)* you begin relaxing upward *(open)* from the root of that substantial leg. As the muscles soften up the right leg, the right ankle and knee adjust, resulting in the body being pulled to the right, steadily increasing weight in the substantial leg. As this relaxation continues to move up and under the gluteal folds, the gluteal muscles let go, *(drooping the buttocks)* the right buttock slightly more than the left. This causes the right kua to physically open and turn you to the left. *(Figure 27)* Once opening is completed, the closing *(relaxing downward)* process starts in the root of the substantial leg, which is the same leg that you've just opened up from. The closing pulls you back to the centre; as you're being pulled back to the centre by the substantial leg, the right hip reverse rotates helping you to be pulled back to the centre. *(Figure 28)* As you close down the right substantial leg, weight increases in the insubstantial left leg. The moment the left leg becomes the substantial leg, opening and closing is transferred to the newly substantial left leg. The process of opening is then repeated identical to **(Figure 27)** with the only difference you're Opening *(relaxing upward)* from the root of the newly substantial left leg which causes the muscles to gently let go causing the body to draw to the left and turn to the right as the left kua physically opens. *(Figure 29)* The transparent arrows represent the former substantial leg, disengaging from the root, allowing the newly substantial leg to take control of the opening and closing process from the previous substantial leg. **This connection between opening and closing and substantiality is inseparable.**

I feel that over the past few decades this symbiotic relationship between opening and closing, substantial and insubstantial has slowly been lost in Tai Chi. Practitioners have not understood or appreciated this symbiotic relationship, and therefore are not able to apply the principles of opening and closing to create substantial and insubstantial in their Tai Chi. They do not appreciate the negative effect this will have on their Tai Chi, whether it's the form or push hands. Opening and closing no longer being included in the process of creating substantial and insubstantial, will be viewed more as a side effect of moving the body, and not the source. It leaves substantial and insubstantial as nothing more than the means with which describe a concept of where dead weight is positioned in the body during Tai Chi. Without the ability to open and close to move substantial and insubstantial, practitioners are left with no real alternative than to use muscle to propel their body forward and back, left and right to achieve substantial and insubstantial.

We have clarified and defined Tai Chi as the physical manifestation of Taoist principles in action, having qualified the chi that powers all movement in Tai Chi, that being Di Xin Xi Yin Li (gravity). We can now access this power source by applying the Taoist principle of Wu Wei, Non-action to create action. By re-directing your opponent's energy/force (chi) through relaxation back into their own root causing them to become isolated and weak, giving the false appearance of you becoming stronger. Relaxation is the means with which we move the many forms of chi/force around and through the body. Dividing relaxation into two categories, closing (Yin) and opening (Yang) gives us access to a continuous source of relaxation. Both opening and closing emanates from intent. When opening & closing emanates from your intent, root is generated. Have established that opening possesses two different qualities, opening for yielding and opening for issuing what causes these two qualities to change, is the direction opening moves in. Having learnt one of the many byproducts of opening and closing is the ability to generate speed without the need for muscle. This connection between opening and closing and substantial and insubstantial are inseparable and co-dependent. If relaxation moves the chi, then what leads the chi?

What Influence does Intent play in Tai Chi?

10. Intent *(Yi)*

"I'm not a meat rack, don't hang your dead meat on me" was a phrase Yang Cheng Fu would often use. Most Tai Chi practitioners believe it's in reference to students resting the weight of their arm or arms on him during push hands. From my personal experience it's extremely rare for even a beginner of push hands to rest their arm weight on you, let alone a senior student. Besides, I can't imagine Yang Cheng Fu teaching push hands to beginners, this job would be left to his more senior students. And I seriously doubt his senior students would have made the near fatal mistake of resting their arm or body weight on Yang Cheng Fu during push hands. I believe, "I'm not a meat rack, don't hang your dead meat on me" is in reference to the fact the person touching him has no intent, without intent the hand touching him is just that... **dead meat**.

Originally I wasn't going to include a Chapter on Yi *(intent)* in this book, because the quality of Yi is such a hard thing to verbalise, so ineffable that I couldn't do the subject justice. Intent *(Yi)* can only be taught by touch. A single touch with someone who applies intent during push hands, can teach you more than thousands of words could on the subject. However, after much deliberation I came to the conclusion that intent makes up such a critical component of your Tai Chi development, and is far too important to be overlooked, especially when reaching the higher levels of Tai Chi.

So what is Intent? As usual, the best starting point for a definition for any word is the Dictionary.

Dictionary.com states; "Intent is something that is planned, proposed, or intended, purpose, design, intention".
Collins English Dictionary states; "A person's intent is their intention to do something".

For me, the above definitions really don't do the concept of intent justice when used in the context of Tai Chi. Let's have a look at the Classics, they may shed some light on the subject, after all Yi or Will is mentioned regularly throughout the Classics. **The following statement is from Wang Ts'ung-Yueh:** "懂勁後，愈練愈精，默識揣摩，漸至從心所欲。Once dong jin *(understanding the forces/energies)* is achieved, further practice and analysis develop greater refinements. Gradually you will reach the stage where everything flow as one wills without constraint". Also from Wang Ts'ung-Yueh: "The will *(intent)* and the intrinsic energy must change with alacrity to ensure roundness and swiftness in movement. This is termed the interplay of emptiness and solidness" Once again he links intent and the movement of chi, which is expressed in opening and closing to the interplay of substantial *(solidness)* and insubstantial *(emptiness)* which in turn creates speed.

Understanding of the Thirteen Postures states: "意氣須換得靈。乃有圓活之趣。所謂轉變虛實" There should be agility in the interaction of the yi *(intent)* and chi, so the chi will be circular and lively *(I believe this is in reference to the opening and closing)*. This is what is meant by changing substantial and insubstantial *(this is in relation to opening and closing and its symbiotic relationship with substantial and insubstantial which in turn creates physical movement)*. Another quote from Understanding of the Thirteen Postures states: 全身意在精神，不在氣，在氣則滯。有氣者無力。無氣者純鋼。氣如車輪，腰如車軸。 " The yi *(intent)* should be on the spirit, not on the chi, or the chi will stagnate. With the chi there will be no strength. Without chi it is like tempered steel. Chi is like the cart wheel and the waist is the axle". Interesting to note that when talking to most people about the concept of the waist representing the axle of a cart wheel, they always view the cart wheel from above, where you could spin the wheel like a lazy susan. *(Figure 30)* Viewing the wheel from above is not how a cart wheel is used. A cart wheel is used standing vertically on its rim, so that it can roll along the ground. The waist like the axle of a cart wheel can be considered the centre point of the body anatomically and structurally. *(Figure 31)* With the rim representing chi circulating in a vertical circle, which can be used to affect and cut your opponent's root.

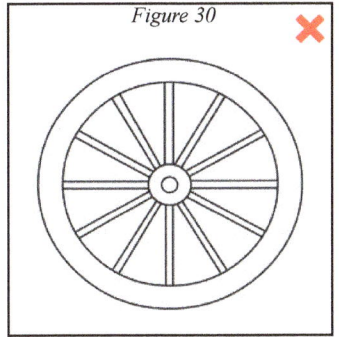

Viewing the cart wheel incorrectly from above.

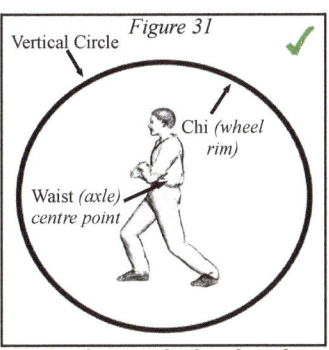

Viewing the cart wheel analogy from the side as it was meant to be viewed.

Important Tai Chi points from the Yang Family Yang Cheng-Fu states; "用意不用力。Use Yi *(intent)* not Li" *(in this case, li is referenced as brute strength and not internal strength)*. If you look through the Classics there is frequent cross referencing between Yi *(intent)*, Shen *(spirit)* and Xin *(heart)* where heart is considered a form of consciousness. These three qualities are often mentioned together. The elements, of Yi *(intent)*, Shen *(spirit)* and Xin *(heart) (consciousness)* have a cause and effect relationship with each other. The will is mentioned regularly throughout the Classics, and is often in reference to the importance of developing the will in your Tai Chi.

Lets us start pulling things apart, starting with will. Are intent and will the same? I believe they are similar, but not the same, although I can understand how intent and will became interchanged in the Classics. Will is closer to determination than it is to intent. For example, someone who becomes lost in the desert *(common occurrence in Australia)* often say, the only thing that kept them going, was wanting to see their loved ones again. It was their intent to see their loved ones again, that gave them the will *(the strength and determination)* to continue, when they very much felt like giving up. Will is more physical, more immediate to the moment. Intent has more to do with a future event or point in time.

There is also a large amount of commentary in the Classics on Spirit, *(TCM has seven sub categories of Spirit alone)*. Statement from *Understanding of the Thirteen Postures* states: "形如搏兔之 鶻。神如捕鼠之貓"。 "Have the appearance of a falcon preying on a hare. Concentrate the Shen *(spirit)* like a cat stalking a mouse". What does the above statement mean? If you've ever watched a documentary on lions, you generally see the lion strolling along looking at nothing in particular. Three things then transpire: the first, the lion's Xin (Heart) *(consciousness)* becomes aware of a zebra; secondly the lion's Yi *(intent)* locks on to the zebra; thirdly the lion's Shen *(spirit)* rises. When the lion's spirit rises, the lion becomes extremely alert, light and nimble, losing any clumsiness, almost giving the appearance of floating above the ground. *(very similar to a Tai Chi practitioner, light, but very much grounded)*. Remember how the lion, creeps up on the Zebra; the lion doesn't physically move up and down, but stays the same height throughout the stalking process. This reminds me of the old Tai Chi proverb: "In Tai Chi the body must expand and contract, but the body must never rise nor fall". The expansion and contraction they are referring to happens in the root. The internal process of opening and closing originates from the root and not from the expansion and contraction of the physical body. During Tai Chi one is constantly contracting *(closing)* into the root, closing *(relaxing downward)* and expanding out of the root, opening *(relaxing upward)* with the body staying still in height. At no time does the body physically rise or fall. Some postures in the form do require you to lower body height such as snake creeps down or bend low and punch, however this is for martial application. The lion has taken on the qualities the Classics often refer to. The Classics state: "精神能提得起。則無遲重之虞。所謂頂頭懸也。 If the Shen *(spirit)* is raised there will not be any sluggishness. This is the meaning of suspending the head from the crown as if you're being suspended from above". Note the order the qualities appeared, first is Xin *(consciousness)* followed by Yi *(intent)* and lastly Shen *(spirit)*

Relating this back to Tai Chi, first expand or open your Xin *(consciousness, awareness)* then extend your Yi *(intent)*, when your intent expands, your Shen *(spirit)* will lift. Don't focus on raising the spirit, just keep your head suspended at all times throughout your Tai Chi; extend your intent and the spirit will rise automatically. Like the falcon preying on the hare, the cat stalking the mouse or the lion hunting the zebra, they all exhibit the same level of intent resulting in their spirit rising naturally. The spirit rising is the result of the head being suspended and extending the intent. Without intent and the head suspended, raising the spirit becomes problematic.

I still haven't been able to define what intent is, after decades of trying. The closest I have come is to realise its function in Tai Chi. Richard Best, one of my senior students, has been an Acupuncturist and Chinese herbalist for the last 38 years, and helped me to define what intent is in relation to Traditional Chinese Medicine, which in this instance is applicable to Tai Chi. I have changed a few words here and there to make it a little more relevant to Tai Chi. "Intent's primary function in Tai Chi is...

"Yi gives you the ability in Tai Chi to lead chi by means of relaxation, to a future point in time and place outside of the body.

Allow me to explain the above definition. Imagine you have a bow and arrow and you're shooting at a moving target. Would you shoot the arrow at the moving target or slightly ahead of the target. I'm guessing you would shoot slightly ahead of it with the expectations of the target moving into the arrow's flight path. So what you've done is you've projected your intent to a future point in time where you think the target will be, releasing the arrow from the immediate moment to a point in time forward of the moment you are presently in. Yi *(intent)* has its origins in the moment, but continues into the future. Intent by its very nature exists between the moment and future; awareness resides only in the moment. Intent isn't really a necessity in solo work if you're training Tai Chi for the purpose of improving your physical and mental health. You really only need to develop relaxation and alignment when training Tai Chi for the purposes of health. However, if you wish to apply Tai Chi as a martial art **intent is absolutely indispensable.**

Intent leads relaxation to a point of your choosing. This relaxation in turn facilitates the movement of various forms of external chi, such as energy from a blow or push *(kinetic chi)* or Di Xin Xi Yin Li *(gravity)* to this chosen point. Intent behaves similarly to the end of a downpipe. Wherever the end of the downpipe is pointed; that is where the water will appear. The pipe itself represents the alignments of your body's: their job is to transport the water *(relaxation)* to the end of the downpipe *(your intent)*. And what is the energy that moves the water through the pipe to its final destination? Di Xin Xi Yin Li *(gravity)*.

Intent is also responsible for the direction and quality relaxation takes on. Whether closing *(relaxing downward)* is used to cut and compress your opponent's root, and to move you physically forward *(advancing)*. Or opening *(relaxing upward)* towards yourself from where your intent is positioned *(forward of yourself)*, resulting in your yielding internally and physically. Or alternatively, you could open *(relaxing upward)* forward of your intent and issue *(fa-jing)* from physical stillness.

We have established that when relaxation and intent are brought together, we have the beginning of root. The next question would have to be: what powers awareness and intent, that makes these two qualities possible? **Simply put, concentration.** Concentration is an absolute necessity in Tai Chi, which of course can be applied to anything you wish to achieve in life. Whether it's studying for a degree, reaching the heights of your chosen sport or even for something as seemingly passive as meditation. Absolute concentration is essential for the maintaining of intent and awareness in Tai Chi.

Often students believe the meditational aspect of Tai Chi is in the concentration that's required to remember the correct order and sequence of postures in the form. Granted this does require a certain amount of concentration, forcing you to switch off from the constant chatter of the mind. The real meditational aspect of Tai Chi is not just remembering the correct sequences of the form, but is a combination of awareness that's needed to generate the opening *(relaxing up)* and closing *(relaxing down)*, and the intent required to lead this relaxation. Both these activities requires an enormous amount of concentration. I feel the following definition best defines the very nature of concentration.

Concentration is the absence of inconsequential thought.

In Tai Chi, awareness and intent can and do occupy the same time frame. But it's not possible for thought and intent to occupy the same time frame. You can have a thought, or you can have intent, not both at the same time. For example when stepping in the form with the functionally empty leg, the second you think or have a thought of lifting the leg, you've lost your intent and with it, your root and control over your opponent's root. Your functionally empty leg **must** step due to relaxation and alignment, without the use of thought. When thought isn't used in the execution of a movement in Tai Chi, intent can be maintained. For those of you who say you can't step without thought, I hold up walking as a classic example of not using it to step. When walking you don't consciously tell the rear leg to step, it steps when the conditions are met, not when you tell it. You may have an intent to walk, but not a thought to walk.

I have also noticed in some Tai Chi books they have written, "The Yi directs the Chi and the Chi directs the Li". Using the word "direct" is incorrect. This one incorrect word changes the relationship and order between Yi, Chi, Li. You may think I'm being pedantic, but these two words "direct" and "lead" completely change the way how Yi, Chi, Li are viewed and interact with each other. For example, if you were to ask me where the toilets are in the building. I have two options; I could direct you to where the toilets are and stay stationary, or I could take you to where the toilets are. In other words I have **led** you to the toilets. Direct and led are not the same, in fact they hold opposite positions to each other *(led in the front and direct at the rear)*. In Tai Chi intent must lead the chi *(relaxation creates the condition for chi to move and Di Xin Xi Yin Li moves the chi)* and the chi must lead the Li *(internal strength)*. When you lead you're at the front of the process, when you direct, you're behind the process. If "direct" and "lead" are not clarified it will have a negative long term effect on your Tai Chi. It is for this reason that I have placed the definition of push and pull in the glossary. A push, is when the energy that moves an object is behind the object it moves. Whereas a pull is when the energy that moves an object is in front of the object it moves. **Gravity (*Di Xin Xi Yin Li*) pulls, doesn't push, so our primary energy source for movement, strength and speed in Tai Chi comes from a pulling action, not a pushing action.**

When you place your intent in front of your physical position *(to be totally honest, I still don't truly understand why it works, I just know it does)* the intent **will lead** the relaxation *(relaxation is created by awareness/consciousness)*, which is pulled by gravity, Di Xin Xi Yin Li, Chi of the Earth along with any energy/force *(chi)* placed on your body to where you've placed your intent. This is hopefully under and behind your opponent. This is why, as stated earlier, if you wait till you feel even the lightest touch on your body and start directing this incoming energy/force into your root, you'll be too late, putting yourself behind the energy instead of leading *(ahead)* the energy/force. I often tell my students during push hands training that they need to start without me. If they wait until they feel my touch, let alone my push, it's already too late. You need to start the closing *(relaxing downward)* process in the root, before your opponent even touches you, this way you're leading the process and not directing the process. By waiting till you feel the energy/force on you, then you're directing this energy/force into your root, placing you behind the energy/force. Leading the relaxation with your intent before your opponent touches you, results in your leading their energy, therefore preventing it becoming a force. Without intent, you're essentially directing/following the force into the ground. **With intent, you're leading the force into the ground to a point where your intent is.** With the earlier process of directing the force, you're not in control and with the latter you are. I would like to relay a story, I was once told about Master Huang. Master Huang was explaining intent to a class and was positioned around 3 metres from the wall of the training hall, when he pointed to a small mark on the wall. Turning his back to the wall, taking a coin from his pocket, he spun around, throwing the coin at the wall, hitting the mark exactly on the wall.

Explanation Of The Thirteen Postures By Wang Ts'ung–Yueh;
"The inner strength may seem slack, but it is not. It may seem stretched but it is not. At times it may seem to have ceased, but at no time does it stop, for in all movements the will *(intent)* is active". Wang Ts'ung-Yueh is referring to intent, and how it needs to be constantly engaged, linking Yi to the continuity of the whole internal and external process of movement.

Continuity Of Intent
It is absolutely imperative you never drop your intent when training Tai Chi, doubly so, in push hands. Why? When stepping in Tai Chi, the leg that moves needs to be completely and functionally empty *(refer to glossary for definition of functionally empty)*. Even if one percent of weight remains in the insubstantial leg when stepping, it will require thought and muscle contraction *(muscle contraction beyond the need for just bearing weight)* to lift this one percent. The second the decision is made to lift this one percent, you will be forced to use thought and muscle to generate this action. Resulting in you instantly dropping your intent causing you to disconnect from your root, positioned under and behind your opponent. At this exact moment your opponent will simultaneously regain control of their root. Wang Ts'ung-Yueh also states; "It is also said that the mind *(intent)* comes first and the body later", referencing the mind is fairly ambiguous. The mind could be in relation to numerous things such as, thought, intent, awareness, emotion, etc but when placed in context with the other Classics, it's pretty obvious he is referring to intent.

Intent in Tai Chi regardless if you're training the Opening and Closing Exercise, Five Loosening Exercises, Form or Push Hands needs to be maintained at all times. This breaking of intent tends to become more apparent when Tai Chi practitioners start to move around. If you watch closely, just before students step forward, they tend to exhibit a slight backward movement first, and likewise, when stepping back, a slight movement forward. This is a very common occurrence, especially when speed is involved. The cause for these small pre-movements forward or back is the practitioner's inability to create physical movement by applying opening *(relaxing upward)* and closing *(relaxation downward)* from where their intent is positioned. Thus requiring them to disconnect from intent before using thought to engage muscle with which to generate forward or backward movement.

During push hands, both parties continuously rock forward and back, looking to take advantage of any mistakes their partner may make when advancing and retreating. Often one party will gain the upper hand by either drawing their partner off their root or cutting into their root. Once their partner's root has been compromised, only then, can they progress to the next stage of the process *(issuing)*. Everything is looking good, their partner's root has been compromised. When proceeding to the next stage of the process of fa-jing, they make the common mistake of pushing from the rear leg, causing them to lose control over their partner's root at the critical moment of release. The first part of the process was performed correctly, they have relaxed *(closed)* past their partner's root, resulting in their partner's root being severed. However, as they moved to the second phase of the process, instead of continuing the process of opening *(relaxing upward)* to issue from where their intent is positioned *(under and behind their partner's root)*, they revert to thought *(a command from the mind)* and muscle to generate power and movement by pushing their rear leg against the ground. The second that thought is used to generate this muscular movement, they have effectively drawn their mind back into their body, resulting in loss of intent. For those who have a mechanical mind, closing and opening behaves in the same way as a piston does in an internal combustion engine. The crank shaft which is constantly travelling in a circular motion allows the piston to go downward which is a linear action. For the piston to travel back up, does the crankshaft stop and reverse direction? No it doesn't, it continues on with its circular motion lifting the piston back up again. This is exactly how opening and closing is performed. If intent is no longer leading relaxation into your partner's root to maintain control, your partner automatically re-establishes connection to their own root, allowing them to re-engage their muscles once again. Having closed *(downward relaxation)* correctly by using intent and having succeeded in controlling and neutralising your opponent's root, to prevent your partner from recovering their root, at the critical moment of issuing you need to have the intent open *(relaxing upward)* from where your intent has been placed *(under and behind your opponent)*. Something to keep in mind, if you maintain your opening and closing and your intent is expanding, then so will your root.

Whenever intent breaks for whatever reason, this can be considered a hollow *(break)* in your intent. A hollow *(break)* or protrusion *(holding)* can appear anytime during the process of Yi Chi Li. This hollow, causes relaxation to disconnect from your opponent's root, allowing your partner to recover their equilibrium, balance and root, just as you issue *(fa jing)*. Yang Lu Chan's grandson Yang Cheng Fu mentions in the Classics; "Apply your Will *(intent)* and not your force". Another reference of using Yi *(intent)* to lead the internal process *(relaxation moves the chi)* and the internal process leads the strength *(internal)*. Remember strength is not muscular, in reality you haven't increased your strength, you've made your opponent weaker, giving the false appearance you possess super human strength. When the **right qualities are applied in the right order** your opponent becomes extremely weak. In the old days, pugilists fighting a Tai Chi exponent, would often describe the sensation of fighting a ghost. When advancing, the Tai Chi exponent would seem to disappear. Yet when withdrawing and retreating, it felt their Tai Chi opponent was unbearably close to them. What they are referring to, is experiencing the effects of a Tai Chi exponent's intent.

Quality Of Intent
What should the quality and nature of your intent be in Tai Chi? The quality of your intent is hinted in the answer Yang Lu Chan gave to a question. When asked how high could he throw someone? His answer was, "How high can I look?" Followed by a second question. How low can you throw someone? His response again, "How low can I look?". No one can seriously suggest that Yang Lu Chan could throw someone 200 metres into the air, simply because he looked that high. His answer to how high and low he can look, I believe is in reference to the nature and quality of his intent. That intent, should take on the quality as if one is looking at an object they're about to walk to, just a light intent. For those people old enough out there, before cell phones were around, do you recall having organised to meet a friend at certain place at a certain time. Maybe you had organised to meet a friend for a lift somewhere or maybe to meet a friend in front of a concert hall, and they had the tickets you needed for entry. You've been waiting for maybe 15 to 20 minutes past the agreed time, you don't know what's happened to them and there is no way to contact them, you're starting to feel anxious. Finally you see them through the crowd, do you remember the sensation you felt, the second you saw them. A wave of relief *(relaxation)* washes through your body the moment you see them, *(your intent locks on to them)*. A wave of relaxation follows your intent to the person you are looking at. This is similar to the quality of intent that's required in Tai Chi, not thought, just consciousness, relaxation and intent. These qualities are mentioned in the Classics; "That in the five direction one should look right, gaze left". Once again there is this reference to the eyes. I believe the Classics are referring to the quality of the intent and not the direction of your eyes. Intent is far too important to your Tai Chi development to only give it a cursory glance. Especially when progressing to the higher levels of Tai Chi, to not give intent the attention it deserves, will be extremely detrimental to your advancement in Tai Chi.

Common Mistake Of Relaxing Towards Your Intent Instead Of Relaxing From Your Intent
I've found a common problem when trying to explain how intent works in Tai Chi, especially from students who are not from my school. Most students make the common mistake of placing their intent behind and under their opponent and then try to relax towards their intent. Students tend to see intent as being similar to that of playing darts. They place their aim *(intent)* on the bullseye throwing the dart at the point they're aiming at. This is not how intent works in Tai Chi. You don't relax towards your intent, it will result in you pushing even if relaxation is used. The correct way is to place your intent behind and under your opponent and then start the relaxation process from where your intent is, not to your intent, regardless if it's closing or opening.

The Song of the Thirteen Postures state; "若言體用何為準, 意氣君來骨肉臣。 *If asked the principle of the understanding and its application, answer; the yi (intent) and the chi are the Emperors, while the flesh and bones are their subjects.*

The hardest part by far, is training the intent in Tai Chi. However, your first priority in Tai Chi is to train relaxation and alignments. Relaxation for the purpose of making your body soft enough so the many forms of chi can pass through the body uninterrupted and unopposed. The second priority is to train the alignments of the body so relaxation can move the alignments in a way that follows the principles of Taoist philosophy of not insisting or resisting. For example, not dropping your rear knee into the rear foot which results in you pushing against the ground. In comparison to the correct way, of allowing the rear knee to move forward which pulls you forward and has the added affect of rolling the pelvis under and elongating the spine. Once having resolved these two issues; relaxation and alignment, only then, can you really start to develop your intent *(you never really stop developing your relaxation and alignment, you're always refining relaxation and alignments, it's a work in progress)*. Intent is the emperor, the body the servant, *(relaxation and alignments)*. The body *(the servant)* needs to be trained so well, that it can respond to the commands of the intent instantly *(the emperor)* without the need for the mind *(awareness)* to come back to the body to supervise the action the emperor has ordered. The intent *(emperor)* always stays in front of your physical position and gives the command to open or close, which causes the body *(servant)* to instantly obey. Depending on whether it's opening or closing will result in the body's alignment to change in a way that the body either retreats, advances, turns left or right. The problem is, the intent *(mind)* always wants to come back to supervise that the order has been carried out. The second this happens communications between intent *(emperor)* and the body *(servants)* is severed and you now have the mind directly moving the body. The hardest quality to train in Tai Chi is maintaining your intent in front of the body. **Master Huang once said; "Tai Chi is physically hard, mentally nearly impossible".**

I can't emphasis this point strongly enough: all relaxation, opening and closing starts at the point of intent *(mind)*. Allowing you to control your opponent's root, the instant contact is made.

We have clarified and defined Tai Chi as the physical manifestation of Taoist principles in action, having qualified the chi that powers all movement in Tai Chi, that being Di Xin Xi Yin Li (gravity). We can now access this power source by applying the Taoist principle of Wu Wei, Non-action to create action. By re-directing your opponent's energy/force (chi) through relaxation back into their own root causing them to become isolated and weak, giving the false appearance of you becoming stronger. Relaxation is the means with which we move the many forms of chi/force around and through the body. Dividing relaxation into two categories, closing (Yin) and opening (Yang), both opening and closing emanates from intent, when opening and closing connects to your intent, root is generated. Having established that opening possesses two different qualities, opening for yielding and opening for issuing, what changes these two qualities, is the direction opening moves in. Having learnt one of the many byproducts of opening and closing is the ability to generate speed without the need for muscle. The connection between opening and closing and substantial and insubstantial are inseparable and co-dependent. Opening and closing are connected to your intent through the substantial leg, allowing intent to lead relaxation, resulting in relaxation leading the many forms of chi. One form of chi is (gravity) (Di Xin Xi Yin Li) causing substantial and insubstantial to interact with each other which in turn moves the body. How do you apply all the above into a practical method of application?

Do you actually Push in Push Hands and if you don't, then what's the source of the Push?

11. Push Hands *(Partner Work)*

In this chapter, I will outline the primary purpose of push hands, explaining the qualities, mental, energetic and physical, at play in achieving this one goal in push hands. This one goal is achieved by the application of Taoist principles learnt, trained and experienced in the form and solo work, which are transferred to your push hands. I will cover common misconceptions that have been repeated so often, they are now deeply ingrained into the theory of Tai Chi. This Chapter is written for the purpose of giving you an outline, an overview of the aims and means of push hands. The cause for push hands to fail are too numerous, making it impossible to list them all in this Chapter. It would require a separate book to list all the various symptoms, causes and faults in push hands. When applying Taoist principles to push hands, you can be 99% right and still be 100% wrong.

The term Push Hands is not my favourite terminology for describing a process which uses the chi of the Earth *(gravity)* by means of relaxation to draw *(pull)* an energy/force *(chi)* through the body, led by intent to a point forward of the body. This energy movement can be expressed during physical movement, or in stillness. Most Tai Chi practitioners refuse to believe or even contemplate that internally and externally you literally don't push in push hands. To be fair though, it does look a lot like the two parties are pushing each other if you're not familiar with the principles and processes at work in Tai Chi. Some Tai Chi teachers have even tried to change the word push, in push hands to negate the inference of the word pushing by changing the name to sensing hands, listening hands, soft hands, cotton palm etc, etc, to no avail. My teacher Wee Kee Jin refers to push hands as partner work, which is much more of an accurate description for push hands. I feel the horse has already bolted when it comes to the name of push hands and it's possible misinterpretation. The saddest part in all of this, the term push, in push hands, literally points the practitioner in the very opposite direction they need to move in. I have noted over the years, students in general tend to make judgements and determinations on the direction their training methods take, from what they observe physically. Which often doesn't correspond to the results they are hoping for.

If reputable Tai Chi Masters are physically positioned in front of the person they have just thrown across the room, then it is self-evident to the observer that this outcome was achieved by the Master pushing. In Tai Chi, it is prudent to never assume the obvious from what you **see and feel**. For example, Tai Chi is an internal art, close to 70% of the processes is hidden and non-visual. This process starts with intent, which can't be seen, awareness, which can't be seen, followed by relaxation which also can't be seen. However, the last part of the process which is physical movement, can be seen, with the hands being the last part of the physical process to move. This is in comparison to most push hands, where the hands are usually the first things that engage rather than the last. This results in most Tai Chi practitioners starting push hands at the wrong end of the process, **the physical**, when they should be starting their push hands with their mind *(intent)*. They start the physical process of push hands by pressing their feet against the ground. This results in the practitioner pushing, instead of pulling to initiate physical movement *(refer to the glossary for the definition of pulling and pushing)*.

Don't mistake effect for cause.

If you're not aware of intent and relaxation being applied first *(non visual)* then you're left with the last third of the process, which is physical with which to try to and understand and make sense of the whole entire process. If you don't believe in training intent, even though it's mentioned numerous times in the Classics you've already lost 33.33% of your art. Were you to train only downward relaxation *(closing)* and not opening *(upward relaxation)*, you've lost another 16.6% of the art, you're now down to 50% of the art. Of that 50% only 16.6% can be considered internal due to the application of downward relaxation *(closing)*. This doesn't leave much of an internal process, with which to develop a supposedly internal martial art.

So what is the primary purpose of push hands, its very purpose? The usual stock standard reply is, push hands helps you to develop listening, joining, sticking, yielding, relaxation, leading, following and adhering, learning to deal with external forces being placed on the body, etc, etc, all very worthy and necessary qualities to train in push hands. But, for what purpose, what is the end game, what is the result you're hoping to achieve by developing all the above qualities in your push hands? These skills are only a means to an end, not an end to a means. Students often forget the primary purpose for training the above qualities in their push hands is to achieve one outcome...

To gain the ability to capture, control and neutralise your opponent's root through the application of Taoist principles of Wu Wei. After which, you have the added option of concluding the process by releasing your opponent by applying fa-jing.

Is capturing, controlling and neutralising your opponent's root a martial quality or a philosophical virtue even when fa-jing is included? There is a fair bit of discussion within Tai Chi circles whether push hands, even has a martial function. Some say push hands is the martial component of Tai Chi others say the form is. I was taught when I first started Tai Chi, that the form was the martial component of Tai Chi and push hands is the application of Taoist philosophy. Both are separate but interconnected. It took years for me to reconcile these two elements. I thought, as most students, that push hands relates more to the martial side of Tai Chi, rather than the form, probably because push hands and fighting both require an opponent and physical contact. Other martial art practitoners mockingly say that push hands by itself can't be used in a fight "What are you going to achieve with push hands in a fight; give your opponent a pushing they won't quickly forget?". Entirely correct. However, looking at the big picture, in a physical conflict, possessing the ability to control your opponent's root and shutting your opponent down, in the first seconds of a conflict, does place you in a very advantageous position. After controlling your opponent's root, in a conflict there would soon follow the inevitable punches, kicks and blows to your opponent, derived from the Tai Chi form. If you've managed to maintain control over your opponent's root while delivering these blows, this will result in your opponent being discharged quite violently. So to answer the question, is push hands the martial component of Tai Chi? No it's not, applying Taoist principles in push hands for the purpose of taking control of your opponent's root does not make it the martial component of Tai Chi. Establishing control over your opponent's root, and then applying techniques derived from your Tai Chi form, such as Brush Knee or Step and Punch Low, would make the form the martial component of Tai Chi.

Push Hands is just one of many modalities in Tai Chi with which we need to physically apply Taoist principles of softness overcoming hardness, the weak overcoming the strong, the slow overcoming the fast, etc, etc. Without Taoist principles, push hands becomes nothing more than a mechanical action where one person performs a specific technique and their training partner then applies the counter technique. Roles are then reversed and the defender becomes the attacker and the attacker becomes the defender. This method of training is not exclusive to Tai Chi, and can be found in most of the harder external martial arts. After learning a push hand set, what next? Do we just keep performing the same push hand set for the next 40 years in the hope that something will happen? This is the difference between 40 years of experience and one year *(the same year)* forty times over.

The means with which to achieve the goal of controlling your opponent's root, lies in applying the qualities that are first experienced and learnt from the form and other solo work. Qualities such as Opening and Closing, Relaxation, Alignment, Awareness, Timing and Technique. If we're training and hopefully achieving these qualities from the form and other solo work, then why is it that we even need push hands? One of the many benefits that push hands offers, is allowing your partner to apply an external force to your body. The second thing your partner brings to push hands, which is easily more important than the application of an external force *(which can be achieved by a mechanical mechanism)*, is the source of the external energy/force, which is often overlooked. **Your partner brings their root to the push hands process.** The external energy/force they apply to your body is generated from their root. Learning how to lead and return your partner's energy/force back into their root, without question is the prime objective of push hands, all achieved by applying Opening, Closing, Relaxation, Alignment, Awareness, Timing and Technique. All this is learnt from solo work which is critical for you if you are going to learn how to accept energy/force and lead *(deflect, return)* it back to your partner's root.

In push hands there will always be at least one point and limitless entry points on your body for energy/force to enter from your opponent's push, with only one exit point for this energy/force, back to your opponent's root. The exit point for this energy/force is our root *(intent)*, which is under and behind our opponent. However, our exit point for returning your opponent's energy *(the energy from their push)* is the starting point for your opponent's push, which is in their root. *(Figure 32)* This energy is returned by means of relaxation, alignment, intent and gravity *(Di Xin Xi Yin Li)* to your partner's root. The process and pathways for push hands and solo work are identical. The form, solo work and push hands uses the same process. You would think transferring these qualities from solo work and form into your push hands would be a straight forward affair... you would be wrong.

Figure 32

Entry point of your opponent's energy/force

Exit point for you was the starting point for your opponent's energy. Resulting in their energy being returned to their root

Establishing your intent behind and under your opponent's root, closing from your intent allows you to return your opponent's energy/force back to it origins. Resulting in your opponent's root being severed.

I was taught early on in my Tai Chi, that what you learn in the form such as technique, posture, alignment, relaxation, opening and closing, you then apply or stress test in your push hands. If there are any faults or errors, they'll show up in your push hands. When a fault is discovered in your push hands, I can guarantee you, you'll find the source of the mistake in your form and other solo work. If a mistake or fault is found in your push hands, the correction needs to be made at the source, which is your solo work and form and not in your push hands. For example, after you sit for an exam or test, your paper is marked and returned. You then return to the classroom where you make the necessary corrections, there is no point in sitting another exam until you've corrected the previous mistakes. You return to the class room *(the form)* and having made your corrections, you then sit another test *(push hands)*. An exam or test is exactly that. A test. Exams only confirm what is correct and what is not. An exam doesn't teach you how to correct these mistakes; it only shows you the faults. Alternatively, imagine your solo work and form as the circuitry on a circuit board. If you want to see if there is a weakness in the circuit, you increase the current through the circuitry *(energy, chi or force from your opponent)*. If there is any resistance or weakness within the circuit, the circuit will blow *(you'll get pushed out)*.

Training the Cause not the Effect
A common fault in push hands is the mistake of training the effect and not the cause. For example we all rock forward and back repeatedly in push hands and the form. The focus is often on the rocking back and forward, which is wrong. The focus should be on the opening and closing, which is the cause of your rocking forward and back. **The effect** *(remember what I said earlier in this Chapter, about practitioners training the last part of the process, the physical, rather than the first part of the*

process, intent and relaxation). The following Tai Chi saying now begins to make sense, "You open to yield *(rocking backwards)* and you close to follow *(rocking forward, following your opponent's retreat)"*. If opening is performed correctly when rocking back *(yielding, retreating)* your partner's energy/force will slip off into the emptiness *(void)*. Your partner will experience the sensation of you disappearing into thin air when you've fully rocked backwards. It's this exact moment you need to start the closing process *(relaxed downward)* in and behind your partner's root where your intent should have stayed when you were internally and physically yielding. This results in instantly cutting your partner's root without the need for you to even physically move forward. Having cut their root, your partner will instinctively go into a defensive mode, trying to recover their root by retreating backwards, mentally, energetically and physically. By continuing the closing process in your root, you'll follow your opponent's retreat. When your partner runs out of physical and internal room and with no root, it's pretty much game over for them.

To quote from the little orange book, Tai Chi Chuan Ta Wen, Questions and Answers on T'ai Chi Chuan by Chen Wei Ming *translated by* Benjamin Pang Jeng Lo *and* Robert W. Smith on the bottom of page 28; "The pursuit of the opponent's long and short distance is based on my level. If my level is low I must follow him long and only when his force is spent I attack him *(this is the spot where we all start our push hands from, learning how to physically yield correctly)*. If my level is higher I can follow a shorter distance and wait for his force to break midway before I counter *(From my personal experience, I believe Chen Wei Ming is referring to the fact that opponents will often collapse or create a hollow or break in their shoulders, then rock forward into their arms to physically close the distance and then re-engage the shoulders to push out with the arms)*. If my level is very high I need only to follow him a little, and when his force breaks I can immediately counter *(most Tai Chi practitioners tend to relax from above down into their back leg into their root when rocking back causing them to break from their opponent, allowing you to close from your root and follow them and cut their root. The second that happens their force is broken and at that point you can throw them out)*. Sometimes I can adhere to an opponent and he can't release his force *(you have so fully captured, controlled and neutralised your opponent's root, they literally can't physically move)*. At this level I don't need to follow my opponent and I can make my own decisions". If you don't have this book, I strongly recommend you buy it, it will be the best $25 you will ever spend when it comes to your Tai Chi *(after this book of course)*.

Training push hands is not about rocking back as far as you can, then using your kuas *(hips)* or yao *(waist)* to turn left or right, followed by an upper body technique to take the force off your body and then simply rock forward so your partner can repeat the same process. This is once again, the same one year, 40 times over. No, you open *(relax upward)* trying to draw your opponent out *(drawing out is defined by your partner moving ever so slightly forward of their bubbling well, usually caused by pushing)* by yielding *(opening)*. At the moment when opening is ending, but hasn't quite ended this is the moment you apply the two thirds rule in Tai Chi and start closing *(relax downward)* in your root which hopefully at this stage of the push hands cycle is under and behind your partner. This has the effect of cutting your partner's root instantly, without the need for even physical movement. For your partner to recover from this perilous situation, they will have to apply the above process to you.

Being Competitive in Push Hands
Some Tai Chi practitioners wrongly believe that the only time you can be competitive, is in free push hands and even this is sometimes frowned upon. Some students view being competitive in set push hands as a mortal sin and is actively discouraged. Set push hands can be very competitive and there is nothing wrong with being competitive and it should be encouraged up to a point, providing Tai Chi principles aren't sacrificed. In this way you are sharpening your skills up against your partner who is doing likewise. This is how you improve, not by doing the same thing over and over. With time and correct training, both parties listening, joining, adhering, following, yielding, sticking and leading

will improve, resulting in their overall ability and speed in capturing, controlling and neutralising their opponent's root. To be honest, I'm extremely competitive by nature, over the years I have learnt to restrain and temper this part of my nature. As much as I hate losing, there is only one thing I hate more, and that's breaking the principles of Tai Chi.

If you're going to learn how to capture, neutralise and control your opponent's root you're going to need a few extra qualities that solo practise can't offer. In push hands you'll need the customary qualities that you've learnt and trained from your solo practise and form work. However, these are mainly physical and energetic attributes, for example, Alignment *(physical)*, Relaxation *(energetic)*, Timing *(internal and physical)*, Posture *(physical)*, Opening and Closing *(energetic)*, Awareness *(mental)*, important as these qualities are, all but one is either energetic or physical. In the performance of push hands your body needs to be extremely soft *(relaxation)* internally, so various energy/forces can pass through your body unimpeded. Your alignment has to be perfect in stillness and in movement so forces don't settle on the joints. Opening and Closing needs to have no hollows *(breaks)* or, protrusions *(holding)* so relaxation doesn't become stagnant or broken. Changes from closing to opening and opening to closing *(timing)* must be seamless otherwise you'll become a victim of double weightedness. Opening and Closing which creates substantial and insubstantial, also needs to be seamless. Substantial and insubstantial creates all physical movement in Tai Chi *(and not muscle)*. All the above is achievable through your solo training, such as Opening and Closing Exercise, Five Loosening Exercises and Form. Push Hands trains qualities solo methods just can't, attributes such as Intent, Listening, Sticking, Following, Joining, Leading and Adhering these are mental qualities. **To learn these qualities, they need to be felt and experienced and can't be taught visually. These qualities of push hand aren't physical, they're mental.**

Controlling and neutralising your opponent's root not only requires the physical qualities derived from the form and solo practise, you'll also need the mental qualities that only push hands can provide. When both physical, energetical and mental attributes are brought together, you will have the means with which to control and neutralise your opponent's root. **Control your opponent's root, you control your opponent, you control the situation** *(if your not in control, then they are)*.

These mental qualities can't be learnt and realised from your form or solo practise, only from push hands. There is a saying in the West; "A picture is worth a thousand words" Similar in Tai Chi, a single touch in push hands can teach you more than a thousand words can. Only after these sensations have been experienced and learnt in push hands, can they be transferred into your solo work, such, as Opening and Closing Exercise, Five Loosening Exercises and Form. Without the combined physical and energetic qualities of solo work and the mental qualities of push hands, controlling, neutralising and, issuing just isn't possible. Only when these mental qualities are experienced, learnt and applied in push hands, can you hope to bring them into your solo practise. Having experienced these mental qualities in push hands you need to, <u>**no you must**</u> transfer these qualities into your solo practise. How is it possible to transfer aspects from your push hands which requires a partner into your solo work which has no partner?

I've mentioned previously that what you train in the Opening and Closing Exercise, you carry into the Five Loosening Exercises from the Five Loosening Exercises into the Form and from the Form into Push Hands. This learning process can and does flow in the opposite direction, from Push Hands back to the Form, from the Form back to the Five Loosening Exercises and finally back to the genesis of Tai Chi, the Opening and Closing Exercise. These qualities discovered and trained in your push hands need to be applied to your solo work.

I remember being given this advice, when first starting push hands, "When practising the form imagine someone is in front of you, when practising push hands imagine there is no one in front of you". At first thought, you may think this advice is in reference to imagining an opponent in front of you when training the form. That you're fighting an imaginary opponent, dodging imaginary punches and kicks while simultaneously delivering your own counter punches and kicks to this invisible foe. I later realised the above advice is in reference to the fact that when training the form, you need to imagine that there is an energy/force constantly being applied to you. With the need for you to continuously feed this energy/force through your body by means of relaxation, led by your intent into your imaginary opponent's root. Though this process is purely imaginary, it still develops your Listening, Sticking, Following, Joining, Adhering and Leading. However, when it comes to push hands the opposite is true. There is a tendency in push hands to overly focus on your partner in front of you, rather than focusing your intent, behind and under your opponent. By focusing on your partner, there is a real tendency to push rather than close *(relax downward)* and pull behind your partner to sever their root. Basically, you've mistakenly placed your intent on your push hand partner rather than behind and under your partner, which requires intent. Some Tai Chi practitioners correctly say, never focus on your opponent's root. When you lead with your intent it's not for the purpose of finding your opponent's root, this would be considered a thought forcing a result. Leading with your intent creates the conditions for your opponent's root to be cut and controlled. There is a difference between these two actions.

Master Huang stressed that the form was extremely important to your Tai Chi development. It's easy to believe that he was only referring to the physical aspects such as technique, posture, alignment timing, continuity of movement, etc, etc which, in itself is extremely important in Tai Chi. However, I believe he was also referencing the training of non physical aspects such as your intent, only after establishing intent will you be able to train, Sticking, Listening, Following, Joining, Adhering and Leading. With correct training, your intent within your solo practise and push hands will result in the form and push hands merging and becoming literally indistinguishable. The form and push hands uses exactly the same internal and external process. The only physical difference between the form and push hands, is that push hands has a partner applying an external energy/force powered by their root to your body, and the form has only your own personal mass to move. By bringing the same mental qualities that are used in your push hands into your form, you will without question lift your push hands to such a high level. By applying the mental qualities to the form you'll be literally training your push hands at the same time. Whether you have a partner or not becomes irrelevant. Regardless if it's the form where there's no force on the body or in push hands where energy/force is placed on the body, the process is identical. Remember the difference between energy and force, energy only becomes a force if it encounters resistance. Three hundred kilos of force stays in a state of energy as long as it encounters no resistance and the same for one gram of force, neither are allowed to convert to a force and therefore both stay in a state of energy making the size of the energy/force irrelevant. Push Hands and the form respond in the same way to a real energy/force regardless of the size of the energy/force or if its an imaginary force. The primary purpose of push hands is learning how to lead energy/force from your opponent through your body and returning it to your opponent's root by means of Intent, Relaxation, Alignment and Di Xin Xi Yin Li. Optimally, over many years of correct training, the form and push hands, becomes indistinguishable, becoming one and the same.

Peng

I remember Patrick Kelly *(a senior Western student of Master Huang)* telling me decades ago, that on one of his visits to Master Ma Yeuh Liang, Master Ma had explained to him the qualities of peng *(pronounced pang)*. Master Ma stated most Tai Chi practitioners have misunderstood the meaning of peng. In Chinese, peng can mean two things. It can mean to carry something heavy, such as a heavy vase. A large number of Tai Chi practitioners have literally applied this definition of peng to their push hands. They hold their arm outwards, rounded and stiff, locking their arms as if they were holding something heavy in front of them. These practitioners have explained to me their rationale for holding their arms locked into this position. Their arms are similar to the front fence of your home. Behind the fence is your front yard, and you mustn't ever allow anyone to enter your front yard. The second and correct meaning of peng can also mean to take on the quality of water. Master Ma explained the nature of water possesses a number of qualities. One of these qualities is it will adapt and mould around whatever it comes into contact with. For example, if you place your hand into a bucket of water, the water will encompass the hand completely, making a perfect mould of your hand. Master Ma went on to say "Water will also float a leaf or a large ship". This reference, to the leaf and ship is the clue to the nature of peng. Placing your hand in the bucket of water will cause two thing to occur. The first, being the water will totally encompass the hand and secondly and more importantly the water level in the bucket will rise, caused by my hand displacing the water in the bucket. It is this displacement effect that I believe Master Ma was hinting at when he used the analogy of the leaf and ship. The leaf displaces maybe less than a gram of water, where a ship will displace hundreds of tonnes of water. The water displacement of the leaf is in perfect harmony for what the leaf requires and the same goes for the ship. The displacement of water is always in exact proportion to the size of the object it comes into contact with and encompasses, never more, never less. Peng is adaptive. Peng is neither soft nor hard, always in perfect balance with what it encounters. This can be related back to Tai Chi, specifically push hands. There is an old Tai Chi proverb which I never really liked and on the surface seems to contradict Tai Chi principles. The proverb states; 彼有力，我亦有力；彼無力，我亦無力。 "When your opponent becomes soft you become softer, if the opponent becomes hard, you become harder". I now realise, it was badly translated and relates to peng. What I believe it was meant to convey is when your opponent, becomes softer you also have to change and become softer to match your opponent, to maintain peng, not softer than your opponent, just enough to match them. If your opponent becomes harder, your structure also needs to become harder, more structured to match your opponent to maintain peng. Peng is always in relation to the structure of your body when in contact with your opponent, always changing like water, depending on the force that you encounter. As a side note, when you open *(relax upwards)* in push hands to draw your partner out, it is often expressed in Tai Chi that you've floated your opponent off their root. Very much like when a ship or a leaf is floating.

Students love to say Tai Chi flows like water, in reality water doesn't flow or move, unless there's an external forces acting on it, such as gravity or wind. However, it does conform to the shape of the object it comes in contact with, but doesn't move it. Peng, like water, will first mould itself around an object, Peng adapts to what it comes into contact with regardless if the energy/force is soft or hard, large or small, it will conform and accommodate. Water adjusts and is dispersed in relation to the size and shape of the ship's hull it supports. If the ship is less dense than the water, it floats causing the water to be displaced resulting in the ship becoming buoyant. The water isn't so soft *(collapsing)* as to have no substance *(peng)*, causing the ship to fully pass through the water and sink to the river bed. Peng is an aspect of relaxation that behaves in the same way as water, supporting, blending and matching with whatever it comes into contact with. Another quality relaxation possesses like water, is it not only supports a leaf or ship, it will also move a leaf or ship by means of the river's current *(intent)* which pulls the river, along with anything on or in the river, with the river banks acting as alignments containing the river's energy. In push hands relaxation and intent has the ability to lead energy/force produced from your partner in push hands, without the need for muscle. These Taoist principles will work, provided you train your intent in conjunction with opening and closing and alignment correctly.

Patrick Kelly told me, an amusing anecdote, that he once showed Master Ma a video of Master Huang doing push hands. Master Ma was very complimentary and commented that Master Huang was of a very high standard, the only fault he could see was Master Huang kept his hands too close to his body. Patrick then showed Master Huang a video of Master Ma doing push hands. Master Huang was also complimentary and said Master Ma was of a very good standard, the only fault he could find was Master Ma kept his hands too far away from his body *(everyone has their own personal preferences)*.

Is it Possible to be too Soft in Push Hands?
Yes you can. Relating an encounter I had with a USA Push Hand champion. This particular Tai Chi instructor was invited to Australia to run workshops by one of the largest Tai Chi Schools in Australia. He was given my name by Lenzie Williams who I met a few years earlier. Lenzie being a senior student of the late Ben Lo. Ben Lo was a senior student of Cheng Man-Ching. When Lenzie discovered this Tai Chi teacher would be in Brisbane, he recommended, that he contact me, which he did. We organised to meet at one of his workshops, and do some free push hands during the lunch break. I found him incredibly soft, and physically flexible in fact he was easily the softest push hand partner I had ever touched hands with. At the slightest pressure he would yield, bend and twist his body. However, when I placed my intent and root under and behind him, he lost the ability to bring his softness and flexibility into play, resulting in him gently collapsing on to the ground when trying to yield. Not having access to his own root resulted in him losing the ability to yield and he became stiff and rigid causing him to collapse to the ground repeatedly. We chatted afterwards and he asked me, if I had any tips for him. I suggested that he was too resistant to my touch and he needed to soften. I still remember the look on his face. It was the look of utter disbelief. He told me that he was renowned for his softness and his yielding ability.

He misunderstood me when I said he was resistant to my push. The misunderstanding stemmed from his assumption that resistance, in the context of Tai Chi, pertained solely to a yang quality, holding one's ground, using muscular strength to resist any incoming energy/force. This is the most common form of resistance you tend to see in Tai Chi push hands these days. The Cambridge Dictionary states; "Resistant is the **refusal to accept** or be changed by something". The Collins Dictionary defines resistant as; "Someone who is resistant to something, is opposed to it and wants to prevent it". Both dictionary definitions are accurate, the key words and phrases are, "opposed, prevent, someone who refuses to accept". The fundamental and core principle of Tai Chi is accepting your opponent's energy/force, then returning this energy/force back to them *(specifically their root)*. If you only yield by being extremely physically soft all you've managed to do, at best, is slip your opponent's energy/force off your body. You have to ask yourself, how much of that energy/force did you accept and return to your opponent's root? **Zero**. You can't return any meaningful energy/force if you're not willing to accept it. You can't give what you don't have. In Tai Chi there is constant reference to the need of being soft, which is entirely correct. However, the softness they're referring to is internal softness, softness *(peng)* needs to be relative. There is physical softness which allows joints to adjust in relation to each other, energy/force and gravity. Then there is the internal softness that allows and encourages energy/force to pass through your body. If energy/force doesn't have the ability to pass through your body, then you have nothing for the intent to lead. This teacher was honestly trying to apply the principles of Tai Chi to the best of his ability, which he is to be commended for *(a quality that is sadly lacking in modern push hands these days)*. He had just taken the concept of softness too far, resulting in his becoming resistant *(extreme yin, leads to yang)*. Essentially, he had lost his peng, *(his structure)*, alternatively, too much peng *(to hard)*, you'll create a protrusion and become resistant, putting you out of relation with the energy/force that is in contact with you. Too little peng *(too soft)* will create a hollow. This will also put you out of relation with the energy/force that you're in contact with, negatively impacting your ability to transfer energy/force through your body to your opponent's root.

Three Levels of Push Hand
1. The third most difficult objective in partner work is the capturing and controlling of your opponent's root.

2. The second most difficult objective in partner work, is maintaining control over your opponent's root while shifting from one leg to the other, whether it's forward, back, left or right, while simultaneously swapping the controlling hand or hands.

3. Easily the hardest and most difficult objective in partner work, is maintaining control over your opponent's root while both parties are in motion, stepping and moving, like in Dao Lu and San Shou *(at this level your are as close as you can get to actual fighting)*.

Reaching the last level of control over your opponent's root is considered an extremely high level of skill. Hence the purpose for learning Dao Lu and San Shou last in partner work. If you haven't achieved the previous two levels of root control, there is no point in learning Dao Lu and San Shou. Training push hands does not improve your standard or training an advanced form of push hands such as Dao Lu or San Shou will not improve your skill level. What will raise your skill level is how you train your push hands. An old saying comes to mind; **"Don't train hard, train wise. Once you train wise, then train hard"**.

No matter how good a martial art is, no martial art can possibly cover every angle of a punch, blow or kick that's going to come their way. Controlling your opponent's root takes away the need to even try to cover every possible blow scenario. Controlling your opponent's root limits their ability to move independently which dramatically limits their capacity to deliver blows or kicks. Controlling your opponent's root, contains and limits your opponent's options and their ability to move, including their ability to deliver blows.

Most Tai Chi practitioners during push hands tend to push in the hope of finding their opponent's centre of gravity. This is a dangerous method of finding your opponent's root. To quote The Art Of War that was written over 2,000 years ago. It is one of my favourite books, I have been constantly reading it for the last 40 odd years. Specifically, The Art Of War edited, translated and foreword by James Clavell. Another book on the Art of War I have been reading recently which is just as good as James Clavell version, is The Art of War translated by Thomas Cleary. Other versions of the Art of War, I've found can be very dry and overly militarily focused. Sun Tzu stated; "The general who enters battle and then looks for victory, for every victory he achieves he will have a loss. Thus it is that in war the victorious general only seeks battle after the victory has been won, whereas he who is destined to defeat first fights and then looks for victory". Tai Chi has borrowed so much from Sun Tzu's, Art Of War. I have learnt as much from reading the Art Of War, as I have from the Tai Chi Classics. When a Tai Chi practitioner pushes before their opponent's root is cut, only gives their position and intentions away, making their position extremely tenuous. Pushing to find your opponent's root will end with the same result, that Sun Tzu foretold over 2,000 years ago. For every push that's successful, there will be one that isn't.

Yi Chi Li, the Bedrock of Tai Chi

The Yi *(intent)* leads the Chi *(relaxations facilitates the movement of chi)* and the Chi leads the Li *(strength)*. I observed over 20 years ago and I include myself in this observation, how push hands was being conducted. When starting push hands both parties physically move into their respected position. They then proceed to lift their hands and place them on their partner and start pushing with no or very little preparation of relaxation or intent being applied. The above process is literally the exact opposite to the concept of Yi Chi Li. We've used muscular strength to lift our hand into position, place it on to our partner, then proceeded to relax *(most students just tend to just press their foot against the ground)* to move the chi that moves the physical with no intent being used during the whole process. They have effectively moved the Li first, the Chi second and lastly, if at all, Yi. Effectively we have started push hands in the wrong order, Li Chi Yi instead of Yi Chi Li.

The correct process when training a stationary push hand set is, first move your body into position of the push hand set. Then project your intent *(Yi)* under and behind your opponent, once your intent has been established you then need to relax, specifically, closing *(relaxing downward)* from your intent to raise your hand or hands. This relaxation originates from your intent which moves various forms of chi through your body. Provided intent has been established first, before the relaxation process begins from your intent, it will instantly lead or pull the chi *(energy/force)* to where the intent is. The closing process which starts from your intent *(Yi)*, will cause relaxation to move the *(Chi)*, which will cause your arm or arms to be physically *(Li)* pulled, into position, touching your opponent lightly *(be careful not to lower your hands from above onto your opponent, this will ever so slightly ground your opponent at the critical moment of cutting their root)*.

Establishing intent first, initiates a point for *(adhere)* **the chi** *(Chi of the Earth)* **to gather. This is followed by relaxation which establishes an energetic connection** *(joining)* **to your intent, behind and under your opponent's root. Lastly touching your opponent** *(sticking)* **results in you completing the physical connection** *(circuitry)* **which connects intent and relaxation to your opponent giving you the ability to neutralise and control your opponent's root.**

There are Two Methods of Returning your Opponent's Force Back to Them

Virtually every serious student of Tai Chi acknowledges one of the main purposes of Push Hands is to redirect or return energy/force back to your opponent. There are two methods with which to achieve this result. The first and most common method is based on absorbing your opponent's energy/force through your body, re-directing it into the ground, under the bubbling well of your substantial leg and then releasing, returning *(rebounding)* this energy/force back up through the substantial leg through your body and back to your opponent. There are a few problems with this method. It is slow, cumbersome and exhibits no root control over your opponent during this process and rarely works under real conditions. As you can tell, I'm not a big fan on this theory of absorbing your opponent's force and then returning it back to the same point where their energy/force first entered your body. It sounds good in theory, but very difficult to carry out in practise, even under controlled conditions. This concept of absorbing energy before returning it, is derived from the misconceived assumption from our past biased belief that we are the sole repository of power regardless from where it originates. Therefore we wrongly conclude all energy emanates from us which fits neatly into our pre-established beliefs on how power and energy is created and discharged. Regardless whether this energy/force is first generated, by you or your opponent, it still places you at the centre and source of all power. This flies in the face of fundamental Taoist principles and concepts of building and hoarding power and strength. This misconception of building or absorbing strength and power in oneself whether it's in the root, spine, dan tien or legs before releasing, has been covered in previous Chapters.

Absorbing and Redirecting The Energy/Force Back to your Opponent Method

This first method of absorbing force from your opponent often starts with rocking backwards *(retreating)* and yielding which I am in favour of, if you are not in control of your opponent's root. However, you only physically yield for two reasons, the first to move out of the way of your opponent's force such as a blow or kick. The second reason is to draw your opponent off their bubbling well so you can weaken their structure and take control of their root. All yielding needs to be generated by relaxing upwards *(opening)* rather than relaxing downwards *(closing)*.

The Song of the 13 Postures confirms this; 仔細留心向推求。屈伸開合聽自由 "Pay close attention and pursue deeper meaning. Let the movement of expanding and contracting, opening and closing flow with freedom". Most practitioners start the first method of absorbing their opponent's energy/force by yielding from the areas where they first feel the energy/force or pressure on their body. The problem with this, when relaxing downward *(closing)* into your root, your are only **yielding from the entry point, the contact point is not where the energy/force is being generated** *(yielding from the contact point, is like trying to extinguish a fire by hosing the tip of the flames rather than the base of the flames)*. Yielding from the entry point, results in your running away from your opponent's energy/force. The most you can hope for by using this process of yielding, is that you may have weakened your opponent structure slightly by having them overextend themselves. You can physically yield as much as you like, you still haven't dealt with the source of the problem. Until you neutralise the source of the push, you'll always be yielding in the hope your opponent slips up, so you can then make your counter move.

Yielding from the contact point, result in you quickly running out of internal and physical space in a very short time period, *(possibly a second, maybe two seconds at best)* **(Figure 33)**. When this inevitably happens and you've run out of physical and internal space to yield, you'll become jammed *(double weighted)* in your own root. Leaving you with no alternative, other than to try and re-direct the energy/force back up the rear leg, *(usually achieved by pressing the back foot against the ground)* back to your opponent. **(Figure 34)** The main problem with this concept of absorbing energy/force first, is you

Relaxing downward (closing) and yielding from the point where you feel the force. Will leave you becoming trapped within your own root resulting in you becoming double weighted.

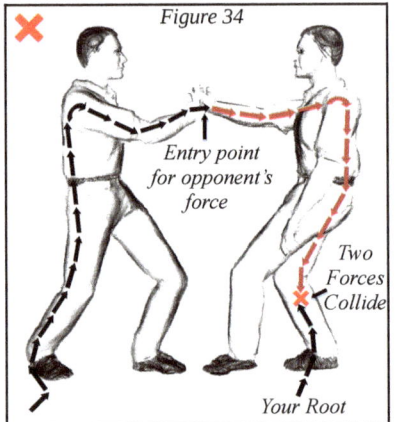

Absorbing force into your root from your opponent and then releasing it back up your leg will result in the returning force colliding with the incoming force of your opponent, causing double weightedness.

still have an incoming force from your opponent being led from above, *(which most practitioners tend do when relaxing)* through your body. This downward force will inevitably collide with the absorbed energy/force returning back up from your root, resulting in you becoming double weighted *(double heaviness)*. It's very hard to make this process work because of so many variables at work such as pushing against gravity *(Chi of the Earth)* timing, direction of force and changing alignments. Due to the very nature of absorbing energy/force into the root or any other part of the body will often lead to a build up of energy/forces within you, where it inevitably becomes trapped and used against you.

Leading your Opponent's Energy/Force Back to their Root

I am a very big fan of returning your opponent's energy/force straight back to your opponent's root without the need of first storing the force in your body or root. You may think the first method of absorbing and returning energy/force back to your opponent and leading energy/force to your opponent's root as the same, they're not. The method of first absorbing an energy/force, and returning it back to your opponent may sound like it's in accordance with Tai Chi principles, I don't believe it is. Where does it say in the Classics, you must first absorb your opponent's force before returning it to your opponent. It's referenced in the Classics frequently about the need to store, direct and gather the Jin or energy before releasing it, we however, automatically assume this energy or Jin is stored in oneself or in our root. This energy or Jin is definitely stored and gathered but, not in you or your root, **but in your opponent's root.** I am convinced of this, and results confirm it, you are in fact gathering the energy, force, jin and chi, whatever you want to call it, in your opponent's root. The only downside of using this method, it only works, when you have intent, that you can project. **Otherwise, it's not possible to lead your opponent's energy/force back to their root,**

Even when students incorrectly use muscle to push, they still require a connection to gravity. Break that connection, and the force you feel on your body instantly disappears. Why? Because the force on your body returns to a state of energy which is led by your intent back to your opponent's root where it converts to a force. Leading your opponent's energy/force back into their root does have its advantages over first storing or absorbing energy.

The first advantage, taking control of your opponent's root is so much quicker than absorbing a force before you can use it. The moment the opponent touches you, their root is compromised, providing your intent and relaxation had been established well before physical contact has been made with your opponent. Intent moves as quick as the mind, relaxation moves as fast as awareness. It's imperative to take control of your opponent's root as quickly as possible *(the longer this takes in a physical conflict, the greater the chance you are going to get hit)*.

Master Huang once gave the following advice; "When engaging in free push hands with someone, if they want to play, then you play. If they just want to push you, just cut their root straight away and issue" *(cutting your opponent's root straight away, doesn't mean pushing first)*. This same rule is applicable in a physical conflict, you don't have the luxury of time, trying to absorb first, before issuing. The second advantage of leading *(deflecting)* force straight into your opponent's root, is the control it gives you over your partner during push hands when yielding. Over the last couple of decades I have sadly noticed the emphasis on winning in push hands, no matter the cost to the principles of Tai Chi and Taoism itself. Some push hand partners will continue pushing regardless, if they're leaning in at a 45 degree angle, they have clearly over extended themselves and are using brute force to continue their push. You on the other hand, have tried to genuinely follow the principles of yielding to an energy/force on your body, only to have yourself become jammed in the back leg with no real alternative other than to eventually push back.

Taking control of your partner's root from the start is like taking out insurance, *(you may not use it, but it's nice to have, just in case)* should your partner decide to throw principles out the window and push forward, regardless. If your root is under and behind your opponent you still have a physical and energetic *(opening and closing)* connection to their root. If you close with your intent you'll shut your partner down instantly. Establishing intent followed by closing from the root, moves the relaxation to a future contact point. When your partner touches you, this completes the circuit, returning their energy/force instantly back to where it originated.

It's for this reason why you need to train intent, so that sticking, leading, joining, adhering, following and relaxation in push hands becomes possible. Establishing control over your partner's root should the need arise; you can shut *(neutralise)* your opponent down instantly. Extremely important to remember in push hands, is that you have an entry point or multiple entry points of energy/force from your partner's push, but only one exit point, *(your partner's root)* for this energy/force to go.

Even before the first gram of force is placed on your body your intent **needs to be** already under and behind your opponent's root and your opening and closing moving. The second intent has been established, start the downward relaxation *(closing)* process from where your intent is. So that when your opponent's hand touches your body, even before they start pushing, their energy/force is instantly led/pulled straight back to their own root, resulting in their root *(strength)* being cut and neutralised. *(Figure 35)* An analogy I like to use when teaching this principle is your opponent steps onto a moving treadmill. We've all seen on YouTube where some poor unsuspecting person steps on a fast moving tread mill. The second they step on the moving tread mill they instantly face plant and shoot into a wall. Closing *(relaxing downward)* from your intent, is similair to the tread mill, the process starts moving before your opponent touches you. There is an old saying in Tai Chi; "The softest person wins" This doesn't mean the person who is physically the softest wins. What is meant by this statement is that if your opponent has just touched you and hasn't started pushing yet, however, you've been closing from your intent before any physical contact is made. You've created an internal downward movement, almost like a vacuum, even though your opponent hasn't pushed it won't matter, you've become more Yin than your opponent, this makes your opponent, Yang by default. You are literally pulling *(creating)* the push from your opponent by being softer. Effectively you've created the push in your opponent by being more Yin *(softer)* which means you've taken control of their energy/force. This means they'll be pulled into their own root, where your intent is located. If you were in free push hands you wouldn't even need to physically yield as you would already have their root, just open *(relax upward)* and issue. *(page 48, Figure 13)* Remember the quote from the little orange book, Tai Chi Chuan Ta Wen, Questions and Answers on T'ai Chi Chuan by Chen Wei Ming; "Sometimes I can adhere to an opponent and he can't release his force. **At this level I do not need to follow my opponent and I can make my own decisions**".

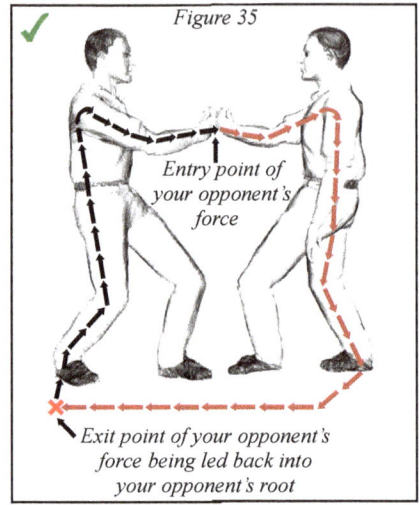

Establishing intent first, followed by closing from the root, to the exit point. When your partner touches you, this completes the circuit, returning their energy/force instantly back to where it started (you have circulated the chi by means of relaxation).

When cutting your opponent's root *(and I can't stress this enough)* the need to be surreptitious when doing so. Your opponent or partner must never feel their root being compromised. Most Tai Chi practitioners tend to rock forward and then push at the end of their rocking forward and in that push, there is their hope, that they may catch their partner off balance or out of position. This is a very hit and miss affair, as stated earlier in this Chapter, quoting from the Art Of War; "Thus it is that in war the victorious general only seeks battle after the victory has been won, whereas he who is destined to defeat first fights and then looks for victory". Most students of Tai Chi, tend to rock forward and start pushing in the hope of locating their opponent's centre. This usually results only in exposing their own position and vulnerabilities in the process.

Master Huang; "In Push Hands You Need To Be Like A Burglar"
My teacher Wee Kee Jin told me that Master Huang often emphasised the need to be like a burglar during push hands. Master Huang explained the burglar analogy in the following; "Does a burglar ring you up at work and tell you that he'll be coming around to your home tonight around 2:30am to rob you? Of course he doesn't. You realise you've been burgled when walking down the stairs in the morning to discover all your valuables missing. You weren't even aware you were being cleaned out". Relating this back to push hands. As a push hand partner, what do you think you're trying to steal from your training partner without their knowledge? Their root of course. Master Huang continues with the burglar analogy: "If the owner of the house hears you trying to break in, they will quickly close the windows and doors and lock them. They may even lean against the door, ensuring, you can't gain entry". What Master Huang is alluding to, if during push hands, your partner becomes aware that you're trying to steal their root, they will tend to dig in and hunker down. As Master Huang said, "once the homeowner discovers he is about to be burgled, he will lock everything down. Master Huang continues with the burglar analogy; "Once the home owner has become aware of your burglary attempt, and

having locked everything down and having locked you out, you've lost the element of surprise. You need to have a change of plans. What you then do is hide behind a bush and yell **FIRE!!**. The home owner runs out of the house, *(I didn't say the home owner was smart)* allowing you to sneak into the house through the open door and start to burgle". So what was the purpose of yelling fire? Master Huang is implying that when your partner has become aware you're trying to cut their root and they have grounded themselves, you need to stop trying to cut their root and start yielding to draw them off their root. Only when your partner has been led or drawn out from their root *(which means they have moved slightly forward and off their bubbling well)*, do you then go back to stealing *(cutting)* their root. I personally feel the burglar analogy is a brilliant way of explaining the process and purpose of cutting and yielding in push hands. It belongs in the Classics.

Continuing with the burglary theme, most push hand competitions these days tend to look more like a home invasion, rather than a burglary. Trying to push through the front door to steal your root, which generally ends in a wrestling match. Speaking from personal experience, the only way you can effectively cut your partner's root is by applying intent and closing *(relaxation downward)*. I've learnt over the years, you can't consistently push an opponent off their root, but you can lead them off their root by using intent. If you push from the back leg, they will feel you coming, if you relax from above, they will feel you coming, if you relax from the back leg *(substantial leg)* straight into the front leg, they will feel you coming. The only way to burgle your partner's root, is by sending your intent under and behind your opponent. Start the closing *(relaxing downward)* process from where your intent *(root)* is, pulling the relaxation through your body from where your intent is. Extremely important: **Don't relax towards your intent but relax from your intent.** This results in the relaxation being pulled by the chi of the earth (*Di Xin Xi Yin Li*) *(gravity)* to your intent.

If you were training a set push hands that required you to yield and rock backwards, you would need to open *(relax upwards)* from where your intent is to where your partner is touching you *(entry point)*. Resulting in your yielding upwards from your root towards your partner's hand, *(entry point)* because you've remained physically and energetically *(relaxation)* connected to your opponent. This allows you to stay in control of your partner's root while yielding, so that at any point through the yielding process, you can internally and therefore physically shut your partner down by closing *(relaxing downward)* from your intent. Achieving this skill in your push hands does take a lot of training, physically, energetically and mentally. Every Tai Chi School regardless of style, has their own particular and unique push hands set. They vary. Some are better than others *(I personally think the Wu style has better push hand sets than Yang style)*. They all share one common aim, taking control of their opponent's root as quickly and as fast as possible. At what stage in your training should you start push hands?

If it's not possible for you to rock forward, backward, turn left or right without using muscle then there is no point in learning push hands, go back to the form. If you can't train the form without using next to no muscle, then maybe you need to go back to the Five Loosening Exercises. If you still can't generate movement without using muscle while training the Five Loosening Exercises, then you may need to return to the Opening and Closing Exercise. Don't make the common mistake of accumulating forms and push hand sets, with acquiring skill *(knowledge, is not necessarily skill)*. Over my time in Tai Chi I have met people who know three to four different styles of Tai Chi. They know so many forms including weapons and endless push hand sets. They have theories upon theories, and yet they still can't rock backwards in a straight line without falling over and they still can't turn left and right without using muscle. My advice is to first become proficient in the fundamentals. This takes time, effort and self-analysis. If you can't apply opening and closing to rocking forward and backward correctly in the form, do you really think you'll be able to do it correctly during push hands with someone hanging off you? When training a push hand set, analyse the set, break it down to its finest detail. Look for the moments when your opponent or yourself are most vulnerable, why are you vulnerable, what causes this vulnerability? What is it that I'm not applying from the form to the push hands? Has my intent broken, has opening and closing stopped, maybe it's my alignments that are causing the problem. The check list is almost inexhaustible.

Choosing Your Partner

Your push hand partner is key to your future advancement in Tai Chi. Choose your push hand partner well. Do they possess the right temperament, are they analytical, methodical, persistent, patient. Can they take and give criticism. This person in front of you will have as much effect on your Tai Chi as your teacher. They can lift your standard up or drag it down. Ego has no place in push hands. You need to be ruthlessly honest with your criticism of yourself and your partner. Push Hands training is far too important for you to just go through the motions without a critical and analytical mind. With the right partner, the load is shared and your chance of finding the errors and mistakes for both of you is doubled.

When things don't work in push hands, it can be incredibly frustrating. The harder you try, the worse it gets. Frustration can lead to anger and bad decisions, such as doubling down on an incorrect method such as pushing. The ancient Greeks came to the conclusion two thousand years ago that anger is caused by disappointment. Disappointment with yourself, your partner, or the outcome of your push hands session. Anger is energy. If correctly channelled, anger can turn into determination. Determination can be used to find the source of the fault *(something I realised from training push hands and it applies to life in general. When nothing seems to work, you haven't failed, you just haven't succeed yet, you've only failed, when you give up)*. In one push hand session, everything works perfectly, the next session it's the exact opposite, nothing you do seems to work. You have such success with one partner and the next partner it all goes pear shaped. Tomorrow is another day. Accept that you are having a bad day and leave it there. As stated earlier anger is caused by disappointment with yourself. The question you have to ask yourself: Is the source of disappointment from the outcome, or something more sinister, such as your ego telling you that you deserve a better outcome. Is your ego writing cheques your ability can't cash? Learn to be gentle with yourself. You are going to have good and not so good days. Try not to take it personally, otherwise you won't last the distance. Training push hands you'll experience incredible highs and unbelievable lows, never a dull moment. If you're finding push hands dull, then you've stopped looking and now you are just going through the motions.

We have clarified and defined Tai Chi as the physical manifestation of Taoist principles in action, having qualified the chi that powers all movement in Tai Chi, that being Di Xin Xi Yin Li (gravity). We can now access this power source by applying the Taoist principle of Wu Wei, Non-action to create action. By re-directing your opponent's energy/force (chi) through relaxation back into their own root causing them to become isolated and weak, giving the false appearance of you becoming stronger. Relaxation is the means with which we move the many forms of chi/force around and through the body. Dividing relaxation into two categories, closing (Yin) and opening (Yang), both opening and closing emanates from intent, when opening and closing connects to your intent, root is generated. Having established that opening possesses two different qualities, opening for yielding and opening for issuing what changes these two qualities, is the direction opening moves in. Having learnt one of the many byproducts of opening and closing is the ability to generate speed without the need for muscle. The connection between opening and closing and substantial and insubstantial are inseparable and co-dependent. Opening and closing are connected to your intent through the substantial leg, allowing intent to lead relaxation resulting in relaxation leading the many forms of chi. One form of chi is (gravity) (Di Xin Xi Yin Li) causing substantial and insubstantial to interact with each other, which in turn moves the body. Push Hands is the means with which to expand the principles of Tai Chi/Tao beyond oneself. So what part does the form play and its function in Tai Chi?

The Form: What's its function? Just a place to keep your Techniques and Postures

12. Form

Young man, "Everything, is in the form". This is what Master Huang, said to my teacher every time he saw him. Wee Kee Jin often attended class a few hours earlier to practise. Master Huang, saw this young man, constantly showing up early for class. Realising this junior student was keen, he would walk over to him and offer this one piece of advice; "Young man, everything is in the form". Not once, but every time he saw him, he would repeat this advice. Now when a Tai Chi practitioner of Master Huang's standing repeatedly offers you this advice, it not only deserves to be acted on, but requires closer examination of the deeper meaning. We will come back to this later and break the phrase down.

The Physical Form

Before discussing the form and its various functions we need to break down the physical attributes of the Tai Chi form to its most basic components. Starting with alignments *(joints)* of the body, bringing a compilation of alignments together we create a posture. These various postures made up of alignments are then brought together to create a singular form. The form performs numerous functions, like the more external martial arts. The Tai Chi form can be used in the delivery of techniques that are of a martial nature. Both external and internal martial arts still require physical contact with their opponents. The primary difference between the two arts is that the external martial art uses its external structure, such as muscle to create speed and power to deliver its force. With the internal martial arts, they use the internal process of chi *(gravity)*, relaxation, alignment and intent to generate their speed, movement and power *(if you can categorise Tai Chi power as power)*. One of the main internal processes of the internal arts would be relaxation, which moves energy/force from your opponent through your body, redirecting it by means of intent, back to your opponent's root, which has the effect of neutralising your opponent's ability to create strength, movement and speed. To use the following analogy, external martial art is the equivalent of whipping your opponent with an electrical lead. With internal martial arts such as Tai Chi you use the same electrical lead however, instead of whipping your opponent with the lead, you plug one end of the lead into a power point, then press the exposed wires of the other end, to your opponent. External martial arts tend to hit you with their physical structure, internal arts use what's inside their structure. Alignments are extremely important, whether they're linear or collective, they are the infrastructure that gives you the means to move energy/force/chi from one point to another.

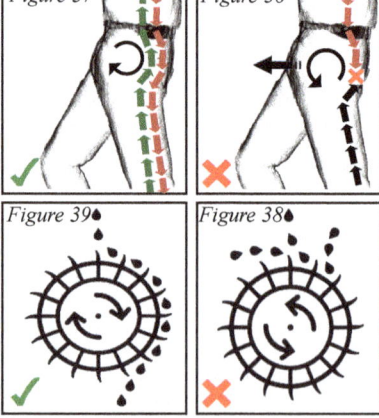

Water wheel turning clockwise accepts and encourages water movement.

Water wheel turning anticlockwise causes water and wheel to collide.

Alignments, linear and collective *(these alignments will be covered in Chapter 13 and 14)* is what makes up the form. If the alignments are defective so will the form be and with it, its ability to move internally and physically. For example, by pressing your rear leg against the ground, or dropping the rear knee into the foot, the hips will forward rotate. This results in the energy/force you are trying to draw downward into your opponent's root, to collide with the force that's being pushed up from the rear leg. *(Figure 36)* The mechanics of the forward rotating hips just won't allow you to return and re-direct energy/force into your opponent's root no matter how much you relax. However, if you open and relax upward, the buttocks will droop, causing the hips to sit and reverse rotate, allowing the two energy/forces to pass each other. *(Figure 37)* It's similar to a water wheel that is powered by an outside force, forward rotating *(anti clockwise)* *(Figure 38)* while water is pouring on the right side of the wheel. This water will work against the direction of the wheel, resulting in water and wheel colliding, causing water to be dispersed and splash everywhere. If the water wheel turns clockwise and the water hits the wheel at the same spot *(Figure 39)* the water is pulled through by the clockwise rotation of the water wheel. This principle is applicable to both ball and socket joints of the hip and shoulder.

You can tell a lot about the standard of a Tai Chi practitioner by how they move in the form. The outside movement of the form needs to accurately reflect the internal movement. The physical mechanics of the form needs be conducive and conform to the internal movement of relaxation and energy/force. Occasionally students join my school from other schools. For me to have an idea of their standard, I ask them to play their form for me. I don't care what style it is, whether it's the short form, long form, fast or slow, large frame or small frame the sequence of the postures or even who they learnt from. All I am interested in is how well they apply the principles of Tai Chi to their form. Usually, I only need to watch up to Ward Off, by the way they move in the form I have a pretty good idea of their standard. After the third or fourth posture I politely ask them to stop. Often they remark, they've only done a few moves. In truth, I only need to see the first four postures, in fact by the time they've finished the Preparation, you have a clear idea of their level *(the more they move their axis to the weighted leg, tells me how much they can empty from their centre)*. How they perform the first movement, will be exactly the same as their last movement. Also how they apply the principles to their form will give you a fair idea how their push hands will be *(if you see them doing their form in a low stance, you just know, they are going to push with their legs when it comes to push hands)*. You see the first movement, you've seen all of them.

Often when speaking with Tai Chi people who come from other schools. I often mention Master Huang's statement, "everything is in the form". Sometimes they tell me in a frustrated tone that they have heard the same advice from their previous teacher, of the importance of the form. They sometimes say that they have been practising the form for over twenty years, and their push hand has not really improved. It almost seems the more they practise their form, the more their level stagnates, especially in relation to their push hands. This could be the reason why so many students drift from school to school, changing styles and wander from teacher to teacher. They are looking for the perfect form. This perfect form will give them all the answers to their lack of progress in their Tai Chi *(The perfect form does not exist; every form has its strength and weaknesses)*. Having established how important the form and alignments are; only when alignments are working collectively and linearly with each other, can the internals and externals have any chance of working harmoniously. What physically moves the form is the internals. The form *(alignments)* channels the internals to move in a certain dirrection, so the body can move.

Back to Master Huang's earlier statement; **"Young man, everything is in the form"**. We need to break this statement down. He didn't say; "Young man, you need to practise the form or "Young man, the form is very important". His exact words, "Everything is **in** the form" the emphasis being **"in"**. Following this statement to its logical conclusion, Master Huang was telling Wee Kee Jin if he wants to advance in his Tai Chi, he needed to develop and train what's inside the form. Master Huang was obviously referring to the internal workings of the form and not just the form itself. The form is the container, which holds the contents and internals *(relaxation, chi energy/force)* processes together. The form is the vehicle which physically expresses the internal working of Tai Chi, it is what's inside the form, that moves the form. A form that doesn't move from the inside is a form that has no substance, it's hollow, a shell and has become an external art. This is a common problem with students of Tai Chi today, students will often train the form, thinking this is all that's required, and their standard will automatically improve. It won't *(this is the case again of one year, the same year, 20 times over)*. The only way to improve your Tai Chi, and this includes push hands, is to train what's inside the form and not just the form. Granted, the form is very important and should occupy at least the first few years of your training, making sure the container you are developing, is fit for purpose. The main purpose of the form, is to facilitate movement of the internal process which generates physical movement, making it the perfect conduit for the movement of energy/chi.

Applications of the Form and Postures as a Martial Art

The most common demonstration of Tai Chi postures in a martial art application usually involves speeding up the postures, then creating a scenario where it can be applied as a strike, be it a palm, punch or kick. This is a perfectly legitimate way of demonstrating the application of the various postures. In reality, the chances of applying these postures in a random situation, on someone who is non compliant is extremely low. It all goes swimmingly, when you are demonstrating on a compliant aggressor. A different experience is had when the interaction is spontaneous and you don't know what's coming your way. Personally, I have never really found Tai Chi postures all that practical, some postures are more practical than others in application, but in general, not all that practical. Maybe a few hundred years ago fighting was done differently, where everyone delivered these very long outstretched punches. In today times with so many different fighting styles, Tai Chi postures don't seem all that practical and can appear quite dated. As previously stated in Chapter 11, the physical martial application of Tai Chi is the form. Push Hands specifically trains the taking control of your opponent's root by means of intent, awareness, relaxation, sticking, joining and adhering. By using the various Tai Chi postures as a means to physically connect *(stick)* to your opponent so the internals can do their job, followed by the postures being used to deliver the blows. Once you have compromised your opponent's root, then different qualities of the postures *(techniques)* can then be applied.

Tai Chi postures may be divided into two categories, entry and execution. Some Tai Chi postures and aspects of postures are used to enter your opponent's space, used to close the physical distance between you and your opponent. Usually, but not always, the first half of a posture is for entry with the second half of the posture for delivering the blow *(executing)*. Such as the second half of the posture Push. The hands or hand extends outward making contact with an incoming punch from your opponent, moving your body towards your hand that's stayed connected *(sticking)* to your opponent's hand, allows you to close the distance. Not just by rocking forward, you may need to step in, to close this distance quickly. This is unlike most external martial arts that tend to bring the hand or fist back to the body to reload for the next punch. In Tai Chi the body tends to move forward to where the hand is, allowing you to achieve three objectives. The first, to reload the punch or palm, the second to close the distance between you and your opponent and thirdly, taking and keeping control of your opponent's root by means of following and adhering to their root. Having entered into your opponent's space, controlling and compressing their root, your posture function changes from entry to execution of a blow. Having moved closer to your hand and your opponent, while maintaining your physical connection to your opponent's arm which also has a connection to your opponent's root, you can now either extend outward as a punch or palm strike, which is usually delivered at the end of a posture *(the difference between a push and a palm strike, is speed, if it's done slowly it's a push, done fast, it's a palm strike)*. Or alternatively you can maintain the physical and internal connection to your opponent's root, delivering the blow with the opposite hand *(cross alignment)*. The choice is yours.

When using Tai Chi as a martial art, it's very rare, nearly unheard of to apply a whole posture exactly as you learnt it, when used in a conflict. For example the posture deflect downward, parry and punch. The chances of using the whole parry and punch in a fight are virtually zero. However, if your arms are slightly outstretched in front of you, you keep the fighting area away from your body until you're ready to close the distance. Making contact with your opponent's arm, your right wrist which stays in contact with your opponent's arm while you step in with your left leg, the left palm takes over from the right fist in controlling your opponent's arm and root. This frees up the right hand to execute a punch. Postures *(form)* will always need to be modified to fit the conditions of the situation.

Fighting is similair to Real Estate it's all about Location, Location, Location

Fighting is similar to real estate. It's all about Location, Location, Location. In my younger days when training Chow Ga Tong Long, sparring was heavily emphasised within the school. I still remember the definition of free sparring; "fighting for one's life with no restrictions of any kind". You train all these elaborate fancy techniques that look really cool, filling you with all this confidence, then when you try to apply these techniques in sparring, they fall apart like a cheap suit. Jeffrey Guishard a friend and student of mine, who teaches in London has a great saying, "The difference between a white belt and a black belt is about four punches to the head". If you've ever watched people spar, neither party wants to get hit, which is totally understandable. *(the first rule in fighting, don't get hit, the second rule of fighting, hit the other guy).* Most people tend to try to hit their sparring partner from a distance to minimise the possibility of getting hit themselves. The only problem with this, your blows are so weak because they're at the extreme point of their reach. Also the chances are, you're not in the most favourable position due to the fact you've launched your attack too soon. My teacher in Chow Ga Tong Long once took me aside and told me, I wasn't allowed to punch or kick when sparing until he told me otherwise. He told me from now on, when sparring, all I was allowed to do was get as close to my opponent as physically possible, literally centimetres from their face. I was allowed to smother them, control their arms and keep them off balance, but no blows. Well, I can tell you the first few months didn't go well. I was knocked out once and came close a few other times. Over time, I got hit less and less to the point over time I could pretty much enter my opponent's space fairly confidentially. Only by getting as close to my opponent as physically possible, did I start to see all these opportunities for striking without really looking for them. Because I was now in a position to see them. The Chow Ga Tong Long school I come from only started teaching Tai Chi, after students had reached a certain level in their Chow Ga Tong Long training.

I had learnt a very valuable lesson, that I never forgot. In any conflict, it's all about being in the right place, at the right time. My Chow Ga Tong Long teacher had taught me fighting wasn't only about launching blows, but getting into position first, *(that was the hard part)* once in position executing the blows was the easier of the two. Sun Tzu said; "The good fighters of old first put themselves beyond the possibility of defeat, and then waited for victory" he also went on to say in the next paragraph. "To secure ourselves against defeat lies in our own hands, but the opportunity of defeating the enemy is provided by the enemy himself". "Thus the good fighter is able to secure themselves against defeat, but cannot make certain of defeating the enemy".

Relating this back to Tai Chi, specifically push hands, most people tend to push first before being in the right position, therefore they are not able to conclude a successful push. I am not only referring to your physical position, but your internal position, where your root is positioned, in what cycle your opening and closing is in, and lastly, where you are substantial and insubstantial.

We have clarified and defined Tai Chi as the physical manifestation of Taoist principles in action, having qualified the chi that powers all movement in Tai Chi, that being Di Xin Xi Yin Li (gravity). We can now access this power source by applying the Taoist principle of Wu Wei, Non-action to create action. By re-directing your opponent's energy/force (chi) through relaxation back into their own root causing them to become isolated and weak, giving the false appearance of you becoming stronger. Relaxation is the means with which we move the many forms of chi/force around and through the body. Dividing relaxation into two categories, closing (Yin) and opening (Yang), both opening and closing emanates from intent, when opening and closing connects to your intent, root is generated. Having established that opening possesses two different qualities, opening for yielding and opening for issuing what changes these two qualities, is the direction opening moves in. Having learnt one of the many byproducts of opening and closing is the ability to generate speed without the need for muscle. The connection between opening and closing and substantial and insubstantial are inseparable and co-dependent. Opening and closing are connected to your intent through the substantial leg, allowing intent to lead relaxation resulting in relaxation leading the many forms of chi. One form of chi is (gravity) (Di Xin Xi Yin Li) causing substantial and insubstantial to interact with each other, which in turn moves the body. Push Hands is the means with which to expand the principles of Tai Chi/Tao beyond oneself. The form is a collection of various internal movements, and alignments, these alignments create postures, postures are then bought together to constitute a form. Which brings us back to the very first question asked in this book, Chapter One. What is Tai Chi? **Tai Chi (form) is the physical manifestations of Taoist principles in action.**

Alignments, do they control the direction Chi takes, and if they do, what controls the Alignments?

13. Alignments

Chapter 11, of the Tao Te Ching, **The Power of the Insubstantial;**
"Thirty spokes meet in the hub of a wheel. But it is the empty space at the centre that makes it useful for a cart. Clay is used to make a pot. But it is the empty space within that makes it useful as a container. Windows and doors pierce the walls of a room. But it is the space within that makes it useful as a dwelling. Thus things with substance are practical. But it is the insubstantial that is productive".

Things of Substance such as Structure and Alignments are critical and Practical. However, for one purpose it serves to move the Internals and the Substantial and Insubstantial.
The above Chapter from the Tao Te Ching is in reference to the fact, that most things in this world require some sort of physical structure to implement its purpose. For example the function of a pipe is to transport the contents of the pipe, it could be water, sewage or gas from A to B. Without a pipe *(structure)*, water couldn't travel from the mains to the house. Laying of the pipe only has one function and one function only, to transport water to the house. Which of the two is more important the pipe or the water? Neither, you need the substance of the pipe to move the water, without the water *(the internals)* there is no need for the pipe. Alignments of the body is the substance that is required to allow the internals of Tai Chi to move freely and unobstructed. The internals can constitute relaxation, that moves the many forms of chi. Some forms of chi are vital to good health. Others could be energy/force from your opponent. Correct structure and alignments are the cornerstone for any movement, be it internal or physical in Tai Chi.

The Cambridge definition of alignment is "an arrangement in which two or more objects are positioned in a straight line or parallel to each other". Nurselabs defines alignment as "the way the joints, tendons, ligaments and muscles are arranged when initiating a position. A line of gravity passing through your base of support while maintaining your balance". What allows physical movement regardless of the sport or activity you do? The simple answer is joints, whether movement comes from the ball and socket joint, hinge joint or the articulated joints of the spine. Were you to fuse every joint in the body you would literally be unable to move. All this sounds rather obvious. Joint movement is what makes physical movement possible. The next question would have to be, what moves the joints? The most common source for joint movement is muscle and sadly it's becoming more common in modern Tai Chi. People never consider an alternative source to the use of muscle in the creation of joint movement. I know of only two physical activities that don't require muscle to create joint movement, walking and Tai Chi. Tai Chi, like walking, uses the relaxation of the muscles which allows the chi *(chi of the earth)* (*Di Xin Xi Yin Li*) *(gravity)* to move weight which in turn moves joints and hence the body by pulling you into position, compared to the more popular method of using muscle to push yourself into position. Using muscle to push yourself into position requires the use of thought and muscle, where alternatively Tai Chi movement requires only awareness, relaxation, intent and the chi of the earth *(gravity)* to pull the joints into movement.

How joints move and behave is totally dependant on the power source that generates joint movement, whether it's muscular or relaxation. It is impossible to separate linear and collective alignment behaviour from the source of energy that moves these alignments. How joints behave in relation to each other whether it's only two joints interacting with each other *(linear alignment)* or numerous joints *(collective alignment)* is all based on the source of movement whether it's relaxation or muscular. Even the tiniest physical movement requires at least one joint or multiple joints to adjust. There are 360 joints in the body. Understanding how these joints interact with each other is absolutely critical in the prevention of injury and understanding how movement, power and speed is generated in Tai Chi. If relaxation is used to create movement, joints will work harmoniously and collectively, resulting in no injuries due to internal and external forces being allowed to pass through the body to generate physical movement. Where muscles isolate and localise, joint movement results in external and internal forces becoming trapped, leading to injury and loss of strength.

Alignments can be broken into two categories, linear alignments and collective alignments. Linear alignment is in reference to two joints in relation to each other. An example of linear alignment would be when the knee and foot stay aligned with each other. The knees regardless whether it's the front or rear leg always points in the same direction as the foot it's above. Sometimes the source of the knee moving out of alignment with the foot isn't the knee's fault, but the foot's fault *(Figure 40)* notice the front foot is turned outward slightly, causing a mis-alignment with the front knee. In *(Figure 41)* the front foot is in its correct position. The same with the rear leg, if the rear foot is turned outward beyond 45 degrees, it results in a mis-alignment between the knee and foot *(Figure 42)*.

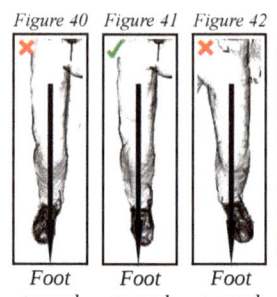

Figure 40　Figure 41　Figure 42　Figure 43

Foot turned outward.　Foot turned inward.　Foot turned outward.　Foot turned in 45°.

Compared to *(Figure 43)* where the rear foot is in the correct 45 degree position which is the same direction as the knee. Sometimes the rear knee going out of linear alignment with the foot can be the fault of the hips. The hips aren't soft enough so when turning to face the front, the rear hip fails to open pulling the back knee inward causing a linear mis-alignment with knee and foot.

There is literally a myriad of possibilities how linear alignment can be lost. Linear alignments are fundamental to Tai Chi and need to be learnt correctly to understand cause and effect, otherwise injury to joint or multiple joints will occur. Linear alignment is fairly easy to learn and is relatively rudimentary, whereas collective alignments are far more complex and subtle. Collective alignment relates to how numerous joints of the body move and behave in relation to each other when in motion. An example of collective alignment would be in the common bow and arrow stance of Tai Chi with 90% weight in the rear leg *(Figure 44)*.

Figure 46

Opening causes a vertical collective adjustment.

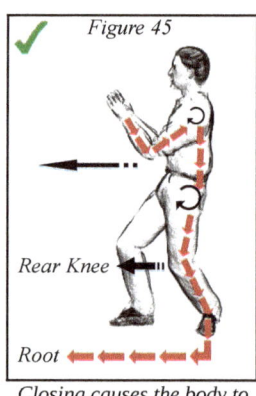

Figure 45

Closing causes the body to adjust forward.

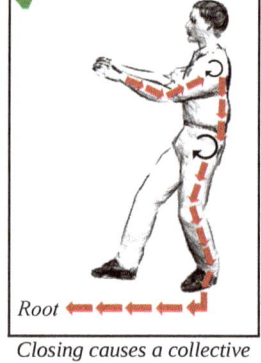

Figure 44

Closing causes a collective adjustment from the root.

Start by relaxing downward *(closing)* in the root of the weighted rear leg. Relaxation being pulled through the back leg will cause the knee to pull forward. The back knee moving forward results in the body physically moving forward. *(Figure 45)*

Internally the energy *(chi of the earth)* is being pulled in a vertical direction down into the root. Forward movement of the back knee causes the head of the femur to simultaneously reverse rotate, resulting in the body moving forward and the sitting of the pelvis which in turn opens the spine and elongates the vertebra. This elongating of the spine not only allows energy/forces to move freely through the body but also causes the shoulder blades to slide downward resulting in both shoulder joints reverse rotating. Upon reaching 55% weight in the rear leg and having reached full compression in the root, you proceed to open *(relax upward)* from the compressed rear root, ***(Figure 46)*** causing a smaller deeper wave of relaxation to move vertically up from the root. Relaxing upward *(opening)* through the collective alignment won't be expressed by any physical forward or backward movement, but through a physical still vertical adjustment *(releasing from stillness)* through the collective alignment. This wave of opening *(relaxing upwards)* travels up from the root through the back of the substantial leg.

In Master Huang lineage we issue from the rear substantial leg upon reaching 55% of weight. ***(Figure 46)*** In most Yang styles they tend to issue *(fa-jing)* when the front substantial leg weight reaches 70%. Regardless whether it's 55% in the rear leg or 70% in the front leg, no principles are compromised by either, as long as the opening *(relaxing upward)* is from the substantial leg. If you are releasing from the substantial front foot then the following will happen up the front leg. Relaxing under the buttocks, causes the hips to reverse rotate slightly. This results in each vertebrae cascading upwards to the shoulder blades, shoulder blades then slide down ever so slightly causing the shoulder joints to reverse rotate which pushes the humerus forward which then pushes the radius and ulna forward, resulting in the hands moving forward and outward. The above process all happens simultaneously and collectively. Collective alignment is referenced in the Tai Chi classics by the following proverbs 一動無有不動，一靜無有不靜。"When one part moves every part moves. But if one part stops all parts stop". Wang Ts'ung-Yueh 周身節節貫串 無令絲毫間斷耳。"The whole body should be connected together, joint by joint like a string. Do not allow the slightest disruption". I believe the above classics are in reference to all joints of the body moving in relationship and in absolute harmony and collectively to each other. It only takes one joint from the above process to stop or even worse, such as the hip forward rotating, instead of reverse rotating, *(hence the reason the buttocks must hang and the pelvis remains seated at all times so the hips can reverse rotate)* then not only do the remaining joints stop, but they actually move in the opposite direction. For example, if the ankle wasn't allowed or prevented from flexing, then the knee wouldn't have the ability to move forward, *(don't make the common mistake of bending the knee for moving the knee forward)* resulting in the pelvis not sitting, the spine not elongating, the shoulder blades not lowering, shoulders joints not reverse rotating and the arms not extending. It only takes one joint from ankle to wrist not to adjust collectively, and the whole body loses its harmony, cohesion and connection to your root and opponent's root. In the following Chapter, linear alignment and collective alignment will be broken down into specific joint movement. Understanding how these two types of alignments complement and support each other in movement is central to understanding how the body mechanics work individually and collectively in Tai Chi.

There is a Tai Chi proverb which explains the importance of linear alignment perfectly; "The chi follows the zig-zag path of the nine pearls". The nine pearls represents nine joints of the body. They are: ankle, knee, hip, shoulder, elbow, wrist, crown of the head *(baihui),* lower back *(ming men)* and coccyx. If you lined up these nine pearls in a straight line, with all the holes also perfectly inline with each other, you could thread a string *(chi)* through the nine pearls. However, it only takes one pearl to be slightly out of alignment or position with the other eight pearls and the string would be stopped. Also, if there is muscle tension around the joint, it's the equivalent of the hole in the pearl closing up, preventing the thread from moving through the pearls. What Chi is it? It could be gravity, Di Xin Xi Yin Li, energy/force from your opponent, vital chi or all of the above.

I was recently speaking with Roger Cotgreave who shared a story about a push hands session with Master Huang. Roger was being thrown around, and Master Huang, communicating through Wee Kee Jin, explained the principle at play. He said that a single misaligned joint is like putting a handle on a suitcase, making it easy for someone to take control and move you. Master Huang was demonstrating this very concept by using Roger's misalignment to gain an advantage.

14. Linear and Collective Alignments

Bubbling Well to Foot

Starting from the bubbling well and moving upwards *(The bubbling well is not a joint. However, it behaves exactly as a joint. Therefore I'm including the bubbling well under linear and collective alignments)*. The bubbling well is easily the most important point on the body in relation to alignments. It's the first and primary point that connects the physical body to your root *(intent and relaxation)* through which all relaxation passes. If the weighted leg *(substantial leg)* at anytime moves off the bubbling well for any reason, the root is instantly severed resulting in the joints of the body becoming isolated and misaligned. **I can't over emphasise the importance of maintaining relaxation whether it's opening** *(relaxing upward)* **or closing** *(relaxing downward)* **through the bubbling well.** Moving off your bubbling well even by a millimetre or two will result in the severing of your root, hence the importance of staying connected to the bubbling well at all times in Tai Chi.

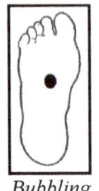
Bubbling Well

When teaching the importance of the bubbling well to my students I have them perform this simple task to highlight the importance of the bubbling well to collective alignment. I have the student sit in the preparation posture *(Wu Chi stance or neutral stance)* where the feet are hip width, feet parallel to each other and weight is 50/50. The knees are directly in line with the feet *(linear alignment between feet and knees)* **(Figure 47)** I ask the student to relax downward *(close)* through the bubbling well **(Figure 48)** while keeping the pelvis in the sitting position. I then ask the student to go as low as they possibly can whilst maintaining their alignment such as the hips seated and the spine straight. They generally lower quite a distance, in most cases their knees move well forward of the toes, in this posture, knees moving forward of the toes is allowed. They need to stop before they break alignment. I then ask them to repeat the same task however, **(Figure 49)** this time I ask them to feed the weight through the centre of each heel instead of the bubbling well, when lowering while at the same time as

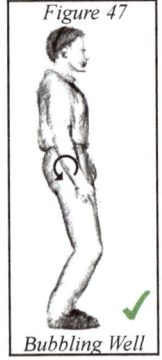
Figure 47 — Bubbling Well ✓

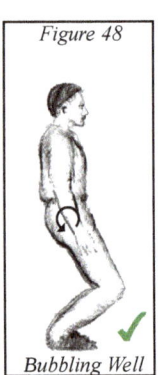
Figure 48 — Bubbling Well ✓

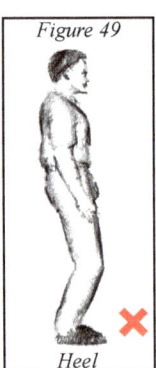
Figure 49 — Heel ✗

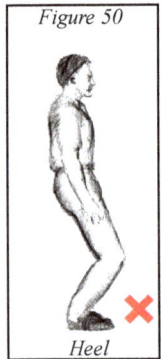
Figure 50 — Heel ✗

Figure 51 — Ball ✗

Figure 52 — Ball ✗

previously, maintaining their alignments such as the hips seated and spine straight. What they quickly discover is that they can only lower half the distance **(Figure 50)** compared to the previous one of relaxing through the bubbling well before their hips, knees and ankles become locked and need to stop lowering. For the third task I once again ask them to start again from the original starting position, **(Figure 51)** but this time, feed the relaxation and weight through the balls of both feet with the same conditions of keeping the pelvis seated and the spine straight, as they lower. **(Figure 52)** The student once again only lowers half as much as figures 47 & 48 before their hips, knees and ankles again become locked once more causing them to stop lowering.

The above example confirms that moving weight and relaxation through the bubbling well allows the body to physically adjust the most, by means of allowing collective joints of the body to move freely while still maintaining correct posture. Drawing weight and relaxation through the heel or the ball of the foot limits the ability of joints to collectively adjust which in turn restricts physical movement. Moving weight and relaxation through the bubbling well is of the utmost importance to your Tai Chi. Also worth pondering: does the bubbling well have a Traditional Chinese Medicine connection to Tai Chi? Or is it nothing more than the optimal point in the foot to feed weight and relaxation into your root, while giving the joints of the body the greatest ability to collectively adjust and continuously adjust whilst still maintaining the integrity of the posture. From personal experience in push hands once you've led your opponent's weight off their bubbling well by only a millimetre or two, either forward or back from their bubbling well, their root is effectively broken, half of the work is done. The other half is keeping their root broken, making sure they don't recover their connection to their bubbling well, either by your pushing *(protrusion)* or collapsing *(hollow)*. People often speak of breaking their opponent's root. Breaking your opponent's root is 50% of the work. Keeping the bubbling well broken is the other 50%.

Foot to Ankle

The foot has 26 bones and 33 joints. When relaxing through the bubbling well the foot needs to relax so the 26 bones and the 33 joints can align with each other. When relaxing the foot correctly there is a strong sensation of the foot splaying or spreading. I used to think the splaying of the foot was from the weight pressing down. I now believe when intent is engaged under the ground and outward, it has the sensation of creating a suction-like sensation which pulls the foot flat causing it to flatten out and splay. Should your feet not relax, or worse you, mistakenly try to grip the floor with your toes, or turn the feet outward so the outside edges of your feet bite against the floor, you will only create tension in the feet, preventing relaxation passing through the bubbling well into the root.

Ankle to Knee

The ankle is a hinge joint and has a fairly limited range at best. The two bones that connect the ankle to the knee are the tibia and the fibula. The ankle is the first real hinge joint that really starts the ball rolling when it comes to physical movement. In the following section, I will break down the relationship the ankle plays in relation to the knee. Starting with 90% weight in the rear leg *(Figure 53)* as the rear knee moves forward both rear and front ankles will flex. The rear knee moving forward will cause weight to decrease from 90% to 55% in the rear leg *(Figure 54)* the rear ankle will flex to a 45 degree angle *(this angle will vary depending on how much weight is in the front or rear leg)*. Movement between ankle and knee is critical in maintaining alignment and connection with the bubbling well of the weighted leg, regardless whether weight is in the front or the rear leg. The relationship between the ankle and knee is key to moving the body forward, backward and maintaining collective alignment with the rest of the body. Over the years teaching Tai Chi I've taught students with various joint injuries, *(spinal, knee, hip and ankle)* all to varying degrees. Ankle and knee injuries are the hardest to work around,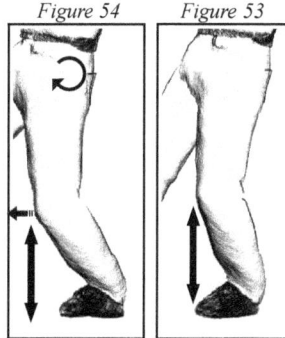

Figure 54 *Figure 53*

Rear leg at 55% weight knee has moved forward. Rear leg weight at 90%, weight behind the foot.

because these two joints are critical in keeping the upper body and lower body connected to the bubbling well and root. These two joints are in constant adjustment to each other and if the injured ankle can't adjust due to mobility issues or pain then your range of knee movement will also be greatly reduced. There will be a need to modify to accommodate this lack of mobility in the ankle such as a higher stance to compensate for the limited movement in the ankle. When teaching Tai Chi I always emphasise, you can only go as low as your least flexible joint. If the ankle is injured then the whole body's alignment is restricted to that of the ankle's flexibility. If it's the knee, then movement is restricted to that of the injured knee. If you were to press the rear foot against the ground to compensate for the limited movement in the rear ankle this would straighten the back knee, resulting in the hip forward rotating. *(Figures 57)* During World War II there was a saying in ship convoys: "The convoy is as fast as the slowest ship". In Tai Chi your range of movement is dictated by the least flexible joint. I am constantly amazed that, over time, with correct alignment and softening of the connective tissue and muscle around the affected joint, there can be significant increases in the range of movement of the injured joint.

Foot to Knee

At all times the foot and knee must stay in linear alignment with each other. **There are no exceptions to this rule.** This means that whatever direction the foot is pointing, regardless of it being the back foot or front foot, the knee must point in the exact same direction as the foot. The knee may move forward past the toe in some instances, however, there can be no lateral movement of the knee in relation to the foot it's above, if you want to prevent knee injuries. The foot, knee linear relationship is extremely important in Tai Chi. Once again to emphasise to my students the importance of the foot direction is to the stability of the knee, I ask them to perform this experiment. I ask the student to take a small bow and arrow stance where the right front foot is pointing straight ahead and the back left foot is at its usual 45 degree angle to the front foot with the shoulders facing square to the front foot, weight being 60% in the front foot. Make sure the outside edge of the right foot is pointing straight ahead and not the toes, leaving you slightly pigeon toed. I ask the student to make sure the front foot stays flat on the ground and that it doesn't roll. I then ask them to see how much they can move their front right knee from side to side laterally. *(Figures 55)* The knee will move side ways by 2 to 3 centimetres. I then ask them to turn the front right foot outward *(away from the body)* by about 20-30 degrees. I again ask them to see how much they can move their front right knee side to side laterally again, to their surprise their knee moves at least 6 to 7 centimetres laterally. *(Figures 56)* This proves foot direction is very important in the prevention of knee injuries. In various Tai Chi books, when they say to point the front foot straight ahead, is it the toe or the outside edge of the foot? They never say. Make sure it's the outside edge of the foot and not the toe, for the above reasons.

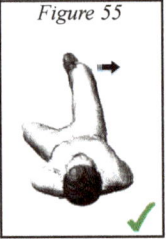

Figure 55

Figure 55

Lateral knee movement limited.

Lateral knee movement limited.

Figure 56

Excessive lateral knee movement.

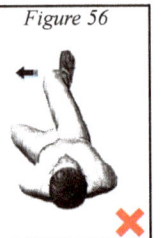

Figure 56

Excessive lateral knee movement.

Front Knee moving forward of the Toes

In Tai Chi it is generally considered incorrect and injurious to the front knee when the knee is allowed to move forward of the toes. Nearly every Tai Chi book you pick up mentions this common fault. When first learning Tai Chi, it's best to keep the front knee behind the toes to play it safe. However, does the knee really have to stay behind the toe? In some cases, yes, the rule is absolutely correct. However, in some cases this rule is not applicable. When is it applicable and when is it not? A biblical saying comes to mind that I have applied throughout my life and to Tai Chi "Rules and laws are for the guidance of wise men and the total obedience of fools". When you understand the purpose of the rule, then you'll understand when the rule can be bent or even broken.

When does the knee have to stay behind the toes of the front foot?

We have been told continuously that the front knee must stay behind the weighted front foot when in the bow stance. Basically, it's not true, what's far more important is the weight moving through the bubbling well, regardless if the knee is past or behind the toes of the front foot. When in the bow and arrow stance, where the outside edge of the front foot is pointing straight ahead and the back foot is hip width apart from the front foot and is at a 45 degree angle to the front foot with the soles of both feet completely flat on the ground. Shoulders square to the front foot, weight is 60% to 70% in the front foot which is the most common weight distribution in most Tai Chi styles when forward. In this position, it's best to play it safe, keep the front knee behind the toes. However, what is more important than the knee moving forward of the toes is the weight moving through the bubbling well. Over the years I've seen Tai Chi practitioners with their front knee well past their front foot and still managed to keep their weight moving through their bubbling well, which keeps them within the principles of Tai Chi. I have also seen practitioners with their front knee behind the toes of their front foot, with their weight, forward of their bubbling well, resting on the ball of their front foot, which puts them in breach of Tai Chi principles. Students have been taught that by keeping their front knee behind the front foot everything will be fine, which isn't entirely true. The real culprit isn't the knee moving past the front foot, it's the weight moving forward of the bubbling well *(if weight isn't moving through the bubbling well, then the weight is in the front knee)*. You can have your knee positioned behind the toes of the front foot, with weight forward of the bubbling well, resulting in the severing of your own root and injuring the front knee. When weight moves forward, off the bubbling well, joints in the leg begin to lock. Remember what happens when you allow weight on to the ball of the foot in *(Figure 51 & 52)* leads to ankle and knee injury. Once joints can't adjust, forces build within these joints. The reason why joints lock is because you have the early stages of loss of balance, you may not feel it yet, but its started. Muscles around the ankle, knee and hip have started to tighten trying to lock the joints into position attempting to create more structure in the hope to keep the body's position stable. Once muscles around the joints begin to tighten and lock the joints, forces such as gravity or force from your opponent *(kinetic energy)* becomes trapped, which ultimately leads to joint injury, loss of balance and power.

The real cause of injury to the ankle, knee and hip isn't the knee moving beyond the toes of the foot, it's the weight shifting forward, of the bubbling well. What causes weight to move forward of the bubbling well? It could be as simple as trying to move the body too far forward or going too low which pulls the weight past the bubbling well. The knee moving beyond the front foot is not the cause but rather the symptom. Another source of weight moving forward of the bubbling well is the back leg pushing against the ground, *(Figure 57)* causing the rear leg to straighten which tilts the pelvis causing the hips to forward rotate *(anterior pelvic tilt)*. The rear knee straightening changes the tilt of the pelvis, causing weight to move forward of the bubbling well, of the front foot which can move the knee past the front foot, but not always. If the rear leg is straight and you've managed to keep the front knee behind the front toe, I can guarantee you the weight will be forward of the bubbling well and on the ball of the foot. Even though the front knee is behind the front foot, the result will be the shearing of your own root and injury to the knees.

For this reason, the back knee needs to stay bent at all times so the pelvis remains seated. So the bubbling well of the weighted front foot stays connected to your root. You may still damage the joints of the front leg, even while keeping the front knee behind the front foot. It's not the knee that's the problem, but the weight moving off the bubbling well. Keep in mind the reverse is true. When the majority of weight is in the rear leg and

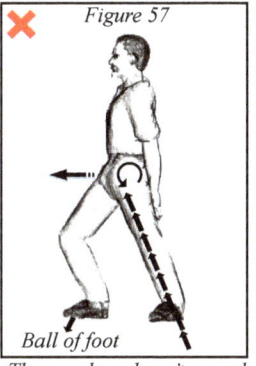

Figure 57

Ball of foot

The rear knee hasn't moved but the femur has, causing a knee extension, the hip forward rotates. Pushing weight onto the ball of the front foot.

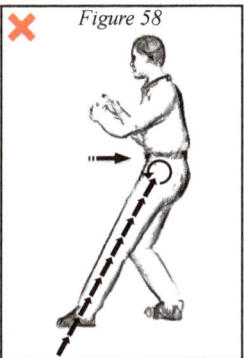

Figure 58

With the front leg straight, will protrude the buttocks. Resulting in forward rotation of the hips and severing your root.

the front knee straightens, the pelvis to also forward rotates *(anterior pelvic tilt)*. This prevents the hips from sitting, causing the buttocks to protrude. **The main reason for the hips to remain seated at all times, throughout Tai Chi, is precisley so the hips can reverse rotate.** This results in the weight moving off the bubbling well towards the heel, severing your root. *(Figure 58)*

The ultimate cause of most injuries to the knee is the inability of the hips to reverse rotate *(posterior pelvic tilt)*. If the buttocks can't droop, the hips can't sit or reverse rotate. The ankles and knees can't adjust this will move the weight forward of the bubbling well to the front of the foot Resulting in ankles, knees and hips locking. The practice of weight moving forward of the bubbling well can be traced back to the method that is used to transfer weight from the back leg to the front leg. Applying the most common method used. These days, the most common Tai Chi method of transferring weight is to press the rear foot against the ground. The moment the foot presses against the ground *(Figure 57 & 58)* you have broken the first cardinal rule of Tai Chi. You have engaged muscle to generate movement. The top half of the knee, the femur moves forward. Causing the rear hip and pelvis to push forward. The hip is forced open, pushing the weight onto the front foot. Preventing the rear hip from reverse rotating *(posterior pelvic tilt)*. This prevents the chi, relaxation, gravity and your opponent's energy/force from passing through the bubbling well into the root. The result is that gravity or your opponent's incoming energy/force will collide with your muscular force which is coming up from the ground and propelling you forward *(double weightedness)*.

All the above is the result of a single act of pressing the rear leg against the ground. To prevent injuries to the lower joints of the body, the pelvis needs to remain seated at all times so the weighted hip can continuously reverse rotate. If hips remain seated the bubbling well of the substantial leg *(forward or rear)* will stay connected to your root. When opening *(relaxing upward)* from the root through the bubbling well to the hip joint, the lower joints must work harmoniously and collectively. *(Figure 59)* It only takes one joint not to adjust, for the collective alignment to malfuction and fall into disarray. In this case, it's the back knee straightening, caused by the pressing of the rear leg against the ground. *(Figure 60)*

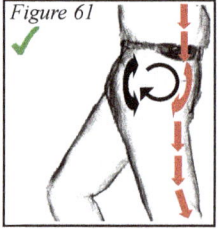 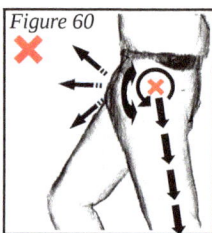 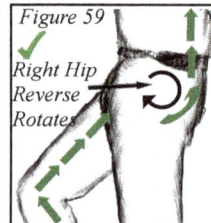

Relaxing down the weighted rear leg droops the buttocks, pulls the weight forward and opens the rear hip.

Pressing the foot against the ground pushes the weight and pelvis forward and forces the rear hip to open.

Relaxing the weight up the substantial front leg droops the buttocks results in the front hip reverse rotating.

Knee to Hip

The relationship between knee and hip is extremely important when moving weight from the substantial rear leg to the front leg. For example, if the rear leg is the substantial leg with 90% weight; transferring this weight forward so that the weight of the rear leg is reduced to 55% still makes it the substantial leg. As stated earlier in Master Huang Sheng Shyan lineage we tend to keep our weight 55% in the rear leg when issuing, whereas in most Yang styles it tends to be 70% in the front leg when issuing. Both are correct because both methods are releasing from the substantial leg. Moving weight forward from the substantial rear leg must be executed by means of closing *(relaxing downward)* *(Figure 15 & 61)* through the rear leg, through the bubbling well under the ground forward of the body led by intent *(root)*. This process pulls the rear substantial knee forward which reverse rotates the rear *(substantial)* hip pulling the pelvis forward and under. The buttocks drooping assists both hips to reverse rotate, the substantial hip more so than the insubstantial hip, the rear substantial kua, physically opens. This allows all forms of chi, whether it's the opponent's force, vital chi or gravity to pass through the pelvis and hip area to continue harmlessly through your bubbling well into your opponent's root. The rear substantial hip reverse rotating is critical in funnelling any incoming force into your root. All the above action was performed by disengaging muscle *(Wu Wei)*. I acknowledge muscle is used to bear weight, nonetheless, no muscle was used in the creation of movement. Muscle use in Tai Chi is limited to weight bearing and creating alignments, but not in generating movement. Pressing the foot against the ground will cause a forward hip rotation **pushing and not pulling the pelvis forward**. *(Figure 57)* Transferring weight from the rear leg to the front leg by means of pressing the rear foot against the ground will result in the contraction of muscles in the rear leg to create this forward movement causing two things to transpire. The first is you are effectively pushing your body against gravity and not borrowing the chi of the earth. Therefore you are pushing against any incoming force, creating double weightedness, instead of re-directing your opponent's energy/force through your body into your root. This helps fuel your collective joint movement *(one part moves every part moves)* causing a forward movement that results in the severing of your opponent's root, eliminating any physical resistance *(double weightedness)*. Secondly, you've isolated the weighted kua from the other joints of the body, effectively creating an isolated body movement. This causes joints of the body to move in isolation to each other, (*but if one part stops every part stops*) causing the chi, opponent's force, gravity or your own vital chi to become trapped within the body resulting in double weightedness.

Hip to Pelvis

The hips play a major part in keeping the pelvis seated which is the correct position for Tai Chi. If the substantial rear knee has been allowed to move forward correctly, this will keep the pelvis seated. The hips and pelvis is the junction point where the upper body and lower body connect. If the pelvis forward rotates *(also known as an anterior pelvic tilt)* this will sever all connection to the lower half of the body and root. If muscle is used to move the body forward by means of pressing the rear foot against the ground, then it really doesn't matter what your hips do, your hips won't be able to reverse rotate. Because muscular energy has been used to create this forward movement, collective alignment will cease and the joints will lose their ability to harmonise and work collectively. Pushing against the ground will trap a large amount of force within the whole body, especially ankles, knees and hips, resulting in the probable injury to these joints. Either using the chi of the Earth *(gravity)* when performing the form or adding the kinetic chi *(energy/force)* of your opponent when doing push hands will enhance and generate freedom of movement and so-called power. Both substantial and insubstantial hips must remain seated at all times. **There are no exceptions.**

The most overlooked muscle in Tai Chi would be the gluteal region, specifically the gluteal fold. If the buttocks are tight then the hips won't sit, or reverse rotate. The waist will stiffen. Hence the reference in the Classics, Wu Chien-Chuan states; **"Loosening the waist and drooping of the buttocks"**. When the buttocks droop the spine will open, which will soften the waist, but even more importantly, both hips will be able to reverse rotate.

Softening the gluteal fold encourages the hips to sit and reverse rotate. In the West everyone wants buns of steel. In Tai Chi it's preferable to have buns of marshmallow. As stated earlier, softening and drooping the buttocks will greatly help in keeping the hips seated. When hips are seated reverse rotation is at least possible. Because the hip joint is a ball socket it has the capacity to reverse rotate which means muscles around the hip area never have to push against the ground when physically rising. It takes a lot of training and correct practice, but over time you'll realise the hip joints can and must continually reverse rotate in Tai Chi to prevent pushing.

I had an interesting experience when teaching Tai Chi at a gym that was frequented by Pilates instructors. I was explaining and demonstrating the beginning of the Tai Chi form. The starting posture of Begin, how the buttocks need to relax under so the hips can be seated, otherwise the buttocks protrude *(anterior pelvic tilt)*. The cause of the buttocks protruding is weight not moving through the bubbling well therefore preventing knees having the ability to move forward enough. One of the Pilates instructors in the class disagreed and claimed it was impossible for the hips to be seated (*posterior pelvic tilt*) without using muscle. She claimed that to achieve this position you need to clench and tighten a combination of core muscles, quadriceps and the glutenous area to bring the bottom back under. She stuck her bottom out and showed me how that by tightening the above muscles the pelvis moved back under and seated the hips. I asked her again to stick her buttocks out slightly, causing an anterior pelvic tilt again. This time I asked her to keep her weight in the bubbling well and imagine her knees were being pulled forward while maintaining weight in the bubbling well. She did what most people tend to do, she bent her knees more, which is not what I asked. I gently coached her to move the knees forward which she did, but she also moved her weight forward onto the balls of her feet. Once again we tried, knees moving forward and the weight staying in the bubbling well. When she performed this action correctly, her buttocks dropped under and the anterior pelvic tilt disappeared. Without the use of muscles.

She wasn't impressed and claimed you still need to activate muscles to sit the pelvis. I asked her to protrude her buttocks once again and to use any muscles that she wished, with one exception. She wasn't allowed to move her knees forward. To ensure her compliance I lightly placed my index fingers on the front of each knee. The moment she used muscle to bring her pelvis back under, her knees moved forward. She tried at least 3 to 4 times before finally giving up. Each time she tried, her knees moved forward. I explained what was happening when she engaged isolated muscles when trying to bring her pelvis under, without moving her knees. The contracting muscles weren't bringing the pelvis under, the pelvis was in fact pushing her knees forward which then allowed the hips to sit. *(try this next time when sitting down in a chair, don't let your knees move forward as you sit, you will literally fall back into the chair).* The difference between Tai Chi's method of sitting the hips and using muscle to sit the hips is that Tai Chi disengages muscles *(non action)* allowing the knees to move forward *(creating an action)* into their correct position which seated the hips, whereas muscles *(isolated body movement)* use muscular force to push the pelvis forward which in turn pushes the knees forward causing a posterior pelvic tilt. It is for this exact reason why the weighted rear knee in Tai Chi needs to be allowed to be pulled forward when rocking forward. The Pilates instructor finally conceded that it was the knees adjusting forward that caused the posterior pelvic tilt *(sitting the hips)*. I remember her last comment on the subject. She said; "That by allowing the knees to move forward to sit the hips you don't obtain any muscular workout of your core muscles. **Exactly!! good thing Tai Chi is not based on muscular generated movement.**

Pelvis to Spine
The whole pelvic area is key to collective spinal adjustment. The spine is not your typical joint, but made up of many joints called vertebrae also known as facet joints, making the whole spine an articulated joint. Thirty three vertebrae make up the spine of which 9 fuse together by the time adulthood is reached. This leaves 24 vertebrae that have the ability to adjust. The pelvis position is key in allowing the vertebrae to adjust collectively and harmoniously. When talking about the spine adjusting, I am not referring to the ability of the spines to flex forward, backwards, sideways or even turning of the waist. Spinal adjustment is in reference to the 24 adjustable vertebrae that make up the spine and the muscles that hold all the vertebrae together. It's the muscles and vertebrae which give you the ability to physically and energetically open and close *(relaxing down and up)* vertically in relation to each other. For the spine to have this ability to adjust between each of the 24 vertebrae, three things must transpire. The first being, the head must be suspended from the crown of the head. Secondly, the pelvis needs to be seated at all times, so that relaxed energy can pass unrestricted, through the joints. Thirdly, energy/force needs to be connected to the root. A plumb bob is a perfect example. It gives you the straightest line possible. All you need is a string, a weight attached to one end, and your hand at the other end of the string. *(Figure 62)* The hand holding the string is **Heaven** *(crown of the head)* the string represents **Man** *(human body)* and the weight is **Earth** *(root)*. All three

are needed to create a plumb bob. If you have a string and a plumb, but no point to hang the string from, the string and plumb lay on the ground. No string then plumb lays on the ground. No plumb and you hang the string and the string dangles and is not fully straight and elongated. In Tai Chi you're effectively a plumb bob on two legs, however, the plumb is always under the substantial leg.

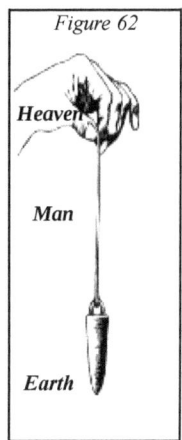

Figure 62

Heaven

Man

Earth

It's common to see students of Tai Chi leaning forward when engaging in push hands by as much as 45 degrees. *(Figure 66)* Once the spine deviates from being vertical it's nearly impossible for the vertebrae to adjust correctly. When the pelvis is allowed to sit in its correct position during Tai Chi it has the effect of elongating the spine provided the crown of the head is kept suspended. Elongation of the spine is conducive for energy *(chi in its many forms)* to travel up and down the spine. One of these energies is relaxation, closing Yin *(relaxation downward)* and opening Yang *(relaxation upward)*. This energy could also be your own intrinsic chi, chi of the earth, Di Xin Xi Yin Li or your opponent's chi which is the energy from a push or blow. These energies are often referred to as a force. I personally don't like this description, because energy only changes into a force when it's blocked or encounters resistance. The whole purpose of Tai Chi is to keep the many forms of chi *(energy)* in a constant state of energy by means of awareness, relaxation, alignment and intent which is led behind and under the opponent's root.

Muscles around the spine need to remain activated enough to hold and maintain structure *(posture)*, but still soft enough to allow these many forms of energy *(chi)* to pass through the body due to relaxing downward *(closing)* from the root. After many years of training relaxation will eventually begin to relax upward *(open)* from the root. Muscles of the spine will adjust in accordance with closing *(relaxing down)* or opening *(relaxing up)*. Relaxing downward originating in the root will elongate the spine causing the majority of the vertebrae to physically open in relation to each other. When opening is used to physically yield the vertebrae will open ever so slightly more, however, when opening is used to issue, the vertebrae will slightly physically close caused from the opening *(relaxation upward)* from the root. Muscle relaxation, specifically opening and closing, is key for the 24 vertebrae adjusting which is instrumental in the creation of arm movement in Tai Chi.

In the Tai Chi Classics there are various references to the back or spine. For example an explanation of the Thirteen Postures By Wang Chung-Yueh states *"Strength is delivered from the back"* another Classic The Understanding of the Thirteen Postures states *"Force is released through the back"*. I personally prefer The Understanding of the Thirteen Postures because it correctly states the force is released through the back and not from the back which implies the energy is generated from the back *(body)*. Sometimes in Tai Chi we're told to spread the back or raise the spine which is in reference to the vertebrae adjusting vertically. When issuing energy forward of the root it is also released from the root travelling up through the body and is **not generated by the body.** The body is just a conduit for the many forms of energy moving through the body. Misalignment between any two joints of the body is considered a breach of linear alignment and will restrict internal movement of the many forms of chi. When joints move in isolation to each other and not harmoniously and collectively, all movement reverts back to isolated body movement, and your years of training will be for nothing.

As mentioned earlier, all of us bring preconceived concepts and beliefs into our Tai Chi from previous experiences in life. An example is strength and power. Past experiences tells us we need muscle from which to generate strength and power for everyday activities, such as lifting and moving objects, which is entirely correct. **However, it's this previous belief and experience that you bring to your Tai Chi, that, will inevitably hold you back.** As your skills and understanding improve over the years you quickly come to the sad realisation that you are in effect your own worst enemy. Bringing incorrect assumptions based on past experiences of muscle based strength and movement into your Tai Chi will impede or negate any progress in your Tai Chi. Understanding how the spine releases energy is critical to understanding Tai Chi. Our belief of how our back works is not helped when it comes from our biased preconceived past. For example in the West we often say *"Put your back into it"* implies strength and power is generated from muscles in the back to get things done. Another one comes to mind *"put your shoulder to the wheel"*. You assume power is created from muscles in the back and shoulders when delivering power to the arms. **(Figure 66)** Recall this Tai Chi proverb *"There is no forward, there is no back, there is no left and no right, there is only up and down, with no top or bottom with no beginning and no end"*.

Of course the up and down is in reference to opening and closing. Remember the previous section, from the ankle to the knee that explains the process of moving forward. When 90% of your weight is in the rear leg and you close *(relaxing downward)* to generate forward movement, the relaxation downward *(closing)* pulls the rear knee forward, which reverse rotates the head of the femur which pulls the body forward. It also elongates the spine pulling the vertebrae straight. If any force is encountered while moving forward it will be instantly pulled through the body into the root of your opponent *(led by your intent)*. Relaxing upward *(opening)* from either the front substantial leg or the rear substantial leg can release fa-jing from the root. This opening *(relaxing upward)* can create fa-jing or yielding, depending on which direction you direct opening. Regardless both yielding and issuing travels up through the back of the substantial leg under the buttocks causing the buttocks to droop, allowing the hips to reverse rotate, continuing through the sitting pelvis, upward through the spine causing the first vertebrae to physically ever so slightly close which creates an upward domino effect through the spine. This results in the vertebrae collectively adjusting up to the shoulder blades. This is what's meant when referring to *"Strength is delivered from the back"* or *"Force is released through the back"* or *"Spread the back"*. The force isn't released from the back into the shoulders to drive the arms forward, instead it's released upward by means of relaxation *(opening)* **through the back**. This results in a deeper relaxation *(opening)* travelling up the spine causing the vertebrae to collectively adjust upward to the shoulder blades.

Spine to Shoulder Blades

The spine adjusting vertically whether closing *(relaxing downward)* or opening, *(relaxing upward)* results in the shoulder blades sliding downwards causing them to act as a counter weight to the arms. This makes the arms functionally empty *(don't mistake momentum for emptiness)* and light, minimising the need to use muscle to generate arm movement. Something to consider: how much muscle is required to move something that has no weight, how fast can you move something that has no weight and how much energy is required to move something that has no weight? The shoulder blades in conjunction with the spine and shoulder joints is what creates all physical arm movement in Tai Chi. This shoulder blade movement is referred to in the Classics. Important Tai Chi points from the Yang Family state 含胸拔背 *"Contain the chest and spread the back"*. Movement of the shoulder blades is vital for the creation of movement in the arms minimising the use of muscle. If you study and train the first four of the Five Loosening Exercises you'll realise and experience how shoulder blade movement cancels out arm weight, making the arms functionally empty.

Shoulder Blades to Shoulder Joints

Most Tai Chi students when performing their form manage to keep their back relatively straight, but all that changes when they encounter an incoming force during push hands. They tend to lean their upper body into the incoming force and tighten their upper back muscles so as to lock their shoulders and arms into position to withstand an external push. **(Figures 66)** Yet in all of the Classics I have ever read, there is no mention or encouragement to use your body weight, or to lean forward or hunch the upper back. On the contrary the Classics constantly promote keeping the spine upright and vertical. Why is that? Because shoulder joints are a ball and socket joint and like all ball and socket joints they behave at their best when the spine is straight and are allowed to move freely in the way nature intended. Ball and socket if allowed, will behave exactly like a pulley *(pulleys are considered levers. A lever magnifies a small force into a larger force).* Therefore it's essential not to lock the shoulder joints, but to allow the shoulder joints to move freely. If your spine is upright and vertical the shoulder joint will sit comfortably in the shoulder socket. When the spine is vertical and you are relaxing downward *(closing)* or relaxing upward *(opening)* the vertebrae will adjust, resulting in the shoulder blades sliding downward. **(Figures 63) If the shoulders are relaxed and sitting they will naturally reverse rotate (Figures 63) and behave as a pulley causing the arms to extend forward and out.**

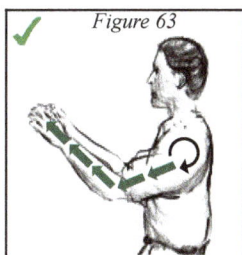
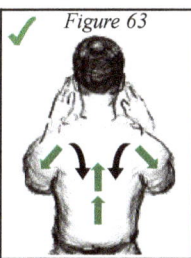

Shoulder blades slide down causing the shoulder joints to reverse rotate, extending the arms.

Shoulder blades slide down causing the shoulder joints to reverse rotate, extending the arms.

For example, if you physically take the position of the 6th movement which is Press in the Yang Form. You are about to start Push the 7th movement of the form, where you rock forward by closing through the back leg pulling the rear knee forward which in turn pulls the body forward. Physically stopping when 55% of weight is in the rear leg *(in Master Huang Sheng Shyan lineage we keep our weight 55% in the rear leg when issuing, whereas in most Yang styles it tends to be 70% in the front leg when issuing. Either weight distribution is correct).* With weight at 55% in the rear leg or 70% in the front leg you should be at full compression in your root. Then open *(relax upward),* this opening can travel up the back leg or front leg, under the buttocks resulting in the buttocks drooping, allowing the hips to reverse rotate, continues through the sitting pelvis up through the spine causing the first vertebrae to ever so slightly physically close, which creates an upward domino effect through the spine. This results in the vertebrae collectively adjusting upwards into the shoulder blades. Shoulder blades then slide downward resulting in both shoulder joints reverse rotating causing the humerus to extend forward and outward completing the 7th Posture Push. Interesting to note that in Master Huang's lineage when you open *(relax upward)* to release you are always physically at your most still, but internally you are at your most active. Which confirms the old Tai Chi proverb *"Release from stillness".* Or as Master Huang often said, *"The more external the movement the less internal the movement, the more internal the movement the less external the movement".* Once again the alignments in Tai Chi are working collectively. The shoulder blades adjusting causes the shoulder joints to reverse rotate. **Like the hips, shoulders always reverse rotate and never forward rotate.**

Shoulder Joints Forward Rotating

What is forward shoulder rotation and why is it so detrimental to your Tai Chi? Forward shoulder rotation is when the shoulder joint as in *(Figures 65)* rotates anticlockwise. The shoulder joint, like the hip, is a ball and socket joint and behaves in the exact same way and must never forward rotate during Tai Chi. This forward rotation will result in your pushing against any incoming force, even if the source of the forward shoulder rotation is generated by relaxation. When joints misalign it often causes injuries to the joints and changes the direction of incoming and outgoing energy/forces. This results in pushing or resisting, even when the movement is generated by relaxation and not muscle. Incorrect joint alignment or joint rotation will cause you to generate a push without realising you are even pushing. In comparison to using muscle to push or resist, you'll instantly become aware of straining muscles pushing against the incoming force and ground. Two things will cause shoulder joints to forward rotate. The first is the elbows holding the same position when rocking forward. This is a common fault in my lineage of Tai Chi. In my lineage we are taught the hands often don't move, either when rocking backwards or forward. The rationale being, your opponent doesn't feel you moving towards them while cutting their root. Your opponent also won't feel you rocking backwards away from them when yielding, drawing them off their bubbling well. However, when moving forward and back and you want to keep the hands stationary the elbows need to lower and move forward. Lowering and moving the elbows forward, encourages the shoulder joints to reverse rotate *(Figure 64)*, helping to draw any force you may encounter to be re-directed into the root. When rocking backwards the elbows will need to rise, which once again helps reverse rotate the shoulder joints. The second and most probable cause of forward rotation of the shoulders by practitioners is of leaning the upper body forward into the hands when performing push hands. *(Figure 66)*.

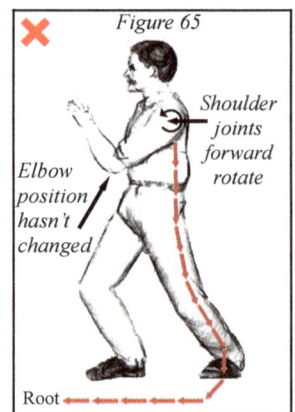

Elbows staying stationary when moving forward, will cause the shoulders to forward rotate.

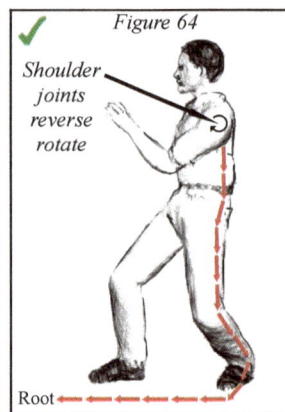

Starting position of the posture Push, the elbows are in their correct position of hanging.

This forward leaning, sometimes up to 45 degrees, is so they can move into their arms and push with their shoulders. This leaning forward breaks so many principles of Tai Chi and Classics, Wang Chung-Yueh's states; 不偏不倚 *"Avoid leaning or inclining your body in any direction"*. Both hips forward rotating causes you to push against the ground, resisting any incoming force simultaneously. Due to the 45 degree angle of the spine, the vertebrae can't adjust in relation to each other causing the spine to become locked and isn't conducive for chi/energy to move up and down the spine. If you are happy to use muscle in your Tai Chi it would be hard to find a better posture for using muscular strength. If you've chosen the Taoist method of applying Taoist principles to your Tai Chi, principles of alignment, relaxation, non action creating action, softness overcoming hardness using intent to direct the chi then this posture is useless to you. For any Tai Chi practitioner who uses this posture in their form or push hands, forward shoulder rotation is the least of their problems. Over the decades leaning forward has become more and more the accepted norm and is commonly seen in push hands competitions. Which doesn't help in the propagation of Tai Chi principles.

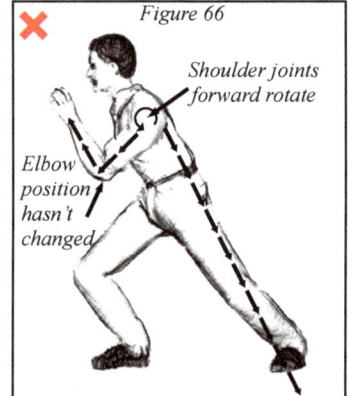

Leaning forward in push hands cause the shoulders to forward rotate, resulting in you pushing against the ground and your opponent simultaneously. This practise is now very common in push hands.

Shoulder Joints to Elbows

The elbows position is key in allowing the shoulder joint to reverse rotate. The elbows need to hang from the shoulders, neither held up nor forced down, if the elbows don't hang from the shoulders then it's impossible for the shoulder joints to reverse rotate. If the shoulders can't reverse rotate they can't adjust and won't behave as a pulley. This lack of adjustment creates a protrusion *(holding)* in the shoulder area resulting in any incoming or outgoing energy/force to settle in the shoulders and upper back *(remember energy stays in a state of energy, until it meets resistance, instantly transforming to a force on your body)*. In some Tai Chi Schools you are actively encouraged to imagine that there is an egg placed under each arm pit. I'm not in favour of this method, as it holds the shoulder out of alignment and doesn't allow the shoulder joint the freedom to reverse rotate. To demonstrate to my students the importance of the elbow position, I have them perform this simple exercise. I have the student take on the posture of Push in the form. I ask them to extend their arm forward as if doing the posture Push. I then tell them to hold that position and to take note of their elbow, shoulder and upper back position and the muscles currently being used. As their arms extend forward their elbows inevitably roll outward pushing their shoulder joints forward, locking the shoulder joints out of position. *(Figures 67)* This locks up and rounds the whole upper back and raises their centre of gravity. They also notice that their chest has collapsed slightly in on itself. Students notice how much muscle is then required to keep their arms and upper back in this position. I ask them to take it from the start again, this time keeping their focus on allowing their elbows to just hang when extending their arms forward, with their elbows hanging and focusing on their shoulder joints gently rotating anticlockwise. *(Figure 63 & 64)* Around 50% of the

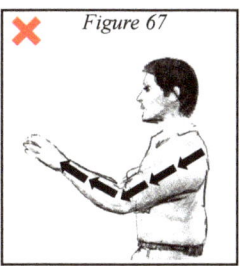

With the shoulders locked it's left to the upper back and arms to do all the work.

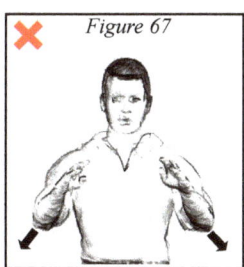

If the elbows are out by 30 degrees the shoulders can't reverse rotate.

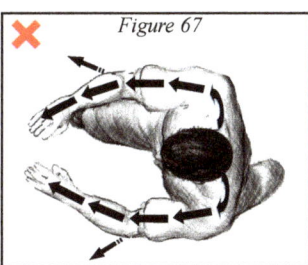

When the elbows stick out, a large amount of energy is redirected out through the elbows.

students try to move the whole shoulder area or just push the arm out. It usually takes a couple of goes before they manage to reverse rotate their shoulder joints. They instantly notice how easy the arm extends outward and is literally unstoppable, no matter how much your opponent pushes or leans on you. I'm not exaggerating, try it and you'll be pleasantly surprised. I never get sick of seeing the look of amazement on the student's face, when their arm naturally and without effort extends forward and out. Repeating this process a few times proves the need for very little arm or upper back muscles to move the arm forward even when encountering an incoming energy/force. If the elbows don't hang the shoulder can't reverse rotate which forces you to push with the upper back, shoulders and arms.

To prove this point I ask them to go back to the start of Push once again, this time instead of the elbow hanging I ask them to move their elbow, laterally sideways and outward by about an extra 15 degrees from where it was previously hanging which makes the right elbow point at 4 o'clock and the left elbow point at 8 o'clock respectively. *(Figures 67)* I then ask them to reverse rotate the shoulder joint once again, to their surprise they discover they physically can't, the shoulders are locked, losing the ability to reverse rotate and extend the arms. All it took was a 15 degree difference to lock the shoulders. Make sure you keep the elbows relaxed, hanging and don't tighten the shoulders. Keep them soft. Don't focus on pushing back against any incoming energy/force. Rather allow the energy/force to pass through the shoulder joints, helping them to reverse rotate, thus preventing the energy/force from settling on the shoulders and upper back. This is the reason there are so many references in the Classics to the placement of the elbows.

Elbows to Wrists

The wrist isn't a major player when it comes to linear and collective alignments. The wrist needs to be firm but relaxed. If the wrist is hyper-extended or hyper-flexed then this will create tension in the elbow which will affect the way the elbow adjusts. The wrist needs to stay comfortably straight so any force it encounters can pass through the wrist unimpaired especially when punching. *(Figures 68)* If the wrist is slightly hyper-extended or hyper-flexed when punching it may cause the wrist joint to buckle either way.

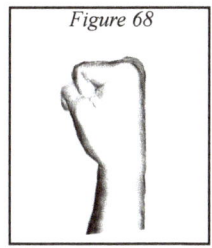

Fist firm, wrist straight

Wrists to Hand

Cheng Man-Ching describes the hands perfectly. He states "the hand should be like that of a lady's hand" *(Figures 69)* neither stretched or limp, but firm and relaxed. I often tell my students your hands should be similar to when patting a dog or a cat, not overly hard or overly soft. The most common problem with the hands isn't physical, but mental. When participating in push hands it's very easy to focus on the result, which is pushing the opponent out with your hands. I often ask students to show me the muscles in the hands that push the hands out. They can't, because there are no muscles in the hands that cause the hands to push out. All this does is focus all your energy on to the hands to achieve the above result. A Tai Chi proverb comes to mind, *"Don't seek what is far, but seek what is near"*. I believe the far they are referring to is the result and the near is the process. The problem is we've become overly focused on results in push hands and neglected the process which delivers the results. The result is achieved by focusing on the process, which is a combination of collective alignment and relaxation *(opening & closing)* which allows the chi of the earth *(gravity)* or energy from your opponent to pass through every joint, muscle and tendon of the body, led by your intent into your root, therefore your opponent's root.

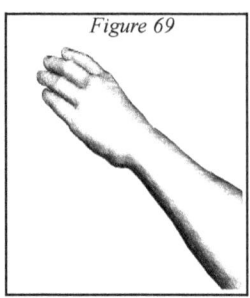

Figure 69

Wrist is firm and straight, the hand is firm, similar firmness to patting a pet.

Applying the Correct Chi *(Di Xin Xi Yin Li)* in Conjuction With The Correct Alignments *(Linear and Collective)* Generates a Virtual Perpetual Exercise.

Imagine a pram *(baby stroller)* rolling down a gentle slopping hill. The energy source for causing the pram to roll is Di Xin Xi Yin Li *(gravity)*. When Di Xin Xi Yin Li is applied to the pram, the wheels of the pram rotate *(hips reverse rotate)* but the pram itself doesn't rotate, just the wheels, resulting in the pram *(the body)* moving forward. Downward energy applied to an alignment that is essentially circular in nature will cause the structure to travel forward. In Tai Chi your alignment has to be perfect, otherwise it's comparable to having square wheels on the pram, the pram won't move, regardless how steep the slope is. If the muscles aren't soft enough to allow Di Xin Xi Yin Li to move the alignments, then it's the equivalent of having the brakes on, The baby stroller doesn't move.

Refering back to page 58 *(Figure 15)* where you're closing *(relaxing downward)* down the rear leg, resulting in you being pulled forward *(rear knee moves forward causing the hip to reverse rotate resulting in you moving forward)*. Until weight reaches 51% in the front leg *(Figure 16)* the front leg now being the substantial leg takes over from the insubstantial rear leg. You now open *(relax up)* up the front leg from the root, resulting in the muscles gently disengaging from the ground up causing the unbroken continuous pulling forward of the body. Opening continues to travel up the body to the crown of the head. Upon reaching the crown of the head, the closing starts again in the root of the front leg, pulling the rear functionally empty leg forward. You then repeat the process *(Figure 15)* again to *(Figure 16)*.

Just think about this for a second. You are not using muscle to generate movement, only using muscle to create a system of alignments that's conducive to creating an internal circular form of energy movement. The energy source for these alignments to move in a circular motion is Di Xin Xi Yin Li *(gravity)*. These circular alignments give the body the ability to move you forward, backward, left and right. In essence, a downward energy causes a circular energy, which creates horizontal movement. I acknowledge, you're using muscle to bear weight so Tai Chi is not entirely energy neutral, but there is no muscular energy used in the propulsion of the body. **Tai Chi would have to be the closest form of a perpetual exercise in existence.**

15. Stepping in Tai Chi

Stepping in Tai Chi whether it be corner stepping *(stepping at a right angle such as Grasp the Ball to Ward Off left)* or forward twist step, needs to be achieved ultimately without thought or muscle. It is also extremely important that you don't physically move up, down or from side to side when stepping in Tai Chi. Using thought and muscle and physically moving up and down or side to side are linked through cause and effect. I realise stepping without using thought or muscle sounds controversial and completely contradictory to everything we know about human movement. In the following Chapter, I will explain the rationale of why muscle or thought must never be used when stepping *(or rocking forward and back)* in Tai Chi, breaking down the numerous reasons why you should never physically move up, down or side to side when stepping in Tai Chi. Towards the end of the Chapter, I will explain the process to remedy these actions.

Why You Shouldn't Move Physically Up and Down or Side to Side when Stepping in Tai Chi

There are two reasons why you mustn't physically move up and down or side to side when stepping or moving forward and back in Tai Chi. The first reason is that it reflects the lack of internal process within your Tai Chi. If you are physically moving up and down when stepping, or just simply rocking forward or back for that matter *(generally it becomes more obvious when stepping though)* is symptomatic of a larger and more serious problem. Physically rising slightly upward when stepping, indicates that you're using muscle to propel yourself forward, caused by the pushing of the rear leg against the ground, **(Figure 70)** resulting in the body rising. In comparison, using muscle to bear weight and maintain a state of equilibrium between you and gravity, is within the principles of Tai Chi. I think you know my view point on pushing against the ground to create movement and how it contradicts the very core principles of Tai Chi, Wu Wei and Taoist Philosophy. Sometimes, not often, students will drop or lower physically in height when stepping, instead of the more common action of physically rising. When a student drops in height this demonstrates, that instead of pushing from their rear leg to initiate the stepping process they have instead, collapsed their weight from above into their front leg to initiate the stepping process. **(Figure 71)** When a student drops their weight into their front leg when stepping, it demonstrates they've disconnected from their root and are now basically relaxing from above into their front foot, generating an isolated body movement. Whether this rising and falling of the body is caused by pushing against the ground or collapsing into the ground, it is a sure sign that the internal process of relaxation has stopped. Specifically the opening and closing process has clearly stopped, resulting in double weightedness. The following Tai Chi proverb confirms the need not to rise, fall or move sideways when stepping'

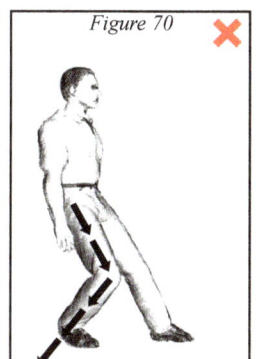

By pressing the rear leg against the ground, causes the whole body to rise.

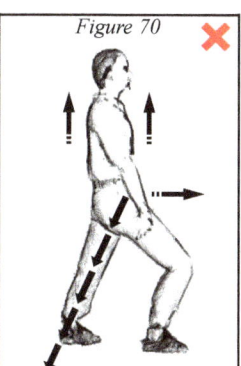

When starting the step forward, you press the rear leg against the ground.

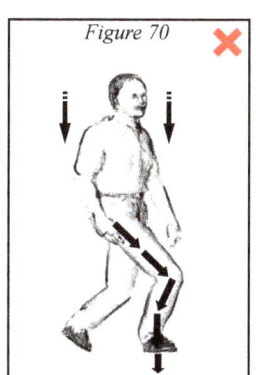

Then dropping back down to pre stepping height, just before stepping.

"When one part of the body moves it shouldn't affect the harmony of the rest of the body". Clearly, the internal relaxation process has broken down, when height change or sideway movement can be discerned, whether stepping forward, backward or just simply rocking forward and back, your height must never change *(of course, there are exceptions to this rule, such as certain postures like Snake Creeps Down or Bend Low and Punch and when your weight is 50/50 such as Begin)* when performing the form or push hands. The following Tai Chi proverb confirms the previous proverb in how the internal process and external movement are linked. **"The body must expand and contract, but the body must never rise nor fall"**. Once again the proverb falls into the typical dichotomy of Taoist philosophy. Breaking the above proverb down, "The body must expand and contract", this is in reference to the internal process of closing and opening. When closing *(relaxing down)* from the root internally *(intent)* while at the same time keeping your head suspended your body will elongate slightly. As the root expands and goes deeper, so will the closing process, and with it, the natural elongation *(expansion)* of the body, the body expands from below, and **not from above**.

After closing has reached full compression, closing then morphs into opening *(relaxation upward)* from the root. When opening *(relaxing upward)* from the root, the body will physically and internally change from elongation to contraction, returning the body to its original previous state. Viewing this process externally, the body will have the appearance of no height change, but internally it has expanded downward with the elongation of the body caused by the closing *(downward relaxation)* and contracted with the opening *(relaxation upward)*. Looking at the whole proverb from a new point of view; **"the body must expand"** this expansion is done internally first through the root by means of closing *(relaxing downward)*, which physically elongates the body *(expands)*. When closing *(relaxation downward)* reaches full compression it changes to opening *(relaxing upward)*, this relates to the next part of the proverb **"and contract"**. The opening *(relaxing upward)* as it travels up from the root, causes the body to internally contract the previous elongation. The second half of the proverb; **"but must not rise or fall"** is inferring that all previous internal movement needs to be achieved without any physical change of height. An analogy I like to use when explaining this proverb. When driving a car and having driven into a pot hole, the car wheel drops into the pot hole causing the car suspension to expand *(elongate)*, keeping the car's height relatively still. As the wheel leaves the pot hole, the car suspension contracts, again keeping the car's height relatively still. This is a similar process that is applied to your Tai Chi.

There are other reasons why you should never push against or drop from above into the ground. By using the previous two incorrect methods of stepping, having made contact with your opponent while stepping, *(which more than likely you will)* you won't have the ability to draw their energy/force back to your opponent's root. If you are pushing against the ground when stepping, and make contact with your opponent in mid step, this will result in your opponent being pushed back into their own root. This effectively makes them stronger, giving them the ability to stop you in mid flight, preventing you from successfully concluding your step *(moving in)*. However, should you step correctly by relaxing downward starting in your root, *(closing)* through your body, and should you make contact with your opponent while in mid step, their energy/force would be pulled *(returned)* back to their own root,

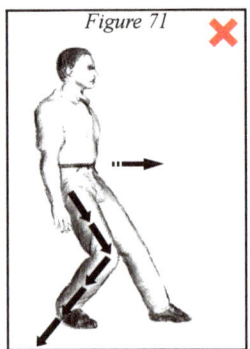
Figure 71
Incorrectly pressing the rear leg against the ground, will move you forward.

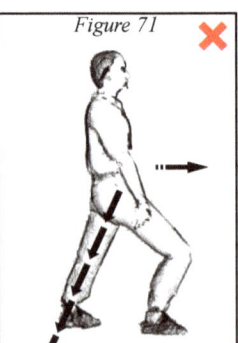
Figure 71
Pressing your leg against the ground prevents your opponent's energy/force, being returned to their root.

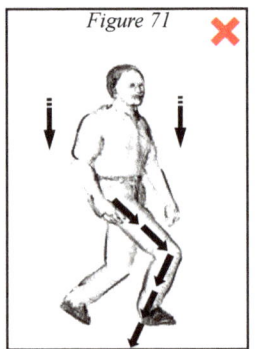
Figure 71
Collapsing from above into the front leg, leaves you with no root and a drop in height.

resulting in them being neutralised. This prevents your opponent from having the ability to stop you in mid step, therefore allowing you to finish the stepping process. Or alternatively, should you drop your weight from above when stepping and once again having made contact with your opponent while in mid step, you could be easily shut down and prevented from finishing the step. When physically dropping from above or relaxing from above, you literally have no root while in mid step, *(don't mistake root for momentum)*. At some point during the step, you'll be on one leg leaving yourself vulnerable to be rolled up. You don't want be caught on one leg with no connection to your own root and therefore your opponent's root. With no root, you've lost the ability to feed or return your opponent's energy/force back to your opponent's root. Closing through the back leg from your root, will have the effect of pulling yourself physically forward. Were you to make contact with your opponent during the stepping process their energy/force would be returned to their root causing them to be neutralised and made ineffectual.

The second reason why you must never move physically up and down when stepping, has more to do with not telegraphing your intentions. When stepping in on someone, rising slightly, especially at the start of the step, telegraphs to your opponent your intentions that you are in the process of moving in on them. When stepping in Tai Chi you must maintain the same height level throughout the stepping process, this way, your opponent at first won't register that you are actually moving. This is because peripheral vision detects movement and motion, central vision distinguishes what your peripheral vision caught, such as shape, colour and other detail. As an example, have you ever seen an object in the sky from a distance, you can't tell if it's a plane or a helicopter or even a UFO, whether it's moving or hovering. The reason for this is if the plane is heading straight towards you, it looks like it's stationary. After a while the object turns slightly, you now realise it's a plane by its horizontal movement across the sky, you may even now have an idea of the plane's speed as it starts to travel laterally to you. Likewise when stepping in Tai Chi, if you maintain the same height your opponent doesn't register movement at first. It may be only half a second, but it's enough to close the distance between you and your opponent. When stepping is performed correctly it should appear as if you're on a skateboard and you've been pushed towards your opponent, there's no vertical or sideways movement for the peripheral vision to catch. By the time central vision has realised something is happening, you've covered valuable real estate. During my Chow Ga Tong Long training, it was considered you were of a good standard, if you could cover your body height when stepping without your opponent realising you were on the move.

The Shortest Point Between A and B is Still a Straight Line

Moving from side to side when stepping in Tai Chi is a very common problem. Why? Because it takes up valuable time, and it telegraphs your intention to step, plus it demonstrates you haven't

Ninety five percent weight positioned in the rear leg. You push the rear leg against the ground.

Having pushed yourself forward you are physically located centrally in the middle of your stance.

Moving forward into the front leg, without fully emptying the rear leg.

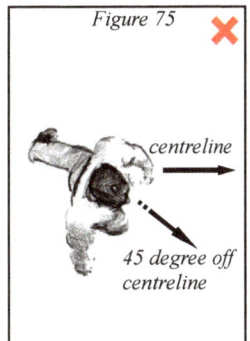
Will cause you to move sideways by up to 45 degrees of your centreline.

functionally emptied the leg you are about to move. Imagine the extra time and effort that's required having to move 45 degrees to the side when stepping *(left or right, depending which leg is forward)*. From my experience, most students tend to step sideways as they move into their front leg when stepping. *(Figures 72, 73, 74 & 75)* Often when pointing this fault out, students will mistakenly claim that it's not possible to stay in the centre when stepping. After demonstrating that it is in fact possible, achievable and necessary, although admittedly not easy and does require a large amount of time, practise, perseverance and analysis. You don't get to choose which principles you follow, you either follow the principles or you don't, regardless of how easy or difficult these principles are. Do we follow the following rule or not: **"When one part of the body moves it shouldn't affect the harmony of the rest of the body"**. If we do, then we need to solve this problem of the body being affected when we move. The choice is simple. This process is applicable to life in general. You have a set of principles that you live by, and these principles are of your own making. You never break these principles regardless of the cost or reward. Master Huang once said: "Only an upright person can do Tai Chi". He was referring to their character and their principles. Back to moving sideways when stepping, this diversion of adding a 45 degrees angle to your step will increase the distance you have to cover by a third, which also means more time is used to cover this extra distance by up to a third. This unnecessary sideway movement when stepping, uses valuable time and space when closing the distance between you and your opponent. Time and space is a valuable commodity in a conflict and needs to be used wisely. The shortest point between A and B is still a straight line.

Moving the Internals and Not the Externals

When moving the internals you'll find the externals *(body)* doesn't need to move as much or at all. Quoting Master Huang again; "The more the internal the less external, the more external the less internal" By working on the internals you'll find there will be less up and down and sideways movement. Tai Chi practitioners love to refer to the internals as if they're mysterious and inexplicable. **Internals just means unseen.** Can you see gravity, oxygen, relaxation, awareness and intent? No. But you can feel the effects of gravity. You can't see oxygen, but you can feel the effects of the lack of oxygen. You can't see awareness or relaxation, but you will the feel the effects of the lack of awareness and relaxation. You can't see intent, but you will feel the effect of intent, when doing push hands with someone who has intent. Often is the case, what stops you from accessing the internals are small things. Such as engaging a small muscle in an area that doesn't seem important, or maybe it's a small joint that hasn't been allowed to adjust. From experience it's the little things that stop internal movement. I often tell students; "Try to look at Tai Chi like an engine. An engine creates energy. An engine is held together by bolts and screws. If you took away all the small screws and bolts from an engine, the motor would literally fall apart and cease to work. No screws, no bolts, no engine, no power.

16. The Classics

The Classics gives us the best means to access the thoughts, insights and thinking of past Tai Chi Masters. They leave behind their thoughts, observations and wisdom for future generations to contemplate and study. Each Master, often at their end of their life, has written down the essence of their art, encapsulating their life long study, to one or two pages.

When reading the Classics, you need to keep a few things in mind. Firstly the Classics like most Taoist literature are written cryptically and riddle-like. The Classics often won't make sense, until you've achieved or passed a certain level in your Tai Chi development, at which point the proverb starts to become clear. **The Classics can also be a check list. It occasionally teaches, but mostly confirms.** For example, Wang Ts'ung–Yueh said; "If your opponent does not move, you do not move. If he makes the slightest move, you move first". I have explained this statement and given an analogy of its meaning on page 36. This statement only made sense to me after personally experiencing the function and purpose of intent in my Tai Chi. I needed to **experience** the effects and sensations of intent, and only then, did Wang Ts'ung–Yueh's proverb **confirm** what I had experienced and understood. Without experiencing the effects of intent, Wang Ts'ung–Yueh's statement just doesn't make sense. Another example of the Classics confirming experience is the statement from The Song of the 13 Postures; "Pay careful attention in your practice of pushing hands. Let the movement of expanding and contracting, opening and closing be natural". Until you understand, experience and apply opening *(relax upward, expand, yang)* and closing *(relax downward, contracting, yin)* the importance of the previous statement is lost.

Most of the Classics are not to be taken literally, but figuratively. Of course, there are quite a lot of instructions in the Classics that are straightforward, such as **Chang San-Feng statement**; "At the moment of movement, the body should be light, agile and most importantly connected together". Fairly self-explanatory. What is also interesting within the Classics, is that they very rarely tell you how to achieve these results. For example Chang San-Feng's above statement could also be applied to the external and harder martial arts. All martial arts should possess lightness, agility and be connected together. Lightness, agility and connectivity are qualities all martial artists should strive for. What is missing is the methodology or the process which will achieve these qualities. The next Classic is not so clear, such as as **Wang Ts'ung–Yueh's** statement; "In movement yin *(substantial, closing)* and yang *(insubstantial opening)* separates and in stillness it unifies"*(notice, no mention of muscle being used to create movement)*. My personal favourite of the Classics is by Wang Ts'ung-Yeuh. From his writings, he really understood the intricacies of Tai Chi. Advice from Wang Ts'ung-Yueh on Yin and Yang is more vague and general compared to Chang San-Feng's previous statement and a lot more difficult to apply to your Tai Chi. Unless you understand the underlying function and principles of Yin *(closing)* and Yang *(opening)*.

Breaking down Wang Ts'ung-Yueh's advice, his reference to yin and yang is fairly vague, it could be linked to nearly anything, he could be referring to Yang advancing, Yin retreating or Yang hard, Yin soft. We need to clarify and qualify the Yin and Yang that he is referring to. The answer may lie in the book written by Chen Wei-Ming, "T'ai Chi Ch'uan" Ta Wen, Question and Answers on T'ai Chi Ch'uan. On page 55, he states; **"Closed is gathering and opening is discharging. When you know opening and closing then you know yin and yang. Reaching this level your skill will progress with the days and you can do as you wish"**. Or, is Wang Ts'ung-Yeuh referring to Yin and Yang in relation to substantial and insubstantial? I believe Wang Ts'ung-Yeuh is referencing Yin and Yang in relation to substantial and insubstantial.

Another thing I have noticed about the Classics is that they seem to have broken into two camps of thought. One camp has a heavy emphasis on chi and the dan tien, the other camp is more about relaxation and intent. Substantial and insubstantial appears to be evenly divided between both camps. It is my opinion that both are talking about the same thing. In Tai Chi, relaxation needs to be viewed as a form of chi in itself. Regardless whether you agree with me or not, one thing is certain. Relaxation facilitates the movement of many forms of chi such as Vital Chi, Yuan Chi, Zong Chi, Ying Chi, Wei Chi, Kinetic energy *(Chi)* from a push or blow and of course, the Chi of the Earth. Without a constant source of unbroken relaxation the above forms of chi will stagnate. Some stagnant chi will result in ill health. Some stagnant forms of chi result in forces building on the body. Other stagnant forms of chi will result in the use of muscle being used to create movement *(breaching Wu Wei philosophy)*.

Explaining the second half of Wang Ts'ung-Yeuh's statement; "and in stillness it *(yin and yang)* unifies". I have also seen this statement written in the following way: "In movement Yin and Yang act independently, in quietude, the two fuse into one and return to the Wu Chi". I personally prefer the latter translation of Wang Ts'ung-Yeuh's statement. It explains the last half of his proverb a little clearer and gives the proverb more structure and direction. Like most things in Tai Chi literature, it comes down to how good the translation is and the translator's level of understanding on the subject. Using the latter statement; "in quietude, the two *(yin and yang)* fuse into one and return to the Wu Chi". At the start of the form, you are still. There is a second time in the form where your weight remains static at 50/50-when you've completed the form and finish in a Wu Chi stance. Having finished the form, all movement ceases. The weight is now 50/50 just as before the start of the form. Yin, *(substantial)* and Yang *(insubstantial)* are perfectly balanced and therefore cancel each other out, and therefore all movement ceases.

When does one plus one equals zero? No it doesn't, I can hear you thinking, it equals two. Not when one is a positive and the other one is a negative. Then it equals zero. When one half is substantial and the other half is insubstantial they cancel each other out and return to the Wu Chi *(zero)*.

When consulting the Classics keep in mind that all Masters are not equal in standard and will vary. Some are more advanced than others and will bring different viewpoints to the same concept. The interesting thing about the Classics is that you will find their meanings will change over time. The Classics don't change, but your interpretations change as your understanding in Tai Chi matures. This is the very nature of the Classics. When I started referring to the Classics over 40 years ago, ninety percent of the Classics didn't make much sense to me. Now the opposite is true, I understand about ninety percent. For example, Chang San-Feng stated, "Power is rooted in the feet, developed by the legs, directed by the waist, and expressed through to the fingers. From the feet through the legs to the waist, should be one flow of chi". Sounds pretty straightforward when first starting Tai Chi. However, I now interpret the above proverb differently from my first reading forty odd years ago. I don't believe power is rooted in the feet. Power, if you can call it power, is in relation to the Chi of the Earth *(Di Xin Xi Yin Li)* and not the feet. The chi, *(Di Xin Xi Yin Li)* may pass through the feet, specifically, through the bubbling well into the ground, led by intent. The second part of the proverb makes two contradictory statements, Chang San-Feng firstly says power is developed by the legs and then later states that power moves through the legs. So which is it, the legs develop power or does the power simply pass through the legs? When I first started Tai Chi, pressing your feet against the ground, engaging leg muscles seemed a commonsense way to develop power in Tai Chi and it fitted neatly into my incorrect preconceived concepts of power generation. I now realise, developing power in the legs was wrong, in the sense of contracting muscle to generate power. However, if you view the legs as a conduit for relaxation to move chi up and down through the legs which if done correctly magnifies this energy without the use of muscle. Then the second part; "through the legs" would be a more accurate description of the proverb. Then we come to: "power is directed by the waist". I don't believe the direction of power is governed by the waist, *(yao)* but by the kuas. When the kuas open and close, this will change the direction of the waist *(the centre of the body)*. Yang Cheng Fu wrote in his book "The transformations of empty and full all result from the turning of waist *(yao)*". Transformation of empty *(insubstantial)* and full *(substantial)* cannot be achieved by turning the waist, it can be achieved only by physically opening and closing through the kua, not by turning the waist. When the kuas open and close the waist will turn. The last part of Chang San-Feng's proverb; "expressed through the fingers" is correct. Translating Chinese into English is a difficult task, the word used could be correct, but could have a different meaning due to the context. Once again it comes down to how good the translator is, and how well they know their subject. Your interpretations of the Classics will change over time, as it should do, as your standard evolves.

As well as using the Classics to help me further my understanding of Tai Chi, I have used analysis to give me direction and this has served me well over the years. My teacher Wee Kee Jin often said: "When in class, you ask the teacher the questions. When training at home, you ask yourself the questions". The questions you ask yourself are ten times more important. The following is an example of the questions I've asked myself. From the very start of my Tai Chi, I was told all movement must come from the root. Causing me to question, what is an isolated body movement in Tai Chi. I came to the conclusion, after much thought, any movement that doesn't emanate from the root can be considered an isolated body movement. I had a choice, either accept the harsh logic of my answer or ignore it. I decided to act on the answer. It literally flipped my Tai Chi upside down. This changed me from relaxing from above, to starting relaxation in the ground. This led me to appreciate the true purpose of intent and fully understand the function of opening and closing in Tai Chi.

The above answer, led me to the second question. What is root? Again after much deliberation, I concluded that root is a combination of relaxation and intent. This led me to ask the third question, what is relaxation? I deduced, relaxation is only using muscle that's required for the moment you occupy *(which is in a constant state of change, similar to the Tao)*. Therefore if relaxation is defined as using only the muscle that's required, for the moment you're in *(which places your action, in harmony with the moment)* then logic dictates, tension is the use of muscle that is excessive to the moment *(any state of excess, contradicts the teachings of the Tao Te Ching)*. The fourth and hardest question is, what is intent? I still haven't worked that one out yet. However, I did discover what function intent plays in Tai Chi. Yi gives you the ability in Tai Chi to project chi by means of relaxation, to a future point in time and place outside of the body. Bringing it all together, relaxing your body allows the chi of the Earth, *(Di Xin Xi Yin Li)* to pull the many forms of chi through your body by means of correct alignment, to a point outside your body which is led by your intent. I still don't know how intent does this, I just know it does, and the results confirm this.

I feel the following statements from two past Tai Chi Masters best sums up the Classics:

Wang Kiu-Yu said: "In the practice of Tai Chi it matters little from what school or what Master one learns, from, the number of movements in a version, a few movements more, a few movements less, and the type of form or circle, high form or low form, big circle or small circle, these are all up to the individual. As long as one does not deviate from the basic principles set forth in the Classics, one can reap the same benefits from the exercise and become a successful practitioner of Tai Chi."

Professor Cheng Man-Ching who died as recently as 1975 said it best; "The Classics are our best link to our Tai Chi past. They are the basis of the art. By their nature they are discursive and redundant, but at the same time, profound. In the present era, when Tai Chi has proliferated into so many schools, the Classics can be used as a model. If any system violates the Classics, then the systems are **wrong**".

17. Following the Cause, Effect and Sequential Order From Wu Chi to Tai Chi

To explain the sequence of events that eventually leads to Tai Chi we need to go all the way back to where it started, with Wu Chi. Leading you through the following, in a sequential order, will give you a clearer understanding of the process at work which is used to generate movement, speed and so called power within Tai Chi. Starting by linking Wu Chi to the first posture of the form, Begin. Begin starts from a neutral stance called Wu Chi *(Wuji)* stance *(feet hip width apart, toes pointing straight*

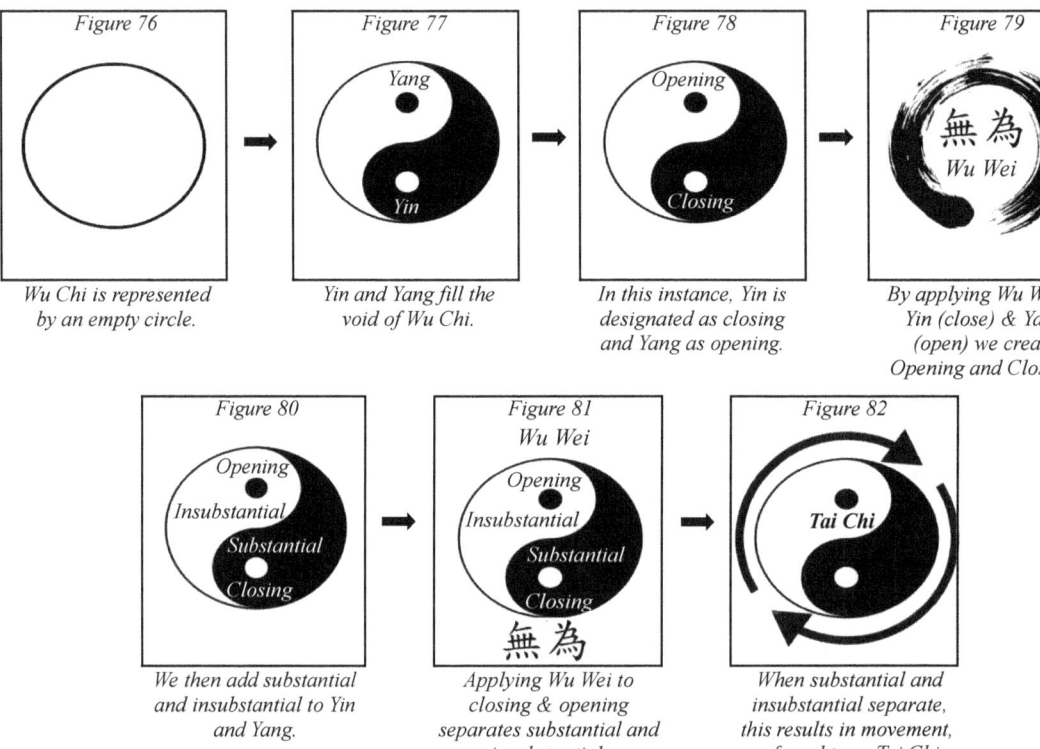

Figure 76	Figure 77	Figure 78	Figure 79
Wu Chi is represented by an empty circle.	Yin and Yang fill the void of Wu Chi.	In this instance, Yin is designated as closing and Yang as opening.	By applying Wu Wei to Yin (close) & Yang (open) we create Opening and Closing.

Figure 80	Figure 81 Wu Wei	Figure 82
We then add substantial and insubstantial to Yin and Yang.	Applying Wu Wei to closing & opening separates substantial and insubstantial.	When substantial and insubstantial separate, this results in movement, referred to as Tai Chi.

ahead with toes level to each other, knees bent, weight 50/50). There's no movement, because we are in a state of Wu Chi *(hence the name, Wu Chi stance)* Yin and Yang is yet to be created, therefore neither has the form, Wu Chi is the void. **(Figure 76)** It helps to view Wu Chi in a similar context to the Big Bang Theory of Western Physics, from which time and matter was created. Wu Chi is the Taoist version of the Big Bang. The next step of the process is the creation of Yin and Yang, which springs from Wu Chi, *(Wu Chi is considered the mother of Yin and Yang)* which fills the empty circle of Wu Chi. **(Figure 77)** Yin and Yang represent complementary opposites such as black and white, hard and soft, male and female. Representations for these opposites are limited only by your imagination. Basically Yin and Yang is a generic term for two opposing but equal opposites. Or if your are a computer programmer, you could view Yin and Yang when applied to trigrams as a Taoist form of binary code. Yin and Yang bring definition. To proceed further in the explanations of the process, we need to assign certain qualities to Yin and Yang. Yin will be designated as closing *(relaxing downward)* and Yang will be designated as opening *(relaxing upward),* relating this process back to the very start of the Tai Chi form with the posture Begin. Having defined Yin as closing *(relaxing downward)* and Yang as opening *(relaxing upward)*. **(Figure 78)** Begin starts with weight 50/50. We then apply the philosophy of Wu Wei *(non action, letting go)* **(Figure 79)** to the process, by closing *(relaxing downward)* first from the root, having achieved full compression in the root *(no physical height change at this stage)*, you then start the opening process *(relaxing upward, Yang)* which causes the body to rise slightly. When opening *(relaxing upward)* has travelled up through the body and having reached chest height *(two third rule is then applied)* closing *(relaxing downward)* starts in the root, and lowers the body back to its original starting position. Yin *(closing)* followed by Yang *(opening)* and then finishing with Yin *(closing)* has been applied to the first Tai Chi posture Begin. Because weight has remained a constant 50% in each leg throughout the opening and closing process, Begin only expresses itself as a gentle raising and lowering of the body. Due to the fact weight has remained 50/50, substantial and insubstantial are yet to be created, only opening and closing happened. Therefore no movement left, right, forward and back is yet possible, only a gentle physical rising and lowering of the body caused by opening and closing. *(similar to the Opening and Closing Exercise)*.

Transitioning to the second posture of the form, Grasp Ball, is when things start to get interesting. Wang Ts'ung-Yueh's proverb; "In movement Yin *(substantial)* and Yang *(insubstantial)* separates and in stillness they unify and return to the Wu Chi" begins to make sense. To proceed further again we need to assign additional qualities to Yin and Yang, adding Substantial to Closing/Yin and Insubstantial to Opening/Yang **(Figure 80)** to the process. Once again applying Wu Wei *(letting go or non action)* to the left leg, as the muscles let go slightly more in the left leg when relaxing upwards this causes the weight to increase in the left leg resulting in it becoming slightly more substantial *(weighted)* than the right leg. **(Figure 81)** With the left leg now at 51%, making it the Yin, substantial leg which in turn makes the right leg Yang, 49% insubstantial leg.

Wu Wei creates Opening and Closing. Opening and Closing creates substantial and insubstantial, and substantial and insubstantial creates movement. *(Figure 82)*.

Applying Yin and Yang to Tai Chi
When applying Yin and Yang to Tai Chi, you need to keep in mind that Yin and Yang are not limited to one definition. Yin and Yang can and does have multiple representations at the same time. Yin is categorised as closing *(relaxing downward)* and is normally associated with substantiality and Yang is associated with opening *(relaxing upward)* and insubstantiality. As confusing as this can be, a Yang quality can sometimes be caused by substantiality and a Yin quality can sometimes be caused by insubstantiality which can go against traditional norms. The reason why will be explained in the following paragraph. When applying the process of opening and closing, substantial and insubstantial to the second posture of the form, Grasp the Ball. I have found that students have difficulty accepting that Yang in relation to opening *(relaxing upward)* can have an expansive empty, yielding quality in body, while simultaneously creating a Yin, quality of substantiality in the root.

Yin and Yang can be and often are subjective, which can confuse the process a little when it comes to defining Yin and Yang. For example using the analogy of the hour glass. As the sand starts to pour into the empty lower chamber, sand falling downward can be considered Yin by nature. Where does the air in the bottom chamber, go? Air compressed by the falling sand rises upward which is Yang by nature. Yin/substantiality creates Yang/insubstantiality. This compressed air moving upward, helps separate the grains of sand, resulting in the sand falling *(Yin)* easier and quicker to the lower compartment *(Yang rising can help facilitate Yin falling)*. Originally the lower compartment which was Yang *(empty and insubstantial)* at first, changes to Yin *(substantial)* as the sand fills the empty chamber, effectively changing the lower compartment from Yang *(empty/insubstantial)* to Yin *(full/substantial)*. On the other hand the upper compartment which was previously Yin *(full/substantial)* has changed to Yang *(empty/insubstantial)*. Effectively changing Yin to Yang and

Yang to Yin. The Tao, if it teaches us anything, teaches that everything is in relationship to each other, and by its nature is in constant state of change. Nothing is in isolation, even opposites. Another example of the constant changing nature of Yin and Yang is water. Water at room temperature of 25 Celsius will stay a fluid, 50% Yin, 50% Yang. Lower the temperature to 0 Celsius and water freezes, 95% Yin, 5% Yang. Raise the temperature to 100 Celsius and water will boil creating steam, steam is 95% Yang, 5% Yin.

You can also relate this to Tai Chi. When cutting and adhering to your opponent's root, your opponent will often describe the sensation of you feeling incredibly Yin, substantial, stable and unmovable. Is this necessarily true? Just because you feel incredibly strong to your opponent, doesn't mean it's true. Your opponent has been weakened so completely due to their root having been severed, a six year old to them would feel incredible Yin, grounded and immovable. In reality you were no stronger than before, all you've done is change the relationship between you and your opponent. If there is a secret to push hands, it would be changing the relationship between you and your opponent. **It's all subjective and perspective-**one person's Yin is another person's Yang. The trick is knowing which qualities Yin and Yang represent at any given time. A word of advice, be careful when using Yin and Yang to conceptualise various theories. It can easily get away from you. I've met people over the years who go too far when explaining and defining qualities and the inter-action of Yin and Yang. It's as if they want to show you how clever they are by the number of situations to which they can apply Yin and Yang. Yin and Yang also have numerous sub-categories. You can have Greater Yang, Greater Yin, Extreme Yin, Extreme Yang, False Yang, False Yin, Young Yin and Young Yang and the list goes on. Yin and Yang can become fractal. If you are not careful you can over complicate the process when conceptualising Yin and Yang causing you to lose sight of the objective, which is to add clarity to the process.

But you could view Yang/Opening as substantial and Yin/ Closing as insubstantial. By applying Wu Wei to the process of opening and closing from the root of the substantial leg (51%). Wu Wei *(non action or letting go)* **causes the opening** *(relaxing upward)* **to travel up the left leg, increasing the weight** *(substantiality)* **of the left leg while at the same making the upper body empty and insubstantial as the opening moves up from the root. Like the roots of a tree which are Yin/Substantial allows the branches to yield and bend which is Yang/Insubstantial.**

Grasp Ball

When substantial and insubstantial start to separate, we have the beginning of left, right, forward and backward movement, a full range of movement which we call Tai Chi. *(Figure 82)* Continuing with the second posture, Grasp Ball, the separation process of Yin *(substantial)* and Yang *(insubstantial)*, caused by opening *(relaxation upward)* continues up the left leg resulting in weight *(substantiality)* increasing in the left side of the body becoming more Yin *(substantial)*. This is where I explain the rationale of Figure 81. As opening travels up the left leg causing the body to empty, turn and yield which is a Yang quality. At the same time the root of the left leg is becoming more Yin and substantial. Essentially the body above ground has become Yang while its root under the ground more Yin. As I stated earlier with the tree analogy, the roots of the tree give the tree its stability, Yin. This Yin quality in the root allows the upper branches of the tree to yield which is a Yang quality. The branches yielding takes force off the tree roots. A tree will always grow its roots first *(Yin)* to gain stability and gather nutrients, before it grows its upper structure *(Yang)*.

Yang opening up the left leg causes the root to become more substantial. When upward relaxation *(opening)* passes through the left gluteal fold, the buttocks will let go and droop, resulting in the left hip reverse rotating, causing the left kua to physically open, resulting in the body turning to the right *(First Loosening Exercise, a vertical circle creating a horizontal circle)*. Simultaneously the right side of the body has become increasingly insubstantial *(Yang)* allowing the right foot to turn outward.

Wang Ts'ung–Yueh's statement; "In movement yin *(substantial, closing)* and yang *(insubstantial opening)* separates and in stillness it unifies"*(notice, no mention of muscle being used to create movement)*. As stated earlier in the Classics, one plus one equals zero, only when one is a positive and the other one is a negative. They cancel each other out and equal zero and return to the Wu Chi *(zero)*. This process is similar in nature to a set of old fashioned balance scales. If you've placed 10 kilos onto each pan, there would be no movement because substantial and insubstantial doesn't exist, **Yet!** *(Figure 83) (Wu Chi)*. However, by placing just one gram on one of the pans creates substantial and insubstantial which generates movement between the two pans. Yin/substantial 10.01 kilos Yang/insubstantial 10.00 kilos *(Figure 84)* are separating, the right pan has become more substantial than the left pan. If you were to remove that same one gram from the right pan, this would cause the scales to move back into balance. *(Figure 85)* Once balance has been re-established the scales cease to move, Yin/substantial and Yang/insubstantial have completely cancelled each other and returned to a state of Wu Chi. Double weightedness does not mean having your weight stationary and placed equally between two feet, *(most people believe having your weight 50/50 is double weightedness which it isn't)*. Double weightedness is when Wu Wei which generates opening *(relaxing upward)* and closing *(relaxing downward)* stops, shuts down and ceases. Regardless where the weight is, it's irrelevant it could be 70/30 or 90/10. Once Wu Wei stops, opening and closing stops, the interaction of substantial and insubstantial stops, and with it, all internal and external movement stops. The many forms of chi and energy stop. **Tai Chi stops.**

Figure 83

Wu Chi

Ten kilos in each pan, no substantial or insubstantial, no movement, only Wu Chi.

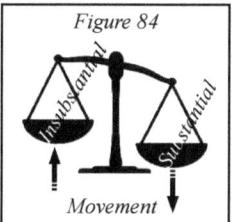

Figure 84

Movement

Add one gram to a pan, creates substantial and insubstantial resulting in movement.

Figure 85

Wu Chi

Remove that same gram, ten kilos in each pan, no movement, a state of Wu Chi has returned.

Now having turned 90 degrees to the right, with 95% of your weight in the left side of the body the empty right foot *(insubstantial)* has turned on its heel 90 degrees to the right, leaving the Wu Chi stance and has now taken on a bow stance. Having fully opened *(relaxed upward)* up the left side, you begin to close down *(relax downward)* the left leg **from the root,** and not from the upper body. This will cause you to move forward through the left leg *(substantial, rear leg). (page 58, Figure 15)* Closing down the left leg *(Fifth Loosening Exercise)* results in the left side of the body becoming less substantial *(Yin)* as the weight starts to shift forward to the right side of the body *(the front leg)* causing the right leg to slowly become more substantial *(Yin)*. You continue to use the bow stance to rock forward until the front right leg reaches 51% of weight and becomes the newly substantial leg *(Yin)*. The moment the front leg *(right leg)* reaches 51% of weight, it is the newly substantial leg *(Yin)* and the left side of the body becomes insubstantial *(Yang)*. At the exact moment the right leg reaches 51%, you must open *(relax upward)* from the root of the newly substantial front leg taking over from the now left insubstantial leg *(Yang)* in a smooth and continuous action. This opening *(relaxing upward)* up the front leg increases the substantiality of the front leg which in turn pulls the body forward. *(page 58, Figure 16)*

As Wang Ts'ung-Yeuh said earlier, when Yin *(substantial)* and Yang *(insubstantial)* separates this will result in movement, it's this constant changing relationship of Yin *(substantial)* and Yang *(insubstantial)* caused by opening and closing, which is created by Wu Wei. Always keeping in mind, what creates substantial and insubstantial and therefore movement is opening *(relaxing up)* and closing *(relaxing down)* through the constantly changing substantial leg.

How Does Wu Wei Create Power?

It doesn't and it can't. Wu Wei is a Taoist concept that plays a large part in a process which allows you to create the conditions, so the many forms of energy/force or what Chinese often refer to as chi can pass through your body unimpeded.

I can't stress enough, the need for you to let go of any belief that you play any part whatsoever in generating, building or storing any form of power in Tai Chi.

I would go as far as to say, it is literally impossible to progress to the higher levels of Tai Chi until you let go of this belief that you create or store any form of energy/power, whether its in the dan tien, root, legs or back and then releasing this energy into your opponent at an opportune moment.

The energy that throws your opponent out, often referred to as fa-jing, is not generated by you or stored by you. The energy/force that throws your opponent out is a result of an imbalance of energy *(gravity)* under your opponent's root. Applying Wu Wei *(which relaxation plays a major part)* creates the optimal conditions for energy/force generated by your opponent's push to be pulled through your body by the Chi of the Earth *(Di Xin Xi Yin Li)*. To a point where your intent is positioned which needs to be under your opponent's substantial foot *(root)*. When closing *(relaxing downward)* originates from your intent *(not the upper body or any part of the body)*. This has the effect of cutting your opponent's root. This results in your opponent's relationship *(equilibrium)* with gravity to be adversely affected. Cutting your opponent's root prevents their ability to re-ground this returned energy/force back into the Earth. Because their connection to gravity has been compromised this creates an imbalance between your opponent and their relationship with gravity. Ultimately, resulting in your opponent excessively tightening muscle to maintain their physical position, making their situation *(imbalance)* worse. Energy from your opponent's push continues to be returned to them combined with their inability to return this energy back to the Earth *(grounding)* causes this energy to become blocked. When any form of energy is blocked it converts to a force. This force, now located between their root and their feet grows. If your opponent can't re-establish a connection to their root, to convert this force back into energy, this results in the force increasing exponentially. When this imbalance reaches a critical tipping point the opponent will need to re-balance from where they physically are, to where they should be *(their centre of gravity)*. At this point your opponent has no other option, but to throw themselves out to re-establish harmony *(balance)* with gravity *(Tao)*.

In Tai Chi, we don't push our opponent off their centre of gravity, instead we move their centre of gravity by means of intent, alignment and relaxation *(Wu Wei)*. If this balance is not remedied, their centre of gravity will eventually move them. In other words, your opponent will eventually need to re-balance *(harmonise)* their relationship with the Tao, *(and gravity is part of the Great Tao)*. Looking at the above process through the eyes of Taoist philosophy, you create no power, you only create the conditions to create imbalance. How violently your opponent throws themselves is entirely up to them. The following Taoist proverb explains it perfectly; "The longer you resist change *(re-balancing of the Tao)*, the more violent the change will be when it happens". So this energy release isn't caused by you. All you've done *(all you've done, I make it sound so easy!)* is facilitate the conditions for an imbalance of energy to happen under the root of your opponent, resulting in them throwing themselves out. This is the very reason why your opponent ideally should never feel any push or pressure from yourself, but rather their own root or body being compressed from the imbalance that's occurring within and under them. As Yang Cheng Fu said over 100 years ago; "Use your will and not force".

To use your will and not force, you will need to let go of established concepts of power and embrace Wu Wei and intent. Without question this will be by far the hardest thing you'll ever achieve in your Tai Chi.

18. Opening & Closing Exercise and the Five Loosening Exercises

In this Chapter, I'm going to apply the theory of Yi Chi Li to Master Huang's Opening and Closing Exercise and Five Loosening Exercises, giving a quick overview into the application of Yi Chi Li to these exercises. My second book, Yi Chi Li of Opening & Closing and the Five Loosening Exercises of Tai Chi is devoted to these six exercises, explaining in detail their methodology, function and aims.

Opening and Closing Exercise

The first exercise you learn in Master Huang's lineage is the Opening and Closing Exercise. Master Huang created this exercise in 1983. Opening and Closing Exercise trains you in numerous qualities. Opening and Closing Exercise teaches and trains a method of relaxation that incorporates downward *(Figure 86)* relaxation *(closing)* and upward relaxation *(opening) (Figure 87)* so the student gains the ability to develop a process of relaxation that freely moves up and down the body. Inside this exercise are timing points. One of these timing points *(Figure 88)* is the two thirds rule for opening. The second timing point is for closing, in your root. *(Figure 86)* The purpose for these two timing points, *(pivot points)* is so relaxation doesn't have a top or bottom *(beginning or an end)*. This allows the student to access a continuous and never ending source of relaxation to apply to their Tai Chi. The Opening and Closing Exercise also introduces the student to the concept of root by means of training your intent. This is achieved by placing your intent 20 centimetres directly below the bubbling well, from which you train to close and open from. Your intent leads the relaxation to where the intent is, followed by opening from your intent position. When relaxation and intent are combined and trained in the right sequence, root is generated. Various alignments are also introduced, such as the training of linear and collective alignments, knees stay aligned with the feet, pelvis remains seated at all time, spine stays suspended from the head, etc, etc. Collective alignment is also introduced to the student through the Opening and Closing Exercise. This is where the student is taught and experiences how the joints of the body harmoniously and collectively move in relation to each other.

First Stage of the Opening & Closing Exercise

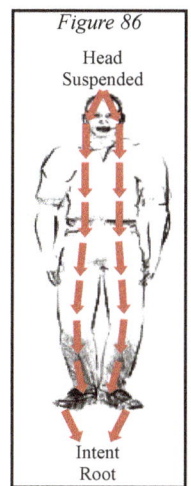

Figure 86
Head Suspended
Intent Root

Starting the closing in the intent (Yi), establishing root.

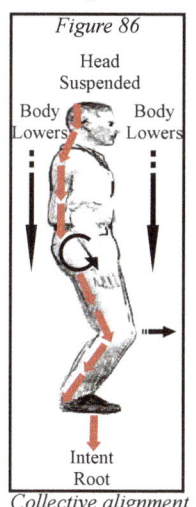

Figure 86
Head Suspended
Body Lowers   Body Lowers
Intent Root

Collective alignment hips reverse rotate and move in relation to the knees.

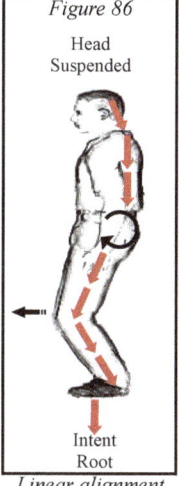

Figure 86
Head Suspended
Intent Root

Linear alignment knees move in the same direction as feet.

Figure 86

View From Above.

Second Stage of the Opening & Closing Exercise

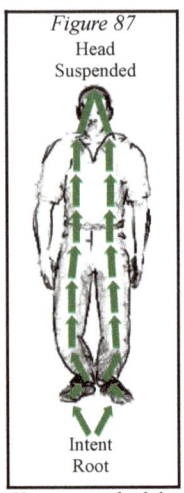

Figure 87
Head Suspended

Intent Root

Having reached the end of First Stage, you begin the Second Stage of relaxing upward.

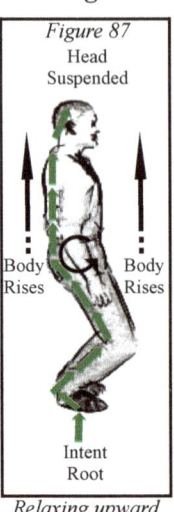

Figure 87
Head Suspended

Body Rises — Body Rises

Intent Root

Relaxing upward from your intent's position causes the body to rise.

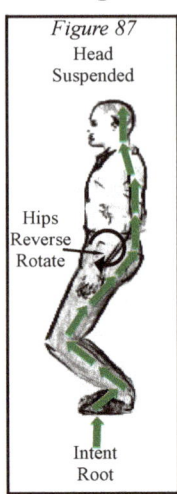

Figure 87
Head Suspended

Hips Reverse Rotate

Intent Root

When opening reaches chest height (two thirds) the closing will start in the intent (root).

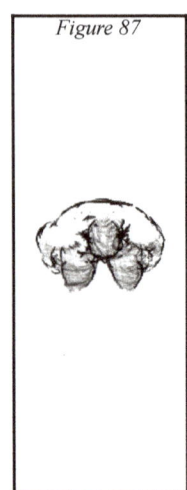

Figure 87

View From Above.

Third Stage of the Opening & Closing Exercise

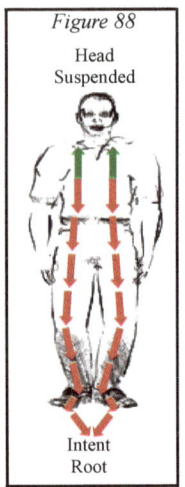

Figure 88
Head Suspended

Intent Root

At the point when opening reaches chest height, closing starts in the root.

Figure 88
Head Suspended

Body Lowers — Body Lowers

Intent Root

While closing starts in the root, opening continues on to the crown of the head.

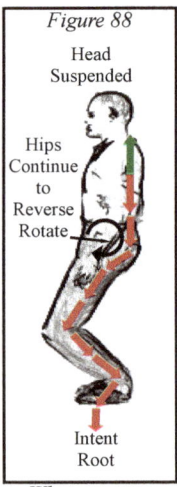

Figure 88
Head Suspended

Hips Continue to Reverse Rotate

Intent Root

When opening reaches the crown of the head, it too changes to closing.

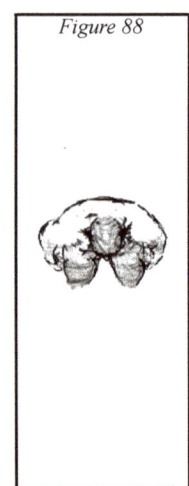

Figure 88

View From Above.

Once the student has achieved a rudimentary understanding and ability to be able to close *(relax downward)* and open *(relax upward)* from their intent under their bubbling well, as the student's training progresses their intent will expand further outward from under their bubbling well, therefore slowly expanding their root. From training the Opening and Closing Exercise the student will also come to understand and develop the timing points of opening and closing, so their opening and closing doesn't have hollows or protrusion *(double weightedness)*, therefore establishing a continuous supply of relaxation with which to power the process. By training the Opening and Closing the student will have established an elementary understanding of linear and collective alignments, such as the continuous reverse rotation of the hips, keeping the bubbling well in alignment with the root, knees remaining in alignment with the feet, etc, etc. Once the student understands and implements these very basic fundamentals to the Opening and Closing they are then ready to apply this same process to the Five Loosening Exercises.

The Five Loosening Exercises

The student now transfers what they have gained from training the Opening and Closing Exercise to the following Five Loosening Exercises. These Five Loosening Exercises were created by Master Huang between 1962–1963. The purpose was to introduce the student to the mechanics of various alignments which creates the five directions of Tai Chi, being, forward, back, left, right and central equilibrium. Having achieved and developed an understanding of the power source of Tai Chi, which is opening and closing, we now need to apply opening and closing to the alignments of body to produce substantial and insubstantial which in turn generates forward and backward movement as well as left and right turns.

First Loosening Exercise

One of the main purposes of the First Loosening Exercise is learning how to create turns by allowing the hips *(kuas)* to physically open and close resulting in you turning left or right, depending on which kua physically opens. The same method of relaxation you've trained in the Opening and Closing is applied to the First Loosening. There are two stages to the First Loosening Exercise. You start in a closed position, *(Figure 89)* you then start the first stage of the First Loosening Exercise opening up *(Figure 90)* the right side of the body causing an increase of weight in the opening side. As the relaxation travels up the right leg to the gluteal fold, the kua of the right leg opens, causing you to turn. The second stage of the First Loosening Exercise when opening reaches chest height, as in the Opening and Closing Exercise you start to close *(relax down)* *(Figure 91)* from the root of the substantial leg, causing the physically opened kua to be pulled closed. This has the effect of pulling you square to the front with weight returning to fifty/fifty in a transitional stage before it moves to 51% in the left leg. Then the first stage is repeated up the left leg. *(Figure 92)*

First Stage of the First Loosening Exercise

Starting with the weight at 50/50 and closing down from the root. Upon reaching full compression, you begin to open up from the root of right leg.

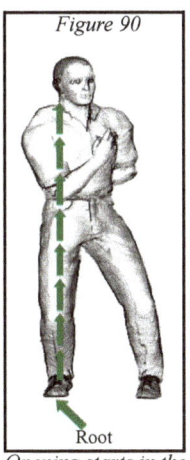

Opening starts in the right root continues up to the crown of the head.

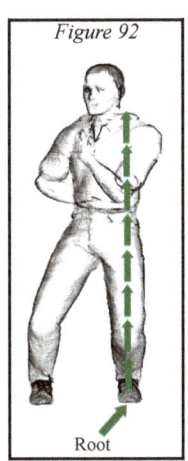

Opening starts in the root and continues up to the crown of the head.

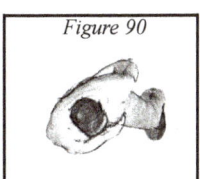

View from above, left turn.

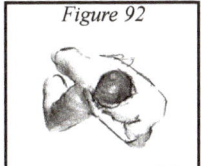

View from above, right turn.

Second Stage of the First Loosening Exercise

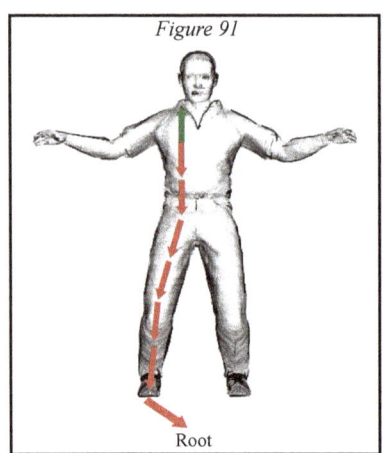

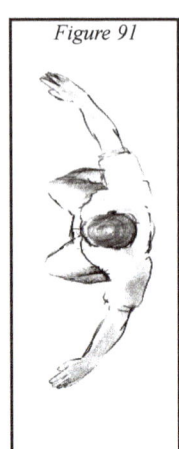

Closing from the root (intent) down the left leg pulls you back to the First Stage of the First Loosening Exercise. *Right Side View.* *Left Side View.* *View From Above.*

Second Loosening Exercise

The Second Loosening Exercise is similar in nature to the Opening and Closing Exercise. In the sense of maintaining central equilibrium throughout the closing *(relaxing downward)* and opening *(relaxation upward)* process while keeping the weight 50/50 in a Wu Chi stance. Due to the fact the weight stays 50/50 in a Wu Chi stance, physical movement such as forward and back or turning won't be possible. Like all movements in Tai Chi, the Second Loosening Exercise's opening and closing always emanates from the intent *(root)*. The Opening and Closing was created 20 years after the Second Loosening Exercise. The alignments, linear and collective as well as timing points used in the Second Loosening Exercise are the same as the Opening and Closing Exercise. It's my opinion the Opening and Closing Exercise was modelled on the Second Loosening Exercise with its similar attributes.

There are eight stages to the Second Loosening Exercise. The Second Loosening Exercise starts with the legs 90% straight, stance is a Wu Chi stance, **(Figure 93)** arms extend outward from the body. The first stage starts with closing from the root, 20 centimetres below the bubbling well pulling the body slightly lower by 3 centimetre, **(Figure 94)** causing the arms to cross in front of the chest. Second stage you continue to close from the root which pulls the body slightly lower by another 3 centimetres, **(Figure 95)** causing the arms to extend back out. Third stage continues to close from the root pulling the body slightly lower by another 3 centimetres, **(Figure 96)** causing the arms to cross in front of the chest. The fourth stage you continue to close from the root. **(Figure 97)** However, this time there's no physical change in height with the arms extending outward. The fifth stage is where you begin to open *(relax upward)* **(Figure 98)** from your intent which 20 centimetres below the bubbling well. This causes the body to physically rise by 3 centimetres resulting in the arms crossing in front of the chest. Sixth stage you continue to open up from the root **(Figure 99)** causing the body to rise another 3 centimetres causing the arms to extend back out. The seventh stage another wave of opening from the root moves up the body causing the body to rise by 3 centimetres **(Figure 100)** resulting in the arms crossing in front of the chest. The last stage, **(Figure 101)** the eighth stage is when the opening *(relaxation upward)* reaches chest height and the body stops rising causing the arms to extend back out, at the same time opening in the root changes to closing.

Second Loosening Exercise

Starting Position

Figure 93

Starting position, stance is Wu Chi, arms extended outward weight 50/50.

First Stage

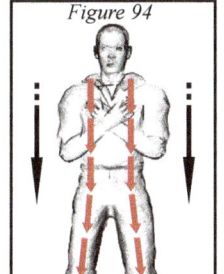

Figure 94

Body lowers 3cm, arms cross in front of chest.

Second Stage

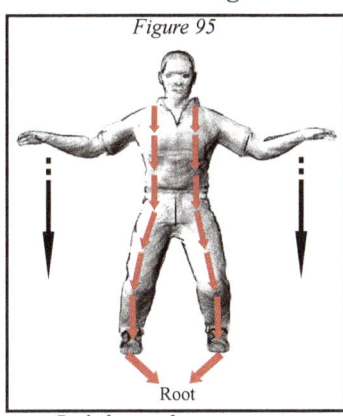

Figure 95

Body lowers 3cm arms swing outward chest height.

Third Stage

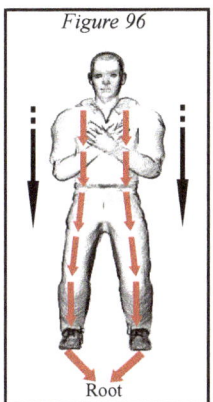

Figure 96

Body lowers 3cm, arms cross in front of chest.

Fourth Stage

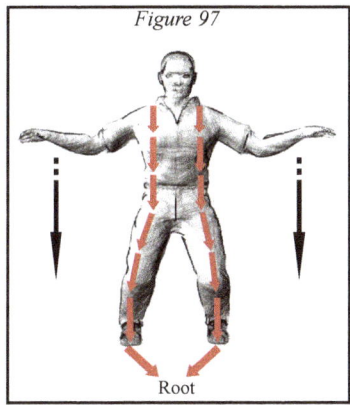

Figure 97

Body lowers 3cm arms swing outward chest height.

Fifth Stage

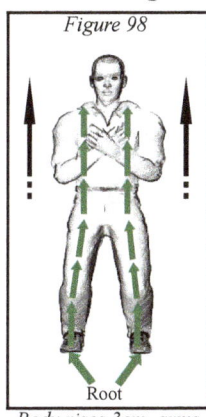

Figure 98

Body rises 3cm, arms cross in front of chest.

Sixth Stage

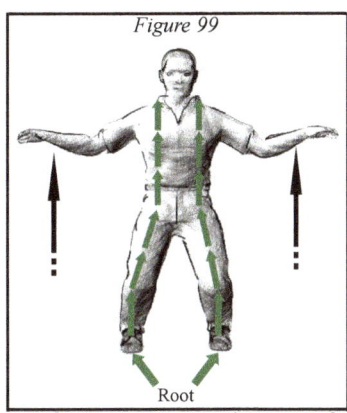

Figure 99

Body rises 3cm arms swing outward chest height.

Seventh Stage

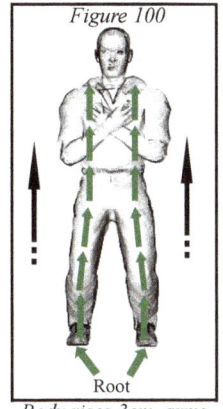

Figure 100

Body rises 3cm, arms cross in front of chest.

Eighth Stage

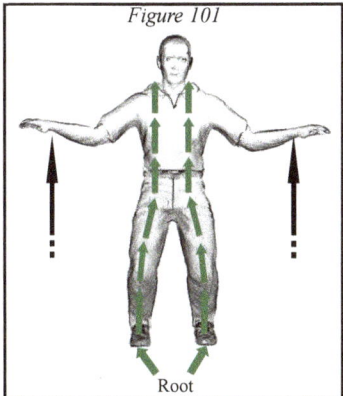

Figure 101

Body rises 3cm arms swing outward chest height.

Third Loosening Exercise

The primary function of the Third Loosening Exercise is for the specific training of cross alignment by applying opening *(relaxation upward)* and closing *(relaxation downward)* and timing points *(two thirds rule)* that was first learnt and trained in the Opening and Closing Exercise. The alignment is slightly different, specifically in the way the hips *(kuas)* work. In the First Loosening Exercise turning is created when upward relaxation from the root passes through the substantial buttock causing the substantial kua to physically open. In the Third Loosening Exercise, the upward relaxation *(opening)* moves up from the root of the substantial leg, through the substantial buttock causing the kua to physically close to create the turn. This physical closing of the kua *(hip)* results in the substantial arm being pulled downward, while on the opposite side of the body, the insubstantial arm raises to chest height. What is cross alignment? In a nutshell, opening *(relaxing upward)* can be used to yield or issue, depending on the direction the opening takes *(I covered this in Chapter 7 Different Qualities of Opening page 44)*. Cross alignment is when you open to yield and issue simultaneously from two opposite arms. When opening up from the substantial left leg, the leftt hand draws your opponent off their bubbling well. While simultaneously the opening *(relaxation upward)* from the substantial left leg crosses over, splits at the shoulder blades causing the right arm to issue. Cross alignment allows you to draw your opponent off their bubbling well with one hand, while simultaneously issuing with the opposite hand. I cover this process in detail in my second book.

Cross Alignment Explained

As stated earlier in this book, cross alignment is usually explained by using Brush Knee in the following example: the weight is in the front left leg and you issue with the right hand. This doesn't explain the process, just the result. Transferring weight from the rear leg, *(refer to figure 15 & 16, page 58)* when weight reaches 51% in the front leg, you open up the front leg, the left hand draws out the opponent, while simultaneously issuing with the right hand. **(Figure 102)** Remember opening *(relaxing upward or sung up)* can be used for yielding or issuing. With cross alignment you are doing both simultaneously.

Figure 102

Opening from your root which is positioned in front you.

Figure 102

Opening splits at the shoulder blades.

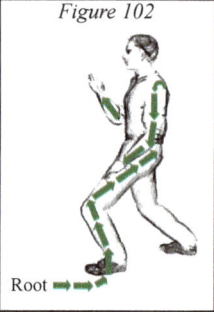

Figure 102

Left hand draws the opponent out, while the right hand issues.

There are four stages that make up the Third Loosening Exercise. The first stage of the Third Loosening Exercise, starts when the left leg becomes 51%, and you open from the left substantial leg causing the left kua to physically close. **(Figure 103)** This turns you slightly to the left pulling the left arm down to your side, while simultaneously lifting the right arm up to chest height. The second stage is more of a timing point when opening under the left foot changes to closing. **(Figure 104)** When opening *(upward relaxation)* reaches chest height or shoulder blade height, closing starts in the root of the left substantial leg, causing the body to be pulled back and squares up to the front with weight now 50/50 for a millisecond before moving to the right leg. The third stage starts when weight reaches 51% under the right foot, making the right leg the substantial leg. The second this happens, opening starts from the root of the substantial right leg. Basically the third stage is a repeat of the first stage but up the right leg, causing the right kua to physically close turning the body slightly to the right resulting in the right arm about to be pulled down **(Figure 105)** and the left arm raising to the centre of the chest. The fourth stage is the same as the second stage, a timing point. When opening reaches chest or shoulder blade height, opening changes under the right foot *(root)* from opening to closing. **(Figure 106)** This causes the right kua to physically open causing the hips and body to square up to the front, with weight 50/50 for a millisecond before moving back to the left leg.

First Stage Of The Third Loosening Exercise

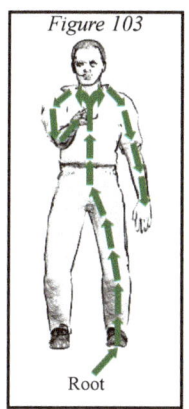

Figure 103

Fifty one percent of the weight under the left foot opening.

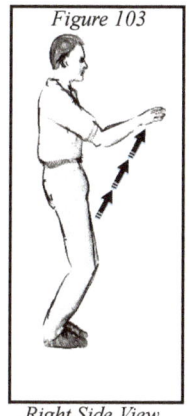

Figure 103

Right Side View.

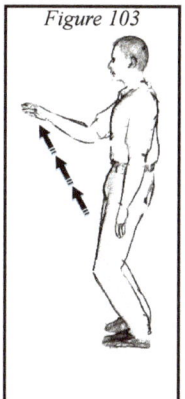

Figure 103

Left Side View.

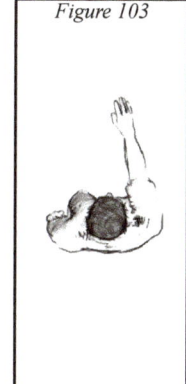

Figure 103

View From Above.

Second Stage Of The Third Loosening Exercise

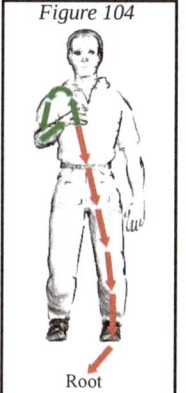

Figure 104

As relaxation travels upwards reaching chest height, begin to close from the left leg (root).

Figure 104

Right Side View.

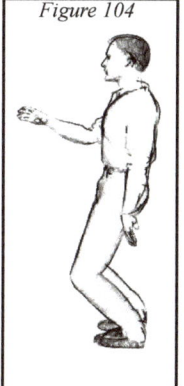

Figure 104

Left Side View.

Figure 104

View From Above.

Third Stage Of The Third Loosening Exercise

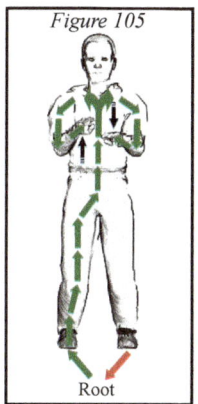

Figure 105

Weight reaches 51% under the right leg. You now open up from under the right foot (root).

Figure 105

Right hand draws the opponent out. At the same time the left hand issues.

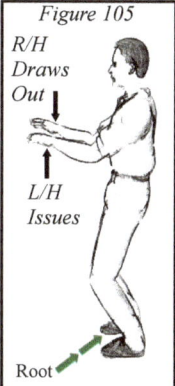

Figure 105

Right hand draws the opponent out. At the same time the left hand issues.

Figure 105

Weight reaches 51% under the right leg. You now open up from under the right foot (root).

Fourth Stage Of The Third Loosening Exercise

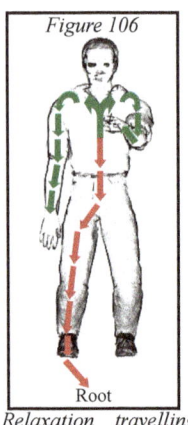

Figure 106

Relaxation travelling up the right leg reaches chest height which is when the left hand at the centre of the chest starts to relax down the left leg.

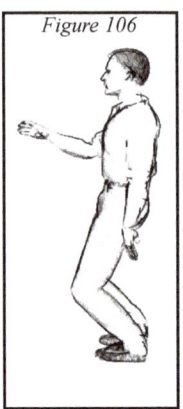

Figure 106

Right Side View.

Figure 106

Left Side View.

Figure 106

View From Above.

Fourth Loosening Exercise

Once again the Fourth Loosening Exercise like the preceding Opening and Closing Exercise and the other Four Loosening Exercises trains specifically the closing *(relaxing downward)* and the opening *(relaxing upward)* process. Applying the same timing points, which for closing is when full compression has been reached in the root. This results in opening from the root. When opening reaches chest height *(known as the two thirds rule)* closing then starts in the root. When the last third of opening reaches the crown of the head the whole body is fully closing. When full compression is reached in the root, the cycle repeats itself. However, where the Fourth Loosening Exercise mainly differs from the previous Three Loosening Exercises is in the way the relaxation process moves the body, which is much closer aligned to how the Tai Chi form behaves. Slower, more structured and deliberate, but with the same application of alignments and same qualities of opening and closing and timing points. The first half of the Fourth Exercise looks similar in nature to the form, with arms extending outward from the centre of the body and returning back to the centre of the body. There are times throughout the Fourth Loosening Exercise where you are bent over from the waist, swinging your arms forward and back, up and down and from side to side. At all times while bent over, you are still applying opening and closing through the body to the arms. In the last section of the Fourth Loosening Exercise there is a much heavier and obvious emphasis on the spine's vertebrae individually and physically opening and closing in relation to each other in comparison to the other Four Loosening Exercises. The rolling of the spine is caused by the opening *(relaxation upward)* travelling up the spine causing the vertebrae to behave in this manner. This requires your awareness to move through every vertebrae without jumping or stopping, causing the spine to roll itself up straight, *(as if you had your lower back against a wall, and you were rolling the spine upward against the wall)* from the lowest point of the spine to the crown of your head.

There are twenty three stages that make up the Fourth Loosening Exercise. The starting position starts with a Wu Chi or neutral stance, stance, with weight 50/50, legs 70% bent, both **(Figure 107)** palms facing the hips. Upon closing and reaching full compression in the root the first stage starts. In the first stage, opening moves up from the root through the body, straightening the legs to 90% and raising the body, causing the arms to extended outward. **(Figure 108)** When opening *(relaxation upward)* reaches chest height, the two thirds rule is applied which instigates the second stage.

In the second stage closing in the root having started, the last third of the upper body slowly finishes opening to the crown of the head. The decreasing opening *(relaxation upward)* slowly moves up through the upper third of the body causing the shoulder blades to lower, resulting in the shoulder joints to reverse rotate causing the arms to be pulled into the centre of the body. The left hand making a fist, and the right hand encompasses the left fist *(Figure 109)* the end of opening has reached the hands and crown of the head. The third stage starts. The third stage starts when opening has fully concluded and closing *(relaxation downward)* is now pulling through the entire body from the root. This lowers the body to where the legs are bent back to 70% *(Figure 110)* and the arms have lowered so the palms are now facing the hips again. In the fourth stage, *(Figure 111)* opening moves once again up from the root through the body, straightening the legs to 90% raising the body, causing the arms to extended outward. When opening *(relaxation upward)* reaches chest height, the two thirds rule is applied which starts the fifth stage in the root.

With the fifth stage having started closing *(relaxation downward)* in the root, *(Figure 112)* opening continues to move up through the last third of the upper body, slowly travelling towards to the crown of the head and hands. The opening *(relaxation upward)* slowly moves through the upper third of the body, causing the shoulder blades to lower, resulting in the shoulder joints reverse rotating causing both arms to be pulled into the centre of the body. When the left hand makes a fist and the right hand encompasses the fist at chest height, the end of opening has concluded at the hands and crown of the head, the sixth stage has begun.

The sixth stage starts *(Figure 113)* when opening has fully concluded and closing *(relaxation downward)* is now pulling through the entire body from the root, lowering the body to where the legs are bent to 70% with the arms lowering so the palms are now facing the hips again. In the seventh stage, opening moves once again up from the root through the body, straightening the legs to 90% raising the body, *(Figure 114)* causing the arms to extended outward. When opening *(relaxation upward)* reaches chest height, the two thirds rule is applied which starts the eighth stage in the root. With the eighth stage *(Figure 115)* having started closing *(relaxation downward)* in the root, opening continues to move up through the last third of the upper body slowly travelling towards to the crown of the head and hands. The opening *(relaxation upward)* slowly moves through the upper third of the body, causing the shoulder blades to lower, resulting in the shoulder joints reverse rotating causing the arms to be pulled into the centre of the body. When the left hand makes a fist and the right hand encompasses the fist at chest height, the end of the eighth stage and opening has concluded at the hands and crown of the head, the ninth stage has now begun.

The ninth stage *(Figure 116)* starts when opening has concluded and closing *(relaxation downward)* is now pulling through the entire body from the root, lowering the body to where the legs are bent back to 70%, as the body lowers both palms open and face you. Tenth stage *(Figure 117)* the arms continue to lower causing the palms to close together at sternum height *(as if your praying)*. At this point when both palms touch at sternum height the eleventh stage starts in the root. Full compression has been achieved and the eleventh stage *(Figure 118)* starts by relaxing upward *(opening)* from the root causing the legs to straighten to 90% as the relaxation continues to move up the spine. When opening reaches shoulder blade height, the shoulder blades will slide downward once again causing the arms to raise upward, forward slightly outward at a 45 degree angle from the centre of your body. As the arms extend forward the outside edge of the palms will open up. Once again, when opening reaches chest height *(two thirds rule)* or shoulder blade height the twelfth stage starts in the root. The relaxation upward *(opening)* continues on up through the last third of the body to the crown of the head. When opening concludes at the crown of the head the thirteenth stage starts in the root. Twelfth stage *(Figure 119)* is when you're fully closing in the root, the whole body is in the closing process to the point where the body has lowered with knees bent, so the thighs are now horizontal to the ground with the elbows resting on the knees. Having reached full compression in the root you start the thirteenth stage *(Figure 120)* by opening from the root *(relaxing upward)*, the legs slowly straighten, with the waist bent over and the fingers are now touching the toes. When the hands are between your two feet the fourteenth stage *(Figure 121)* starts. Opening from the root will cause a ripple *(adjustment)* to move up the spine. When this opening reaches shoulder blade height, closing then starts in the root, resulting in the start of the fifteenth stage to commence causing the remaining opening to travel up the body causing the arms to throw forward. When opening concludes at the finger tips and crown of the head, the fifteenth *(Figure 122)* stage starts in the root. Closing from the root causes the whole body to be fully in the closing process, resulting in the arms being pulled between the legs once again. At that point the fourteenth and fifteenth stage is repeated for one minute. After one minute, the sixteenth stage *(Figure 123)* starts with opening up the right leg. Weight changes to 55% in the right leg, enabling the right shoulder to rotate. This draws the right arm in and higher, and extends the left arm outward and lower. Stage seventeen starts *(Figure 124)* closing *(relax downward)*, down the right leg changes the weight back to 50/50, enabling the right arm to move forward and lower and the left arm to draw in. Now both hands are level with each other.

Eighteenth stage starts *(Figure 125)* opening up *(relax up)* the left leg. This changes the weight to 55% in the left leg, causing the left shoulder to rotate and draw the left arm in closer and higher. The right arm extends outwards and lowers. Then close down *(relax down)* the left leg. This changes the weight to 50/50, enabling the left arm to move forward and lower and the right arm to draw in so now both hands are level with each other and are back in the centre. Stages sixteen, seventeen and eighteen are repeated for one minute. Nineteenth stage *(Figure 126)* starts with opening up *(relaxing up)* the right leg. This changes the weight to 55% in the right leg, causing the right arm to swing in front of the left leg. At the same time the left arm swings behind the left leg. Then close down *(relax down)*, the right leg changes the weight back to 50/50 bringing both arms in between the feet. At that point the twentieth stage starts *(Figure 127)* opening up the left leg causes the left arm to swing in front of the right leg and right arm behind the right leg. Nineteenth and Twentieth are repeated for one minute. After one minute, the twenty-first stage *(Figure 128)* begins with closing down *(relaxing down)* the left leg changing the weight back to 50/50 in both legs,

When the arms are in between the legs and the weight is 50/50 the twenty second stage *(Figure 129)* starts with the whole body closing from the root causing the knees to bend, until the thighs are horizontal to the ground, with the inside of the elbows resting on the knees. The final stage, the twenty third stage *(Figure 130)* starts with opening *(relaxing upward)* from the root, causing the knees to slowly straighten. When the finger tips touch the knees, the pelvis rolls under, continuing the opening *(relaxation upward)* up the spine, causing the spine to roll itself up to the crown of the head. Repeat stage one through to stage twenty three, two more times, three times in total.

Fourth Loosening Exercise

Starting Position

Figure 107
Root

Closing in the root and reaching full compression.

First Stage

Figure 108
Root

Opening from the root causes both hands to lift to two thirds body height. Finishing with palms facing backwards.

Second Stage

Figure 109
Root

Closing in the root pulls the arms together.

Third Stage

Figure 110
Root

Full compression in the root and you're about to open.

Fourth Stage

Figure 111
Root

Opening from the root causes both hands to lift to two thirds body height. Finishing with palms facing backwards.

Fifth Stage

Figure 112
Root

Closing in the root pulls the arms together.

Sixth Stage

Figure 113
Root

Full compression in the root and you're about to open.

Seventh Stage

Figure 114
Root

Opening from the root causes both hands to lift to two thirds body height. Finishing with palms facing backwards.

Eighth Stage

Figure 115
Root

Closing in the root pulls the arms together.

Nineth Stage

Figure 116
Root

Closing causes the hands to open.

Tenth Stage

Figure 117
Root

Closing in the root causes the palms to close together.

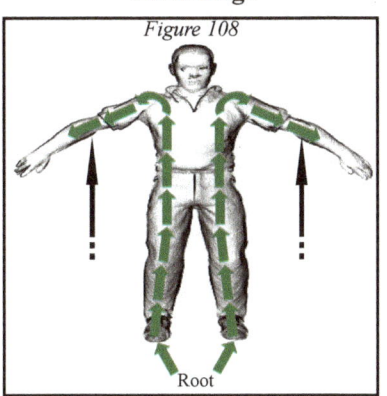

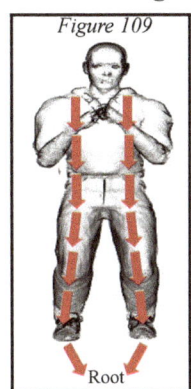

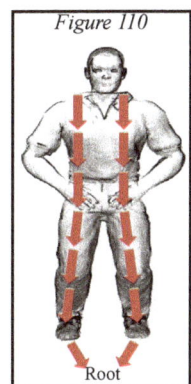

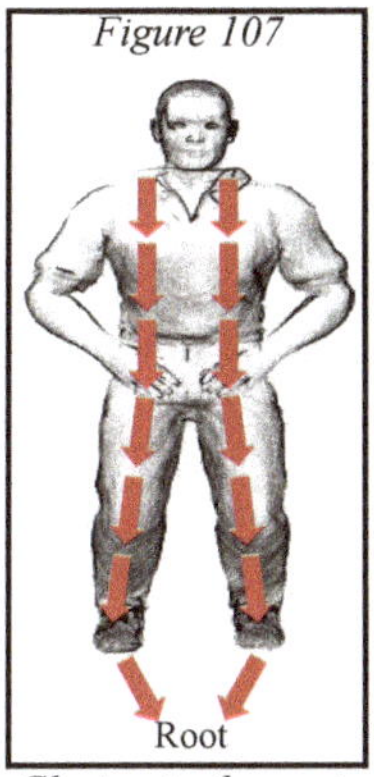

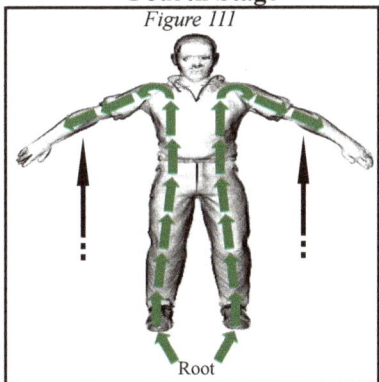

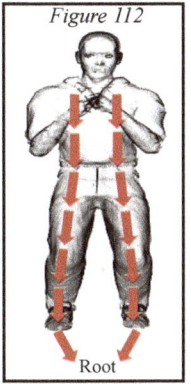

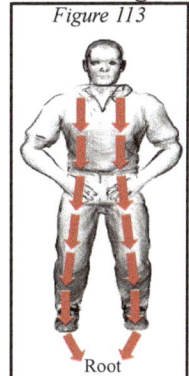

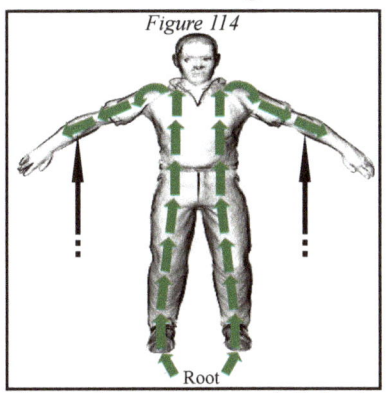

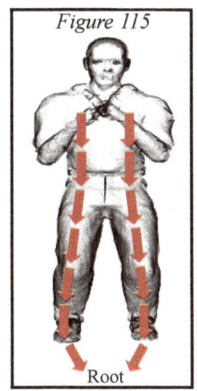

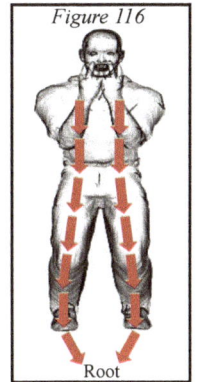

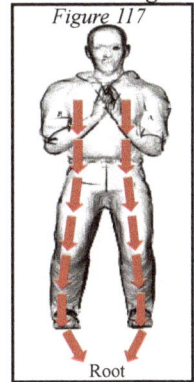

Eleventh Stage

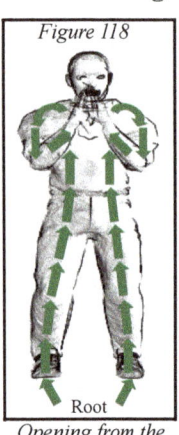

Opening from the root raising the arms.

Twelfth Stage

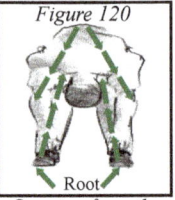

At this point you're reaching full compression.

Thirteenth Stage

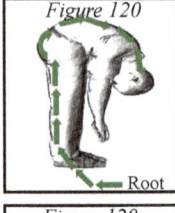

Opening from the root causes the legs to straighten.

Fourteenth Stage

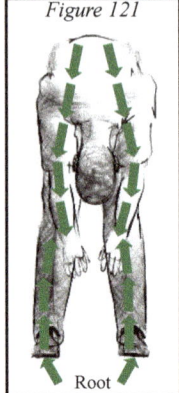

Opening from the root causes the arms to swing forward.

Fourteenth Stage

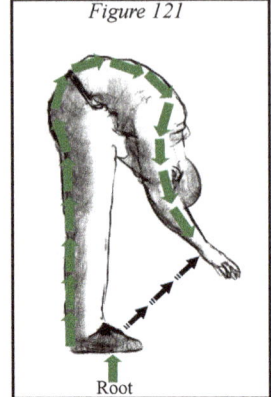

Opening from the root causes the arms to swing forward.

Fifteenth Stage

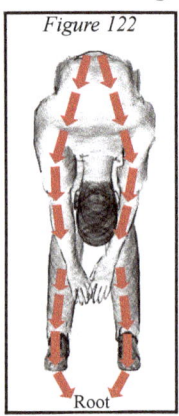

Closing in the root causes the arms to draw downward.

Fifteenth Stage

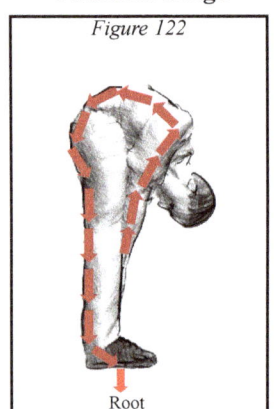

Right Side View.

Sixteenth Stage

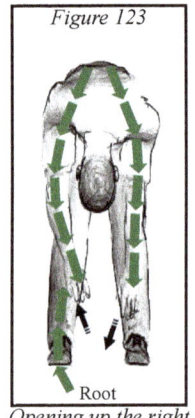

Opening up the right leg moves the arms up and down.

Sixteenth Stage

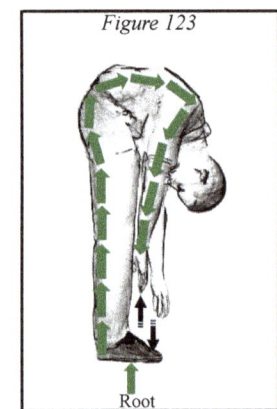

Right Side View.

Seventeenth Stage

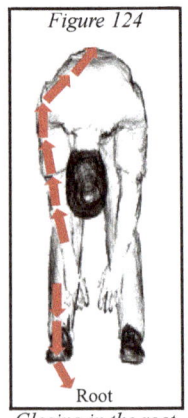

Closing in the root draws the hands between your feet.

Seventeenth Stage

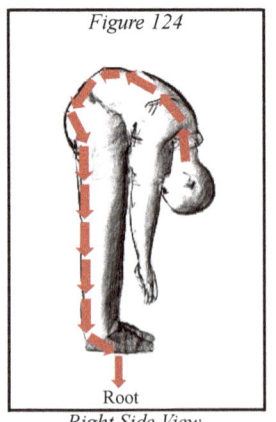

Right Side View.

Eighteenth Stage

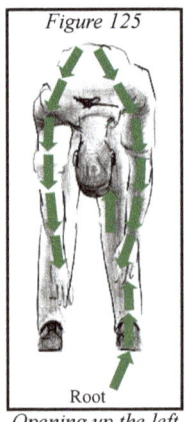

Opening up the left leg moves the arms up and down.

Eighteenth Stage

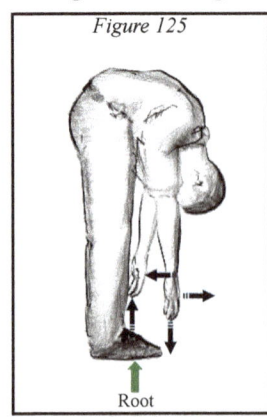

Right Side View.

Nineteenth Stage	**Nineteenth Stage**	**Twentieth Stage**	**Twentieth Stage**
Figure 126	*Figure 126*	*Figure 127*	*Figure 127*
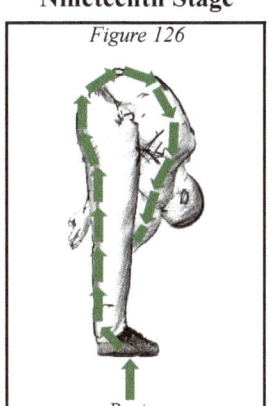		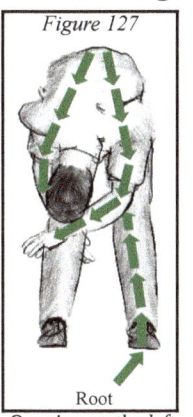	
Opening up the right leg to swing to the left.	Right Side View.	Opening up the left leg to swing to the right.	Right Side View.

Twenty First Stage

Figure 128

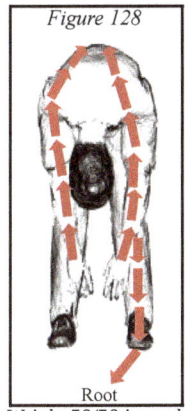

Weight 50/50 in each leg with the arms just hanging down.

Twenty First Stage

Figure 128

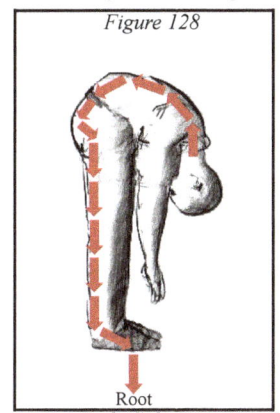

Right Side View.

Twenty Second Stage

Figure 129

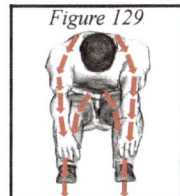

Figure 129

End of the Twenty Second Stage you should be fully compressed.

Twenty Third Stage

Figure 130	*Figure 130*	*Figure 130*	*Figure 130*	*Figure 130*	*Figure 130*
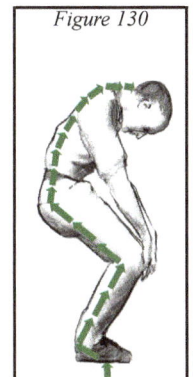	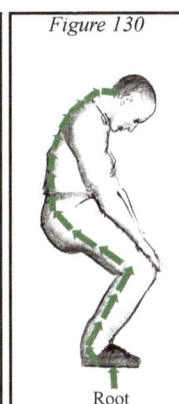	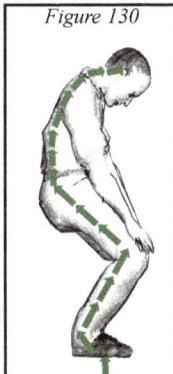		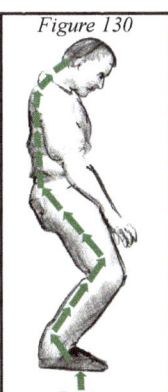	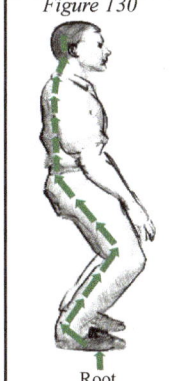
Root	Root	Root	Root	Root	Root

The last half of the Twenty Third Stage, make sure you roll the spine up from below allowing the lower vertebra to pull the next vertebra above into position. Causing the next vertebra above to open, this generates a domino effect all the way up the spine resulting in the spine being pulled erect.

Fifth Loosening Exercise

In the First Loosening Exercise the right substantial knee and ankle physically flexes a large amount, causing the substantial kua to physically open resulting in the pelvis turning in the opposite direction *(the right kua physically opens and you turn to the left)*. This is often known as a vertical circle creating a horizontal circle. In the Second Loosening Exercise the weight stays 50/50 and both kuas physically open and close simultaneously causing the body to rise and lower, which can be considered, central equilibrium. In the Third Loosening Exercise the ankles and knees stay still and it's the kuas that physically open and close, specifically the substantial kua which physically closes due to the upward relaxation *(opening)*, the right buttock lets go *(drooping the buttocks)*. This physical closing of the substantial kua causes the pelvis to turn slightly towards the closing kua *(the right kua physically closes and you turn slightly to the right)*. This is another example of a vertical circle creating a horizontal circle, but in the opposite direction to the First Loosening Exercise. The Fourth Loosening Exercise has elements of central equilibrium due to the fact, weight remains 50/50 most of the time throughout the exercise. It also exhibits elements such as the raising and lowering of the arms in a Tai Chi form-like manner. The underlying cause of arm movement is due to the vertebrae adjusting in a way that results in the scapula sliding downward, causing the shoulder joints to reverse rotate causing the arms to move. The primary emphasis throughout the Fourth Loosening Exercise is clearly to soften the spine so that each vertebra can open and close in relation to each other so arm movement then becomes possible during Tai Chi. The previous Four Loosening Exercises cover the directions of left, right and central equilibrium. The only directions left to cover are forward and backwards.

Hence the need for the Fifth Loosening Exercise, when opening and closing moves through the collective alignments *(the mechanics)* of the Fifth Loosening Exercise a forward and backward movement becomes possible. This completes the five directions of Tai Chi, they being left, right, forward, backward and central equilibrium. Tai Chi is known for its constant rocking forward and backward motion. However, this constant moving forward and back, has to comply and conform with the principles of Tai Chi and chief amongst them is Wu Wei. From my experience most students of Tai Chi achieve this forward movement, by pushing their rear foot against the ground, or by dropping their rear knee into the rear foot, all incorrect. Pressing the rear foot against the ground means you are powering your movement by using muscle to generate movement which violates the very principles of Wu Wei (refer to page 100, figure 60). Dropping your rear knee into the back foot will propel you forward. It's wrong, due to the fact your hips will forward rotate resulting in you pushing against the ground even if relaxation is applied. By dropping the knee into the rear foot you've caused the hips to forward rotate, violating how collective alignments work *(refer to chapter 12 Form, page 88, figures 36, 37, 38, 39)*, which should be collectively and harmoniously.

Due to the pain often experienced in the rear thigh when first training the Fifth Loosening Exercise, some students, mistakenly believe the main purpose of the Fifth Exercise is to develop thigh strength, which it isn't. It's learning how to maintain relaxation *(opening and closing)* in the thighs while under load, so energy/force can still pass through the legs while supporting body weight. One last thing to keep in mind when training the Fifth Loosening Exercise. It's very easy to overly focus from the waist down when training the Fifth Loosening Exercise. The focal point can sometimes be excessively focused on the opening and closing in the lower alignments such ankles, knees, and hips. However, when closing *(relaxing downward)* make sure the closing pulls through the entire body starting from your intent/root to the crown of the head. I think pain plays a major part in causing you to overly focus on the legs. Pain is just another form of awareness and nothing grabs your attention like pain does. Granted the lower limbs do all the heavy work nevertheless, you still need to take the relaxation process from the intent/root moving it through the whole body when closing. Followed by relaxing upward *(opening)* from the intent/root back up through the rear leg and up through the spine to the crown of the head. Don't overly fixate on the legs, remember you need to connect and link the whole body with the Fifth Loosening Exercise.

There are six stages to the Fifth Loosening Exercises. Starting at the beginning with your weight, 95% in the rear leg. *(Figure 131)* The rear knee being bent with back foot turned in at a forty five degree angle, the front foot pointing straight ahead with both heels aligned in a straight line with each other. Buttocks relaxed under, head suspended from the crown of the head, spine straight. Starting the first stage by closing from your intent under the bubbling well, pulling the relaxation through the body. At this stage in the Fifth Loosening Exercise your aim is to cut your opponent's root by means of intent and relaxation, before physically moving *(by moving your opponent's weight slightly off their bubbling well towards their heel, whether it's with a real partner or an imaginary partner the process is the same)*. When the closing *(relaxing downward)* **(Figure 132)** reaches the crown of the head the rear knee starts to move forward causing the rear hip to reverse rotate pulling you physically forward. First Stage is concluded upon reaching full compression in the root/intent with **(Figure 132)** weight now at 70% in the rear leg. Second stage starts in the root opening *(relaxing upward)* from the root/intent, while simultaneously relaxing up *(opening)* through the bubbling well, through the rear foot, calf, hamstrings and gluteal fold *(making sure the hips reverse rotate)*. The body rises ever so slightly. At this point in the Fifth Loosening Exercise, opening *(relaxing upward)* is used for issuing/releasing/fa-jing **(Figure 133)** and not for yielding. As stated earlier in the book you can only have fa-jing when you have an opponent's root. The emphasis is on training the process and not the result. Old Tai Chi saying; "Don't seek what is far *(the result)*, seek what is near *(the process)*".

The gluteal fold under the rear buttock drops away *(drooping the buttocks)*, causing the hip to reverse rotate, resulting in the vertebrae adjusting upward through the spine. When upward relaxation *(opening)* reaches two thirds of body height *(chest height or alternatively shoulder blade height)* the third stage **(Figure 134)** starts, by closing *(relaxing downward)* in the intent/root. Basically third stage starts before stage two is completed. In Tai Chi there is a constant continuous overlap of opening and closing. A Tai Chi proverb states: The ending of one move is the beginning of the next, all movement is based on opening and closing. When closing is coming to an end, opening has already started and vice versa. When the third stage starts in the root/intent, the body remains still, however, the last upper third of body is still adjusting upward, finishing the remaining opening at the crown of the head. When opening finishes at the crown of the head, you've completed the third stage and you've started the fourth stage. When the third stage finishes at the crown of the head and you have reached full compression in the intent/root, you are ready to start the fourth stage.

The fourth stage starts when you open *(relax upward)* from where your intent/root is. If your intent/root is positioned a metre in front of you under the ground, when relaxing upward *(opening)* the relaxation moves towards you. As the relaxation moves up the rear leg, this results in the muscle letting go *(Wu Wei)* enough so the chi of the Earth *(Di Xin Xi Yin Li, Gravity)* causes a controlled rocking back, **(Figure 135)** known as a physical yield and if done correctly, an internal yield. With the opening continuing up through the vertebrae, upon reaching chest or shoulder blade height once again the next stage starts in the intent/root. At the end of the fourth stage you return to the first stage of rocking forward. Stages one to four are repeated five times, after the fifth cycle you move on to the fifth stage. The fifth stage starts when the weight is 95% in the rear leg, opening has reached chest height with the front part of the foot having lifted, the heel is lightly touching the ground. With the fifth stage coming to an end, the totally empty front foot is pulled in. **(Figure 136)** Closing having started in the intent/root signals the start of the sixth stage. When the fifth stage finishes at the crown of the head and the whole body is closing *(sixth stage)*, the empty front foot is pulled out with the heel lightly touching the ground. **(Figure 137)** Stages five and six are repeated eight times. Stages seven, eight and nine are dedicated to turning the body 180 degrees, so you can repeat stages one to to six on the opposite leg. For expediency I won't be covering that in this book.

Fifth Loosening Exercise

Starting Position
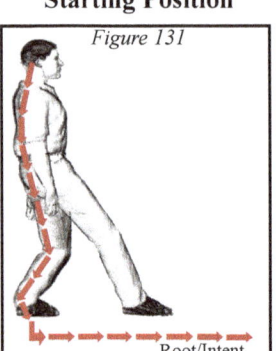
Figure 131

Weight 95% in the rear leg. You close in the root pulling your relaxation to your intent.

First Stage
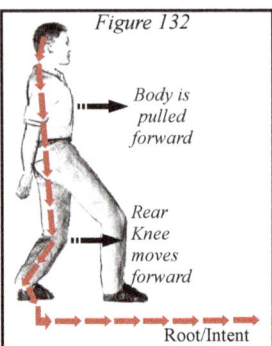
Figure 132

Body is pulled forward

Rear Knee moves forward

Closing down the rear leg pulls the rear knee forward causing you to move forward.

Second Stage
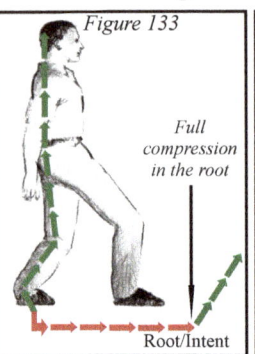
Figure 133

Full compression in the root

Reaching full compression in the root, open from the root and body simultaneously.

Third Stage
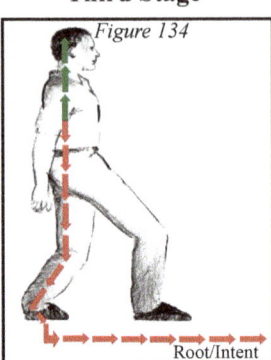
Figure 134

At the two third point, begin to close in the root.

Fourth Stage
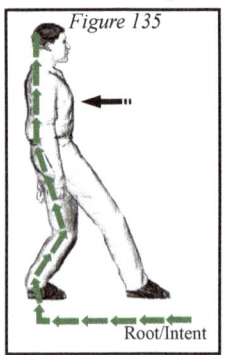
Figure 135

Opening causes you to move backwards.

Fifth Stage
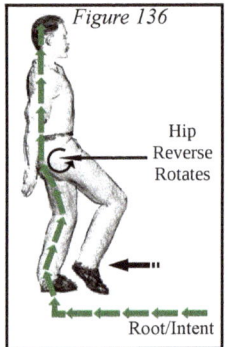
Figure 136

Hip Reverse Rotates

Opening up the rear leg causes the front leg to draw inward.

Sixth Stage
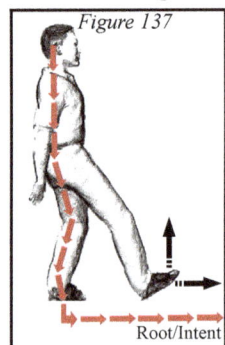
Figure 137

Closing from the root draws the empty front foot forward.

Conclusion

I sincerely hope, having read this book, your understanding of cause and effect is a little clearer, giving you a more coherent and precise direction in which to take your Tai Chi. It's easy to be confused with the competing theories and information being offered out there.

There are a few things I can suggest that may help you to successfully pilot the maze of Tai Chi theories. Firstly, check with the Tao Te Ching. If the theories contradict the Tao Te Ching, then you need to question the theory further.

Secondly, if the theories contravene the Tai Chi Classics, then these theories need to be viewed with suspicion. The best form of quality control over Tai Chi theories is through careful analysis. Asking the hard questions goes a long way in helping to eliminate the contradictions that permeate Tai Chi.

To quote pop culture: There is a scene at the end of the movie in Pulp Fiction, where John Travolta and Samuel Jackson characters are discussing Samuel Jackson's decision to retire from his profession. John Travolta is becoming increasingly agitated by Samuel Jackson's ambiguous answers to his questions. It ends with, Samuel Jackson telling John Travolta, "If you don't like the scary answers, don't ask the scary questions". In Tai Chi, you need to ask the scary questions. The answers will inevitably lead to more questions. That's okay. This is the basis for learning, understanding and finally realising. In Tai Chi, there are times to follow what has been left behind from past teachings, and there will be times where you need to ask the hard questions. Get the balance right between these two points, and you will make progress. At some point in your training you will ultimately have to take responsibility for your Tai Chi.

I'm occasionally asked, "What's the most important quality in Tai Chi. Is it awareness, intent, relaxation, alignment, etc, etc? My reply is always the same. **HONESTY** and **CHARACTER.**

If your are not honest with yourself, then you have no point of reference. If you tell yourself lies, you will lose the ability to discern between fact and fiction. Having decided what is factual, you then require the character to implement these changes in your training, your honesty has led you to. This is a scary time in your Tai Chi, this is when you take full responsibility and control for your future Tai Chi direction. To progress in your Tai Chi you need to eliminate the contradiction. This is not possible without honesty.

Master Huang said' "Only an upright person can do Tai Chi".

Only when you improve your character *(honesty plays a big part in character)* will you be in a position to answer the hard questions, Tai Chi is going to throw your way.

I hope you've enjoyed reading this book and it has furthered your understanding and practice of Tai Chi.

Good Luck in your Tai Chi.

Glenn Blythe.
29th July 2025

References

One of the main books I use in referencing the Classics is a book written by my teacher; "Tàijíquán – True to the Art". This is an excellent book on Tai Chi covers his personal experiences and insights of Tai Chi. The book includes astute writings of the Tai Chi Classics. It can be purchased as a PDF for NZD30 at www.taijiquan-school-of-central-equilibrium.com/shop/

Another book that references the Classics is; "Tai Chi Ch'uan The Technique Of Power", by Tem Horwitz and Susan Kimmelman with H.H. Lui. First published in 1979.

I have frequently referenced "The Art of War" by Sun Tzu. There are many different translations:

"The Art of War" by Sun Tzu translated by Thomas Cleary.

"The Art of War" by Sun Tzu, edited and foreword by James Clavell.

I've found these two books to be the clearest and easiest to read. Some translations of "The Art of War" can be very dry and overly militaristic.